VISUAL FORM DETECTION IN 3-DIMENSIONAL SPACE

JOHN M. MacEACHRAN MEMORIAL
LECTURE SERIES

Sponsored by
The Department of Psychology
The University of Alberta
with the support of
The Alberta Heritage Foundation
for Medical Research
in memory of John M. MacEachran
pioneer in Canadian Psychology

VISUAL FORM DETECTION IN 3-DIMENSIONAL SPACE

WILLIAM R. UTTAL
Perception Laboratory
Institute for Social Research
University of Michigan

LAWRENCE ERLBAUM ASSOCIATES, PUBLISHERS
1983   Hillsdale, New Jersey   London

Copyright © 1983 by Lawrence Erlbaum Associates, Inc.
All rights reserved. No part of this book may be reproduced in
any form, by photostat, microform, retrieval system, or any other
means, without the prior written permission of the publisher.

Lawrence Erlbaum Associates, Inc., Publishers
365 Broadway
Hillsdale, New Jersey 07642

Library of Congress Cataloging in Publication Data

Uttal, William R.
  Visual form detection in 3-dimensional space.

  (The John M. MacEachran lectures; 1982)
  Bibliography: p.
  Includes index.
  1. Visual perception. 2. Form perception. I. Title.
II. Series. [DNLM: 1. Form perception. 2. Visual
perception. WW 105 U93v]
BF241.U87 1983   152.1'423   83-1677
ISBN 0-89859-289-5

Printed in the United States of America
10   9   8   7   6   5   4   3   2   1

Contents

PREFACE ix

1. FORM AND PROCESS 1
    Introduction   1
    What Is A Form?   9
    What Is "Form Perception?"   12
    Earlier Work In Two Dimensional Form
       Detection   20
    A Brief History   23

2. THE EXPERIMENTAL PARADIGM 35
    General Procedure   36
    Observers   40
    Apparatus   41
    The Perceived Cubical Space   45

3. EXPERIMENTAL DESIGN AND RESULTS 46
    Dots   48
        Experiment 1   48
        Experiment 2   52

Lines   55
    Experiment 3   55
    Experiment 4   62
    Experiment 5   64
    Experiment 6   68
Planes   71
    Experiment 7   71
    Experiment 8   77
    Experiment 9   79
    Experiment 10   81
    Experiment 11   85
    Experiment 12   89
    Experiment 13   91
    Experiment 14   95
    Experiment 15   99
    Experiment 16   100

4. DISCUSSION 105

Perceptual Significance   108
    Supplemental Experiment 1   121
    Supplemental Experiment 2   123
A Formal Model   125
Final Comments   142
Acknowledgments   144

REFERENCES 147

The Author's Publications   151

AUTHOR INDEX.................................... 157

SUBJECT INDEX 161

As ever,
　　　　　For Mit-chan

Preface

It is with the greatest appreciation and pleasure that I present to you three lectures concerning visual perception. I feel deeply honored to have been invited to participate in this lecture series honoring the memory of John M. MacEachran, the founder of the Department of Psychology at the University of Alberta and one of Canada's most eminent as well as versatile psychologists. The lecturers who have preceded me in this series make up a distinguished group among whom I am proud to be included.

Before I begin the substance of my presentation, I would like to make a few informal comments. In the last year I discovered that the invitation to present these lectures posed a number of interesting challenges, the solutions to which may be incompatible. First, I appreciate that I am facing an audience of diverse backgrounds. Some of you may know more than I do about perceptual science, while others whose interests and background are in different fields may find some of this material irrelevant, to say the least. How then can I speak to both groups in a way that will neither drug the specialists into a stupor nor overwhelm the nonspecialists? Frankly I have found no way to cut this knot. I have, therefore, chosen to compromise by prefacing the detailed discussion of the esoteric logic, procedures, and interpretations of a series of experiments with general comments on the history and philosophy of perceptual science. I have also chosen to spend more time than usual summarizing, restating conclusions and results, and interpreting findings. Although this is not a complete solution to the problem, perhaps it will alleviate some of the difficulties presentations like these raise.

The second problem is a personal one for which there is really no excuse, but about which I would like to make a brief comment. When I was first contacted by Professors DiLollo and Lechelt to particpate in the MacEachran lectures, my lab had been reopened for only three months after having been closed for three years. Those three years had been spent on a full time writing project that did not involve active collection of experimental data. My research, and research it was, was one of a different kind. Fortunately, this first year has gone very well. In particular, a new generation of equipment has permitted me to carry out experiments with a reliability, dependability, and dispatch to which I was not accustomed back in the olden days of the early and mid 1970's.

Even more important than the hardware, however, was the "peopleware" with whom I worked. John Brogan, a mathematician-computer programmer par excellance, did a herculean job providing the software necessary to carry out most of the experiments that I shall report to you here. (A few experiments from older work, are included so that the story I tell is complete.) Mark Azzato, my research assistant, was equally competent managing the flow of experimental observers and sequencing the large number of experiments that we were able to conduct. Recently Susan Robertson has joined us bringing her high level of skills to our project.

During this last year I also had the pleasure of hosting a visiting colleague from the Institute of Psychology in the Academy of Sciences of the People's Republic of China. Yu Bo-Lin has a distinguished record as a researcher in visual perception in China and joined us this year through the University of Michigan—Institute of Psychology exchange program that has so enriched Ann Arbor's life in the last several years. Our lab also enjoyed the presence of a science apprentice, Millicent Newhouse, who was a high school student and is now an undergraduate at The University of Michigan. Miss Newhouse, by the way, was the senior author of the first paper to come from our newly reopened laboratory.

In general, this last year has been a busy and happy one for all of us. The invitation to give the MacEachran Lecture added incentive, urgency, and impetus beyond that usually associated with such esoterica as I shall report to you here.

Two other acknowledgments must be made in turn to an institution and a man. Our laboratory is now being supported by the Engineering Psychology Branch of the Office of Naval Research of the United States Department of Defense. The Office of Naval Research, the model upon which our National Science Foundation was originally based, has a long history of support of basic science as well as applied science and all of us who have been associated with the Office of Naval Research are proud to acknowledge their many contributions to academic science. The Office of Naval Research was also the organization that supported the three year writing project I mentioned at a time when research support of that kind was unavailable from other agencies. I am especially grateful for the support of the Science Officer who monitored the project, Dr. John O'Hare, whose collegial interaction with us has been one of the outstanding aspects of this project.

Finally, I would like to once again acknowledge my debt and gratitude to my wife May, the *sine qua non* of my professional and personal life.

William R. Uttal
University of Michigan

1 Form and Process

INTRODUCTION

How do we gain knowledge about the external world? This is the foundation question of epistemology. *How do people visually perceive forms?* This is the fundamental question that has guided one branch of psychological thought for centuries (and, incidentally, has directed most of my laboratory research for the last decade). The conceptual similarity of these two questions makes the visual laboratory nothing less than the empirical arm of technical epistemology. One, therefore, has to be awed by the audaciousness, if not the pretentiousness, of what we perceptual psychologists are attempting to do in our laboratories. This is so in spite of the fact that the seemingly silly little experiments we perform sometimes obscure the grandeur of the underlying issues under attack. Make no mistake; what we are attempting is a formidable task even in the light of the powerful new tools and methods of which earlier experimental epistemologists could not have dreamed.

It takes no great historical insight to appreciate that the questions currently asked have been asked by others for millenia. The history of the problem of form perception contains such illustrious (and sometimes unexpected) names as Plato, Aristotle, Democritus, Euclid, Alhazen, Seneca, Galen, Avicenna, Grossteste, Descartes, Da Vinci, Vesalius, Kepler, Locke, Berkeley, Hobbes, Goethe, Müller, Helmholtz, Mach, Wundt, James, Koffka, Wertheimer, and Gibson. A large company of other historical figures, as well as a growing army of our contemporaries have also been concerned with various aspects of the form perception problem. What good company we are in when involved in such a quest! And, how enticing the magnitude of the task makes that quest! Not only is the issue dignified by its antiquity, but it is also broad enough to allow one to pursue almost any kind of scientific activity while remaining within the fold of perceptual psychology. It is possible to fiddle with exotic computers and displays; it is possible to carry out psychophysical experiments; it is possible to manipulate mathematical concepts and logical simulations; it is possible to record electrophysiological correlates; it is even possible to become what Jerry Fodor has called a speculative psychologist and manipulate nothing other than a pen or a typewriter, the enormous published data base, or a few pieces of paper, and still be a contributing perceptual scientist.

This expansiveness is one of the reasons I find this field of research so congenial. Every few years, I become jaded with a task, turn to another, and then later find myself returning to what had been suspended earlier. However inconstant my day to day activities, my professional life for many years has been single minded. My long term goal has been to understand the "input" aspect of human cognition. The urge to achieve this goal has been undiminished for what is now, to my horror, almost a third of a century of a more or less constant commitment to sensory and perceptual studies.

In spite of the long term commitment on the part of so many in the past and present, it is clear that there are many unanswered questions concerning form perception. In fact, most of the relevant and significant questions so far formulated are as yet unanswered. We have hardly begun even to define the vocabulary of the science, much less understand how things happen.

Even more startling (than to appreciate that most relevant questions are still unanswered) is to realize in light of the long history I shall briefly review later in this chapter, how infrequently form perceptionists of the past or present have asked what is perhaps *the* fundamental question. That question, whose neglect a number of our contemporaries (e.g., Sutherland, 1967; Zusne, 1970) have also noted, is—*What are the attributes or characteristics of a form that regulate its detectability or recognizability?* It is important to appreciate that I use the word *attribute* here to emphasize that I am especially concerned with the *global* properties of the form rather the *local* features. I intend there to be a major difference between my use of the term "attribute" and the use of the word "feature." It is the difference between some aspect of the overall *arrangement* of, as opposed to the *nature* of, the component parts of a form that I believe dominates form perception. In short, my thesis in these lectures is exactly that people see forms as a result of the arrangement of, and not the nature of, the component parts!

Since the heyday of the Gestalt tradition, relatively few psychologists have approached the study of visual form perception with such a global emphasis. Among these few are Rock (1973), Brown and Owen (1967), and Garner (1974). Even these globalists have usually emphasized some simple transformation (e.g., orientation), some general feature (e.g., compactness), or the influence of memory (and/or how memory or imagery are influenced by form) rather than the impact of the organizational geometry of the stimulus form itself on detection, discrimination, or classification. Indeed, recent decades have clearly been dominated by a strong elementalist tradition in perceptual theory. At first, spatial domain feature detection concepts dominated theory; currently frequency domain spatial frequency ideas provide the basis for what is clearly a consensus model. Both approaches are alike in stressing the importance of the component part, as opposed to global organization, in the determination of the perceptual response.

It is only in the last few years that the wholistic tradition has been notably revitalized, as evidenced by Kubovy and Pomerantz's (1981) recent book. Even in this extraordinarily thoughtful compendium of papers on perceptual organization—a book with which I felt an enormous amount of sympathetic agreement, and which substantially conforms to the approach, if not the experimental detail, of these lectures—there is relatively little consideration given to the global stimulus attributes involved in form perception. In some cases this is specifically because the authors reject the attribute approach, but in others, the empirical data is simply not obtained in a manner that might help develop an answer to this question.

One persistent and pervasive approach to "data" and "proof" in Kubovy and Pomerantz's book, as well as in classic Gestalt psychology, is the use of compelling demonstrations, rather than parametric experimental manipulation—the approach that characterizes so much of the rest of experimental psychology. Only in the articles written by Julesz, Pomerantz, and Shepard do we see the kind of parametric manipulation that seems to me necessary for understanding form perception. Nevertheless, the neo-Gestaltism reflected in this book is a promising sign that the wholistic tradition's contributions have not been lost and are regaining the attention of contemporary psychologists.

There are three practical reasons, beyond the decline of wholism, for the long neglect of the attribute question. First, there is as yet no adequate means of quantifying what we mean by the word "form;" thus it is difficult to precisely specify the attributes of a form. While some authors have suggested statistical families of forms that are alike in some general way, there is no single dimension along which form may be continuously varied comparable to electromagnetic frequency in color research or acoustic frequency in pitch research. Furthermore, neither the algebra of form proposed by Leeuwenberg (1969, 1971) nor the statistical algorithms for *generating* individual samples of broad classes of form (Attneave & Arnoult, 1956; Fitts & Leonard, 1957) have yet proved satisfactory and acceptable means of *manipulating* form as an experimental variable in the manner that scientific psychology depends upon so much. Such formularizations as Leeuwenberg's may model the psychological propensity to classify forms according to those general properties that are common to a group of forms (as has been pointed out to me in a personal communication from H.F.J.M. Buffart in 1982); nevertheless they do not define form in a specific enough manner to allow us to use these classifications as measures of an independent variable. In a sense all of these form generating methods are prototheories of how the visual system works rather than a practical means of scaling physical stimuli along a continuous dimension.

Perhaps the fundamental source of this difficulty lies in the fact that spatial and temporal forms are intrinsically multidimensional, and in present day psychology we still tend to think mainly in unidimensional terms. Forms, in the absence of a unique descriptive dimension are often generated in a more or less arbitrary manner and are equally often defined as experimental stimuli on the basis of some vaguely articulated ad hoc rule. This difficulty remains; my group has done no better than our predecessors in resolving the problem. As reported later, the stimulus forms we use are also more or less arbitrary, although in some cases a continuous variable (e.g., variance) does satisfy the immediate needs of a particular experiment. I must also acknowledge that it is entirely possible that the search for a precise quantification of "form" may be a search for a chimera; it may never be possible to quantify forms. This issue is yet to be resolved.

The second reason that the specific attribute problem has been ignored is that heretofore there has been no easy way to easily manipulate even arbitrarily defined forms in stimulus displays. Gestalt psychology was damaged perhaps even more by this practical difficulty than the falsification of their neuroelectrical field theories. Those pioneers simply did not have the technical capabilities to carry out the obvious experiments. One must wonder what the state of contemporary psychology would have been if those insightful psychologists had possessed the information manipulation tools now available to modern perceptual researchers. The advent of the laboratory computer, in particular, has ameliorated this practical difficulty. Forms of great variety and complexity in two, three, and even four dimensions (i.e., X, Y, Z, t) are today easily generated in many laboratories about the world.

I believe the third reason the specific attribute problem has been neglected is that the manipulation of the form of continuous figures usually leads to a confounded outcome. That is, changing one attribute of the global arrangement of the parts of a form also often covaries some other local feature. For example, varying the area of a geometrical form also varies the perimeter of that form. Such a confounding often makes the actual causal relationship between any particular attribute of the form and any measure of the perceptual response uncertain. The use of dotted stimuli *sometimes* overcomes this problem. There are, in the case of such stimulus materials, no local attributes other than "arrangement" itself; as long as the number of dots remains constant, all of the other aspects of the stimulus can be subsumed under the single factor called "arrangement." On the other hand, "arrangement," however singular it is as an item in our vocabulary, is itself not a simple term; it is at least as complicated as "form" and arrangements themselves may fall victim to multidimensional confounding in cases in which the intention is to change only a single attribute.

Nevertheless, dot patterns can often be manipulated in a reasonably straightforward manner compared to continuous visual stimuli. For example, a line of five dots may be elongated from one to two centimeters without changing the number of dots in the line. The physical stimulus intensity is thus kept constant. A continuous line, however, can be elongated only by adding luminous area (the number of pixels along the line), and thus a long straight line produces more total physical energy than does a short line if the elements are kept equally luminous. The stimuli used in the experiments described in Chapter III serve as examples of the extent to which we have overcome this third difficulty.

It is my goal in these lectures to assay the ways in which the visual system responds to a set of arbitrarily designed and highly constrained dotted stimulus forms. It is my hope that by manipulating some of the attributes of these abstract approximations to continuous scenes and measuring their effects on form detection, that a few steps towards a general understanding of the ways in which we perceive geometric forms will be forthcoming. Obviously, this is an ambitious goal and not one that is likely to be fulfilled in the short run. Therefore, these lectures can deal only with a few experiments from which I shall attempt to draw some germane, but highly limited, conclusions as well as partially test one formal model.

Prior to a discussion of conclusions, however, I must direct your attention to some less earth-shaking, but practically important, details of method and some raw experimental results that may seem esoteric and isolated from the grand epistemological question (How do we see forms?). I hope my audience will not despair, because an understanding of these abstract experimental stimuli, technical methods, and empirical results is essential for a scientific (as opposed to an intuitive) solution to the problem of form perception. The absence of such concrete anchors to psychobiological reality would permit us to fall victim to the ruminations of armchair speculation. And, as we shall see, speculation without empirical testing in at least a few instances would have led us wildly astray; some of the results that are obtained in this study are surprisingly counterintuitive.

The specific attribute question is, however, only one of two major epistemological issues toward which our work is aimed. The other is the grand old question of perceptual research concerned with visual *space*—how is it that we are able to construct the third dimension from the two dimensional images projected on the retinae? That this is both a long standing issue and a perplexing one has been most eloquently expressed by my good friend and colleague Dan Robinson (1982) of Georgetown University when he states:

> The very phenomenon of "space" erected so durable a barrier against radical empiricism that Mill, Bain, Helmholtz, and Wundt—these otherwise legendary empiricists—quailed before it. Helmholtz could explain space perception only by invoking the delphic process of "unconscious inference" and, in a similar vein, Wundt had to rely on something called "synthesis." The details of their respective accounts are less important than their theoretical justifications: Since space is not given by any property of a stimulus, it must be constructed (inferred; synthesized) by the nonsensory (intellectual-cognitive) processes of the percipient. What this

1. VISUAL FORM DETECTION IN 3-DIMENSIONAL SPACE

requires of Spencer and the Mills, "intoxicated with the principle of association" (James—Principles, 2:270), is the impossible task of accounting for the sensation of space through a compounding of totally nonspatial sensations. They, with Wundt and Helmholtz, may be lumped as "psychic stimulists," ensnared by the very Kantian principles they so eagerly disown. [pp. 199]

I doubt that the vocabulary with which I am most comfortable (e.g., "perceptual space is calculated by the extraction of invariances existing in the two monocular images") is likely to satisfy Dan Robinson any more than the vocabulary of "unconscious inference" or "synthesis." It should not be overlooked, however, that in some functional way, these earlier theorists may have, in fact, been right! Even though they lacked the modern information processing metaphor necessary to phrase their theories in acceptable contemporary terms, they may have described the process appropriately in the less formal terms of their times. Space *is* implicit in the *relationships* between the two retinal images even if not "given" *directly* by any single attribute of the stimulus. Space is "given" *indirectly* in that it must be made explicit by more or less straightforward computational or transformational processes carried out on multiple aspects of the stimulus. Indeed, as we shall see, the stark reality may be that *nothing is "given" directly*, but rather that the superficial isomorphic relationship of the two dimensional experiences to the physical X and Y axis is no more "direct" than the relationship of the perceived Z axis to the dichoptic invariances. This tenative conclusion cuts through the knot posed by the question of how we see depth when the inputs are only two dimensional by asserting that *everything is indirect* (i.e., all perceptions are mediated by implicit representational mechanisms). Such an approach releases us from the obligation to find any special manner by which the mysterious Z-axis becomes like the apparently unmysterious X and Y axis by suggesting that all three are equally mysterious! One line of evidence would support such a seemingly far fetched and initially repugnant suggestion. If observers performed as well vis a vis the X, Y and Z axis (even though two of them are "direct" and one is "indirect") then we should be able to accept as plausible the idea that all three perceived dimensions are governed by the same natural laws.

As we shall see, this is exactly the kind of evidence that I have obtained in this study and the conclusion toward which I have been inexorably propelled. This resolution of the issue is quite different from William James' proposed solution to the perplexity of depth perception. He attempted to make depth (Z) a direct rather than an unmediated dimension and in this manner make it compatible with the other two spatial dimensions (X and Y). Quite to the contrary, my analysis (and, among others, that of Hermann Helmholtz and Thomas Reid) makes *all* three perceived dimensions indirect constructions resulting from the activation of complex internal processes of which we still know very little.

Whether either approach (i.e., making Z direct or making X and Y indirect) resolves the perplexity proposed by depth is, of course, still an open issue. But it is clear that any determinist and empiricist theory based on unmediated and direct transformations is unlikely to be able to solve this problem. Interpreted in this way, it is obvious that current space and form perception research is but the most recent focus in a longstanding controversy between classic empiricism and classic rationalism. (See my discussion of this issue in Chapter 2 of Uttal, 1981).

The perception of form and the perception of space are obviously closely intertwined. This interaction is the main reason that I have chosen to carry out the experiments reported here in stereoscopic space rather than on a plane. The interactions between the spatial attributes and the form attributes, as we shall see, are instructive in solving some of the puzzles posed by form perception and space perception. The recent work of Robert Fox and his colleagues, (Fox & Patterson, 1980; Fox, 1981) and of Walter Gogel and Donald Mershon (Gogel 1969; Mershon, 1972) makes it clear that what happens perceptually on a two dimensional plane need not necessarily predict what will happen in three dimensional visual space.

Specifically, the program of research I report to you here is aimed at the elucidation of the factors influencing the *detection* of dotted forms in a dynamic steroscopic space. Observers in these experiments perceive what appears to them to be a three dimensional (cartesian) volume in which some of the stimulus dots may appear to be moving or flickering. This temporal property makes our experiments four dimensional, but in a "space-time" rather than a "hyperspace" context. That is, our "space" is one defined by three spatial coordinates and one temporal one, and not four spatial ones. Observers are asked only to say if they saw *any* constellation of dots that is organized in space or time, not to identify, name, or discriminate that constellation. This detection task can be made more or less difficult by varying the density of other irregularly positioned "masking" dots.

The main hypothesis of this study is that the difficulty of the detection task varies as a function of the spatio-temporal form of the stimulus. The suggestion that there should be a shape or time influence on form detection in three dimensional space is an outgrowth of our earlier studies on analogous detection tasks in two dimensional space (which I summed up in Uttal, 1975). As we shall see, this initial hypothesis is supported only in part; the degree of spatio-temporal influence depends on what kind of form is being studied. Some surprising and counterintuitive results have been obtained and will be reported to you in due course.

One of the most important aspects of both the earlier and the present work is that I conceive of it as being quite limited in scope. That is, my coworkers and I are not claiming to study all stages of form perception or all aspects of visual space in these experiments. Our goal is much more modest. As will become evident when we discuss our experimental paradigm, our concern is only with what is the putatively "primitive" stage of visual processing underlying form *detection* and the stimulus attributes that affect that stage. It is also important to appreciate that our goal is to study the perception of geometric form and not the symbolic aspects of perception tapped when one measures short term memory or the conveyance of symbolic meaning. Others such as Hogben (1972), DiLollo and Wilson (1978), DiLollo (1980), DiLollo and Woods (1981), Garner and Clement (1963), Garner (1974), and Jonides, Irwin, and Yantis (1982) all share with me an enthusiasm for the dot as a research tool. However, my goal here is to use persistence, masking, and binocular disparity as vehicles to explore the perception of forms rather than to study short term visual memory, figural goodness, or sorting behavior—the important psychological processes that were the targets of their studies. My goal is one I believe is shared with Nakayama (1981), Fox (1981), Barlow (1979), Barlow and Reeves (1980), Lappin, Doner, and Kottas (1980), Falzett and Lappin (1981), Johansson (e.g., 1978), Rogers and Graham (1982), and others, all of whom use dot patterns as a means of studying one or another aspect of the spatio-temporal geometry of form perception per se. Another area beyond the intended scope of this project is the metric of visual space—Is it Euclidean or non-Euclidean? Many others have sought and are seeking the answer to this important question (most notably, at present, is Joseph Lappin of Vanderbilt University). I am not concerned, however, with this issue beyond the simple matter of the equivalence or nonequivalence of the three spatial dimensions.

My long term goal is thus limited to determining how we see forms in general by examining the detectability of static and dynamic single dots, dotted lines, dotted surfaces, and dotted solids in a variety of masking environments in particular. As such, I will be attempting to determine what attributes of the spatial and temporal arrangement of dotted forms influence their detectability. In the particular studies that are presented in this report I am specifically concerned with determining the effects of the spatial and temporal characteristics of dots, lines, and planes on their detection in a masking noise consisting of arrays of briefly presented, randomly placed, single dots. In later extensions of this work, I plan to deal with more complex surfaces and solid stimuli, and with noise arrays that themselves have some coherent order or texture. The expectation (and, at this point, this is clearly an act of faith I hope to make concrete at the end of these lectures) is that the results obtained in this highly abstract stimulus situation will generalize to other kinds of visual stimuli, and that what is learned here will tell us something about how we see all kinds of forms, including continuous ones.

In some of my earlier work (Uttal, 1975), dealing with the two dimensional analog of the present stereoscopic experiments, I successfully developed a mathematical model based on the autocorrelation function that was capable of predicting the rank order detectability of sets of targets varying along a single dimension. I plan to extend this model, or some modification of it, to the multidimensional case embodied in the dynamic stereoscopic stimulus space in which our observers now operate. The application of this autocorrelation model to some of the data obtained in the experiments is the substance of the final part of my third lecture.

In sum, in these lectures, I report the results of 19 experiments concerned with the detection of dots, dotted lines, and dotted planes in arrays of random masking dots, and I apply the model to the outcome of these data. Before I can do that, however, I must clarify the intellectual foundations of this work by considering a number of other definitional, conceptual, and technical issues.

WHAT IS A FORM?

At first glance, it is a surprising fact that in spite of the enormous past and current interest in "form" perception, there are relatively few reported instances in which form itself has been used as an independent variable in a way that allows us even partially to answer the specific attribute question. It becomes clear immediately upon reading those books that are fully dedicated to the problem of form (most notable among these, of course, are Zusne's comprehensive 1970 review of the field and the extremely thoughtful and recent collection of papers edited by Kubovy and Pomerantz, 1981) that we, as a scientific community, have not succeeded in precisely defining what it is that we mean by the word "form." We have progressed only modestly beyond the Gestalt notion that form is "any segregated whole or unit."

The word "form" tends, therefore, to be operationally defined by psychologists in terms of the particular experiment in which they are currently involved. When precision of definition has been explicitly sought, the concept of "form," more often than not, has been embodied in terms of *classes of forms* rather than a specific form. Indeed, some of the approximations to a precise specification of form used in the psychological literature have been statistical in nature as I have already indicated. Consider, for example, the classic Attneave and Arnout (1956) patterns shown in Fig. 1 or the "random histograms" of Fitts and Leonard (1957) shown in Fig. 2. Each of these statistical devices was intended to provide a graded series of stimulus form classes rather than to generate a specific form. Each does, in a statistical sense, accomplish that goal. However, it seems equally clear that this statistical specification is not adequate. Two forms having very similar statistics may be perceived as being quite different because of global organizational factors that are not distinguished by the generating rule that gave rise to them. I believe this same criticism, nonuniqueness, can be applied to the form "equation" work of Leeuwenberg (1971), as well as to that of Rogers and Trofanenko (1979) who use spatial entropy to characterize the complexity of a shape. Neither model uniquely defines a particular shape; they only provide a metric for classes of shape.

Other global attributes (e.g., organization and arrangement), which were very vaguely defined, were the foundations on which the Gestalt theoretical approach was based. Scholar-scientists such as Max Wertheimer (1880–1893), Kurt Koffka (1886–1941) and Wolfgang Kohler (1887–1967) appreciated that forms possessed attributes that were not easily quantified (e.g., pragnanz and good-

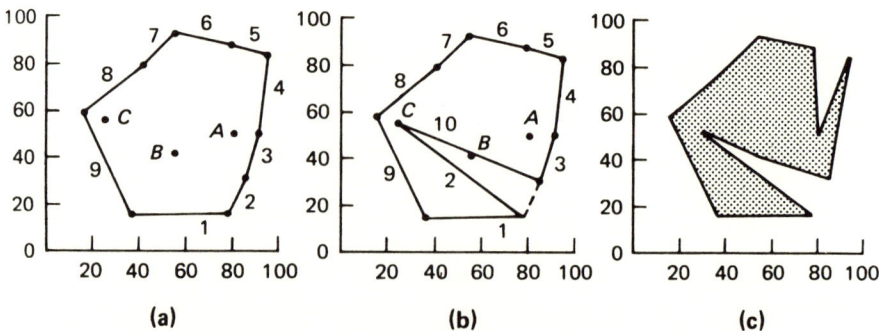

FIG. 1. Steps in the construction of random polygon, using the procedure invented by Attneave and Arnoult. Random points are first plotted, and then the exterior points are connected. Then slices are taken out of the external polygon to connect the internal points, thus forming irregular polygons with both convexities and concavities. (From Attneave & Arnoult, 1956.)

ness) or even defined qualitatively. Indeed, they built their entire scientific system around these unquantified and ill defined concepts. In my opinion, the Gestalt psychologists' inability to precisely specify what they meant by a form and to quantify these vague attributes was the major factor leading to the collapse of what otherwise was their important, and I think, fundamentally correct wholistic approach to perceptual science. (Their total failure to develop a plausible neurophysiology did not help either, of course.) In the absence of measures of their dependent variables, definitions of key concepts, and an efficient methodology, they simply could not carry out the crucial experiments. Thus their approach, however correct in principle, was infertile in practice, and like all such fruitless approaches quite properly was abandoned by scientific psychology.

In recent years there have been renewed efforts to develop nomenclature systems that can specifically define a unique form. But the problem remains refractory. Zusne (1970), in his exhaustive search of the literature of visual form, refers to the influence on psychophysical responses of "variables of the distal stimulus." He shares with me the feeling that form has not yet been adequately quantified, and proposes the following interim definition: ". . . form may be considered both a one dimensional emergent of its physical dimensions and a multidimensional variable" (p. 175). Zusne then turns, unsatisfyingly I am sure to him as well as to me, to discussions of statistical generating rules (pp. 176–189) as the prototypes of experimental forms. For usable descriptions of individual stimuli, Zusne points out that psychologists must invoke such vague, multidimensional "factors" as compactness, jaggedness, or skewness (Brown & Owen, 1967).

Precise definitions and specific quantitative measures of whatever it is that we mean by *form* remain elusive. Hochberg and McAlister's (1953) seriously mistitled paper ("A quantitative approach to figural goodness") makes this argument clear. Their "quantitative" measures of goodness (an aspect of form) are counts of the numbers of line segments, angles, or points of intersection—properties that themselves do not in any way define the arrangement or the form of a visual stimulus.

Recent attempts to quantify form on the basis of two dimensional Fourier analyses have been offered as another alternative, but this approach suffers from the same difficulty. Form, from this point of view, may be represented in terms of the spatial spectral components of the stimulus scene. So far this technique has proven to be extremely useful if one uses stimuli that are gratings or spatial frequency-like in their global appearance. If, on the other hand, the spatial frequency model is used for nongrating stimuli (such as block letters), the analysis does not work well in predicting the outcome of psychophysical experiments (Coffin, 1978). There is, obviously, something more to a visual form than what is captured in the sum of its spatial frequency components (even when phase relationships are considered) just as there is more to a form than its constituent ensemble of local features. Incidentally the unarguable utility of the Fourier approach in defining stimuli and quantifying responses does not necessarily mean that there exist neuroanatomically defined spatial frequency "channels" in the nervous system. But, this is another matter and for a more complete critique of this issue, I refer my audience to an earlier work (Uttal, 1981).

Another difficulty arises from the confusion of the two words *form* and *pattern*. There is a subtle distinction here that makes me quite discontent with the use of the term *pattern*. *Pattern*, according to my dictionary, carries the connotation of a prototype or mold, from which replicas or repetitions are produced. This

FIG. 2. Two histogram-type stimulus patterns formed by random selection of the height of columns in an 8 × 8 matrix. The pattern (a) has been formed by true random sampling with replacement, while the one in (b) was formed by constrained random sampling without replacement. (From Fitts & Leonard, 1957.)

connotation is different from that of the term *form* which specifically speaks, it seems to me, to the attributes of shape or arrangement. The distinction may be small but may have, in fact, had a profound theoretical outcome: *Pattern perception* is often used as a misnomer for *form perception* in a way that leads directly to a particular kind of theoretical explanation that, in fact, is logically and behaviorally unlikely—a template matching process. You can see why definitions are so important—a single misdefinition early on can lead directly to the acceptance of an unsuitable theoretical outcome.

In sum, neither my group nor anyone else to my knowledge has yet provided an operational definition of what is meant by the word *form* that comes close to satisfying the needs of perceptual researchers. Perhaps because of its multidimensional nature, form is intrinsically difficult or even impossible to define and to quantify. At best we manipulate something as simple as the height-width ratio of a rectangle and thus reduce the problem to a level at which the essence of form is ignored; at worst we create complex stimulus scenes, so superloaded with symbolic meaning that they tap cognitive and symbolic processes quite different from the raw and immediate form perception process with which I am concerned here.

This brings me to the next matter of definition—what is it that we mean by form *perception?* As we shall now see, the difficulties of definition are as great in the definition of the word denoting the process—*perception*—as they are in the definition of the word denoting the stimulus—*form*.

WHAT IS "FORM PERCEPTION?"

It is quite clear that just as there is a certain vagueness about what is meant by the word *form*, there is at least an equivalent, and perhaps a greater, nebulousness in the meaning of the word *perception*. This difficulty in definition is compounded by the frequent substitution of other related terms (e.g., *recognition*) in this field. The basic reason for this confusion is that at the most molar level, the act of *perceiving* a pattern always involves a constellation of contributing processes and it is not always made clear exactly what is being assayed in a particular experiment. By carrying out some operations under certain conditions it is possible to measure the ability of an observer to *detect* the presence of a form. Other experimental designs allow us to ask the observer to *recognize,* (i.e., classify) a form by either naming it or the class to which it belongs, thus incorporating this particular stimulus within a more general concept.

It is also possible to ask the subject to *discriminate* between two forms, or to study the interactive effect of some attribute of some form other than the immediate stimulus on any of these processes. As an example of an interactive effect, the detection of a form may be influenced by its orientation or the spatial frequency of some previously or subsequently presented form or by the simultaneous presence of an adjacent form.

Clearly, different experimental tasks assay different perceptual processes. It is entirely possible for an observer to detect a form at stimulus levels that do not allow its classification or recognition. On the other hand, classification in the absence of detection seems to be a logical impossibility. Even though an observer does not report the conscious awareness of a stimulus event, the act of recognition implies some kind of prior or concomitant detection. The absence of explicit detection means only that the observer's attention and efforts are directed toward the measurement of only a part of that total perceptual process; it does not mean that detection is not occurring. Similarly, the experimenter's measurement of recognition processes does not imply that the detection processes are not occurring, only that the task is not designed to measure them.

Of course two assumptions are being asserted here that are, at best, hypothetical and at worst fallacious. First, it is assumed in these remarks that perception is an aggregate of virtually independent subprocesses or levels. Second, it is assumed that it is possible to separately assay these independent processes by appropriate experimental designs. Even though they are fundamental to the present work, I must acknowledge that neither of these two assumptions is yet unequivocal.

M. D. Vernon (1952) is another who has ascribed to this "separatist" or "stages of perception" view. However, today the most active students of this approach, or as they call it "microgenesis," are the Soviet psychologists. Their work is exemplified by Talis Bachmann's fine study of the genesis of a subjective image (Bachmann, 1980).

Obviously other empirical questions are created by the very act of breaking up perception into stages that also have not yet been resolved. Some of these questions concern how separable these processes are. Others deal with what is biologically real and what is just a manifestation of the research methodology. Another set of issues, of great interest to my current work, but first raised by Helson and Fehrer (1932), concerns what, if any, are the differential effects of form on the various stages. Using thresholds for luminosity, just noticeable form, and certain form, they were not able to determine any systematic effect of form on these perceptual tasks. As we shall see, the present experiments, using a very different paradigm, substantiate their findings in part, but refute them elsewhere.

The one thing that is clear, however, is that the current definition of form perception is at once too broad, too restricted, too nebulous, and too thoroughly confusing to our understanding of these processes. In only a few instances do we define what is meant by the words perception, recognition, discrimination, and detection in a way that transcends a simple description of the operations carried out by the experimenter. While acknowledging the still clearly heard messages of behaviorism and operationalism, I believe there is an underlying functional reality that involves more than just the psychophysical methodology and overt behavioral responses. We have an obligation to say what it is that we mean by these key psychological words when we use them. To meet that obligation, I propose the following definitions for this study.

1. Detection.   The perceptual experience of the presence an organized stimulus form. One behavioral correlate of this experience is the correct selection of a stimulus presentation from two alternatives, one of which contains the stimulus and one of which contains only noise.
2. Discrimination.   The perceptual experience of two stimulus forms sufficient to specify whether they are identical or nonidentical. One behavioral correlate of this experience is the correct answer (same or different) when presented with two stimuli that may or may not be identical.
3. Recognition (or classification).   The perceptual experience of a stimulus form sufficient to allow the observer to specify its name or the class of forms to which it belongs. The behavioral correlate of this experience is the correct naming of the form or the class.
4. Perception.   All of the above and more.

One instance in which the specific process of concern is satisfactorily defined is to be found in the content matter of *Pattern Recognition,* a journal presenting papers that are rigorously constrained to the form *classification* rubric. Virtually all papers in this journal deal with the assignment of forms to classes on the basis of criteria that are almost always associated with the constituent local geometric features. But, remember, this journal is guided by what is essentially an engineering approach. *Pattern Recognition* is not a journal of psychological theory or empirical results—it is a corpus of knowledge associated with how to make a special kind of machine—a computer—optimally classify geometric forms into classes using a methodology that is based strictly on local features. *Pattern Recognition* does not deal with either the problem of psychological awareness or the mechanisms of human form perception, or even the problem of signal detection in the communication theory sense: It is purely a journal of automatic classification strategies. For this reason, few psychologists read this journal, and even fewer are influenced by it.

Unfortunately the relevant body of perceptual research is not as well defined and it is sometimes quite difficult to discern which of the several possible microgenetic levels a particular experiment is examining. Furthermore, theoretical matters (explanations of *how* a process occurs) are sometimes injudiciously mixed into the descriptions of *what* a process is. For example, any statement such as "form recognition is the process of classifying forms into categories *on the basis of the extraction of local features*" not only begs the theoretical question of *how* we classify forms, but also confuses the description of the perceptual process with the specific mechanism underlying that process.

If we are to make any sense of the abundant experimental literature it is critical that the level of perception under investigation be precisely specified. It is senseless to attempt to study form perception in general. We are obliged to be as specific in describing what we are trying to study as we are in specifying experimental operations.

In response to this self imposed caveat, I want to repeat that my present research goals are quite limited: They are to understand form *detection* in a three dimensional context—no more and no less. The task assigned to my observers is the key to this limited goal; they are asked only to specify which of two alternative, sequential stimuli contains one of the forms with which they have been pretrained. Our task does not ask the observer to identify that form nor to discriminate it from anything other than a random nonform. My results tell us nothing about discrimination or recognition and my formal model is not intended to deal with these levels of processing. Autocorrelation processes are at least plausible to describe detection processes, but they can not be a total explanation of all of form perception. Categorization or discrimination processes are likely to involve comparisons with conceptual references that may require mechanisms more like cross correlations. Higher level (cognitive) influences are not even remotely associated with these simple transforms.

At this point, I would like to present to you a brief outline of my personal taxonomy of visual processing levels. This taxonomy has been spelled out in far too much detail elsewhere (Uttal, 1981), but it may help in understanding the task I have set for myself if I briefly outline it here.

My taxonomy, as presented in Table 1 is composed of six levels. One, level 0, is preneural and prepsychological. It invokes patently optical (or otherwise physical) and pretransductive mechanisms to explain certain phenomena. Levels 1 and 2 are the explicitly neuroreductionistic levels, while Levels 3, 4, and 5 are patently *non*neuroreductionistic. I believe the phenomena and processes of these latter levels can only be studied through the application of molar descriptions and theories. I believe that any attempt to search for neural equivalents here is certain to be frustrated. Before I start discussing this taxonomy in detail, I would like to clarify some of its attributes:

1. This is a taxonomy of *processes* and not of *phenomena*. By processes I mean the underlying interactions or mechanism invoked in explaining the phenomenon. Some processes are neuroreductionistic; some are explanatory only in a more molar psychological sense. In the latter case, the mechanisms are information, rather than neural signal, processors. By phenomena I mean both mental experiences and any measure (data, table, or graph) of such experiences.

2. This taxonomy assumes that processes like detection and recognition can be separated and isolated *critical levels* identified. *Critical levels* are the points at

TABLE 1
Outline of a Taxonomy of Visual Processes (from Uttal, 1981).

A STEP TOWARDS A TAXONOMY OF PERCEPTUAL PROCESSES

ABSTRACT

LEVEL	EXAMPLES
0-Preneural and Prepsychological Processing	Selective absorption of ultraviolet light by lens and macular pigment
1-Receptor Level Processing	Analysis into trivariant code by three different cone absorption spectra
2-Neural Network Processing	Contour enhancement (Mach Bands)
3-Figure-Ground Organization and Signal Extraction Processing (Prequantitative and unidimensional)	Organization of Ishihara patterns
4-Integration and Construction (Quantitative and multidemensional)	Color constancy and contrast; The Land phenomena; simultaneous contrast and metacontrast
5-Subsequent Mental Image Processing	Shephard and Cooper's mental rotation

←——— Immediate, Preattentive Physicalistic, Deterministic, Neural Model ———→

←——— Molar, Psychological, Rationalistic Model ———→

↑ Subsequent Manipulative Attentive Active

which the meaning or significance of a transmitted message changes, not just the code used to represent information that is otherwise constant in meaning.

3. This taxonomy assumes that *multi level processing* may occur, that all levels of processing are capable of influencing perception; and that effects at different levels may be redundant or compensatory.

4. This taxonomy involves the idea of *information saturation*—no further change in meaning, value, or significance occurs once some threshold has been crossed, even though the nature of the transmission code may change. (For example, semaphore flags in bright light convey the same information as flags in dim light, as long as you can see them at all.)

5. Except for level 5, this taxonomy deals with immediate responses mediated by preattentive, passive, mentally effortless neural processes of various degrees of complexity. Level 5 requires cognitive effort, attentive focusing, and active processing.

6. The taxonomy is *eclectic*, involving both neuroreductionistic and molar processes. It is both neoempiricist and neorationalist. This is both its strength, its weakness, and the plain fact of contemporary perceptual science.

(Parenthetically, I must insert a disclaimer here. Higher levels of processing are nonneuroreductionistic only because of their complexity. We can not reduce them to neural terms only because there are so many neurons involved. In fact, all higher levels are really extensions of Level 2—neural net—mechanisms. I am not subtly introducing some cryptic or covert dualism at this point. All levels are *in principle* reducible to neural terms even if they are not *in practice*.)

Now, let's consider the taxonomy in detail:

Level 0 Processes. From the point that photons are reflected or emitted by an object and begin their course towards the point in the receptor where the primary sensory action occurs, there are innumerable opportunities, both external and internal to the eye, for the stimulus to be modulated in ways that have perceptual consequences. Though these modulations or transformations of the stimulus by the optical and spatial properties of the external environment and of the eye are not, strictly speaking, even physiological processes. They are often confused with transformations occurring within the nervous system and do exert equally powerful influences on our response to the distal stimuli. It is necessary, therefore, to include a separate category for these physical processes in the proposed taxonomy.

Level 1 Processes. Level 1 is concerned with the transductive processes of the photoreceptor. It is almost exclusively influenced by the actual physical energetics of the interactions between the photons, the stimulus, and the photoreceptor chemicals, or by the distribution of the receptor cells themselves. Luminous, chromatic, and acuity thresholds are, at least in part, influenced by processes categorized within this first level. A light must be a certain intensity and wavelength, and the receptor must be in a certain state, before a visual experience can be elicited. However, except for some modest temporal and spatial summation (within the confines of a single receptor), nothing about the geometric form of the stimulus influences processes at this level. Absolute threshold measurements using appropriate psychophysical procedures have generally been the experimental paradigm of choice in studies of Level 1 phenomena. However, there is increasing interest in suprathreshold phenomena associated with scales of perceived magnitude, which, it is not appreciated, are also substantially defined by neural mechanisms within the receptor cell. Some temporal properties of the perceptual response (for example, visual persistence) may also be attributable to this stage of information processing.

Level 2 Processes. Level 2 processes include those specifically affected by neural network interactions in the retina and perhaps in the more peripheral portions of the central nervous system. Both thresholds and the magnitude of the resulting perceptual response may be either suppressed or enhanced as a result of interaction effects between neighboring portions of neural networks more central than the receptor itself. Contour enhancement effects, such as the Mach band or the gray spots in the Hermann grid, are the most clear-cut examples of perceptual phenomena reasonably attributed to Level 2 spatial interaction processes, but spatial summation effects on the threshold and some aspects of visual acuity and the dark adaptation curve also are best explained in the vocabulary of this level. In addition, many temporal properties of vision are now thought to result from Level 2 processes.

Level 3 Processes. Level 3 processes, like those of Level 2, also include critical operations exquisitely sensitive to the detailed geometry and microstructure of the stimulus. However, Level 3 processes do not necessarily result in any change in the apparent magnitude of a stimulus-induced perceptual response. Rather, the effects on form at this third level are more often exhibited as variations in the organization or detectability of an entire form as a Gestalt, rather than in terms of the absolute detectability of its elements.

I believe that the study I am presenting to you dealing with detection of a dotted form within dotted noise, is aimed at elucidating what is essentially a Level 3 process. I believe that recognition experiments are, in the main, explained by Level 5 processes.

Level 4 Processes. Level 4 processes, however, are the first in which nonisomorphisms and nonveridicalities are almost always observed between the dimensions of the most salient stimulus and the dimensions of the evoked perceptual experience. At this level, specific isomorphic relationships must be subservient to other symbolic aspects of the stimulus. Processing of signals at Level 4, I believe, exemplifies the first level of predominantly symbolic (i.e., nonisomorphic) processing and, therefore, is undoubtedly accomplished by even more complex neural mechanisms that no longer even represent the stimulus in a map-like fashion.

The main property of responses affected by processes of Level 4 is that they are characteristically multidimensionally determined; aspects of the percept change as a function of the joint influence of multiple aspects or dimensions of the stimulus. Relationships among the different dimensions of the stimulus are very important at this level. There may be gross discrepancies between what might have been the single physical dimension initially thought to be most closely associated with the phenomena and the perceptual response itself. Another important property is that they produce a quantified dimension of experience. That is, Level 4 processes allow us to say that an object is big, red, far away, or high, instead of just isolating it from its background.

Level 5 Processes. Levels 0 to 4 of psychoneural processing in this taxonomic scheme are collectively characterized by a single criterion—they all represent relatively immediate, even though multidimensional, preattentive responses to the stimulus scene. These four lower level sets of processes set up the raw sensory-perceptual experiences that can be processed by subsequent mental information manipulations. Decisions must be made, criteria evaluated, comparisons carried out, classifications and categorizations established, and discriminations between the raw experiences made; these are the manipulative processes that are characteristic of what I claim is the fifth level of perceptual processing.

Level 5 processes may be distinguished from the preceding ones, therefore, on the basis of the criterion of active or attentive mental manipulation. This stage of visual processing consists of active cognitive manipulations that are carried out subsequent to the more immediate response mediated by the earlier processing levels. Level 5 visual processes may be divided into the following subcategories: (1) acquistion and attention; (2) classification; (3) decision-making; (4) spatial thinking; (5) storage and retrieval.

In brief, then, this is the skeleton of a taxonomy of explanatory process *theories* of visual perception. Table 1 also indicates some of the essential and salient aspects of the taxonomic level theory proposed here. One major dichotomy in this classification system is between the more or less immediate responses of Levels 0, 1, 2, 3, and 4 and the subsequent responses of Level 5 requiring some sort of active mental manipulation by the perceiver. In addition, a second major dichotomy can be discerned between Levels 0, 1, 2, and 3, where it seems likely that a high degree of dimensional isomorphism is maintained between the stimulus and its internal representation, and Levels 4, and 5 that are more likely to be encoded by symbolic mechanisms. A third dichotomy exists between the neuroreductive levels (1 and 2) and the nonneuroreductive ones (3, 4, and 5).

Now, having described the basic ideas behind my taxonomy, its structure, and the level at which I believe the present work falls, I can return to the specific matters at hand. The next section briefly reviews some of the work behind the development of an autocorrelation theory of two dimensional form detection in order that the origins of the present work be understood.

EARLIER WORK IN TWO DIMENSIONAL FORM DETECTION

My general approach (as described in Uttal, 1975) to the problem of two dimensional dotted form detection has been to carry out a series of psychophysical experiments in which sets of dotted stimuli were systematically varied along dimensions that characterized some attribute of form. The effect of these variations was measured by a detection task in which the stimulus pattern was degraded by embedding it in an additional (and variable) number of masking dots distributed in a single two dimensional image. An example of such a two dimensional stimulus set is shown in Fig. 3. The percentage of stimuli that were correctly detected in a two-alternative, forced-choice, computer-controlled tachistoscopic procedure made up the relevant psychophysical data base. This psychophysical data base was then compared to the results of a computer simulation model based upon an autocorrelation transformation that operated on simulated samples of the stimuli. The autocorrelation model was based on the following equation:

$$A(\Delta x, \Delta y) = \int\int f(x,y) \cdot f(x + \Delta x, y + \Delta y) dy dx \qquad \text{(Eq. 1)}$$

where Δx and Δy are shifts in the positions of the points of a stimulus pattern $f(x,y)$. (However, it was implemented in a discrete approximation to this equation.) A family of $A(\Delta x, \Delta y)$ values must be computed for all possible Δx and Δy combinations to fill the autocorrelation space. A sample of two simulated stimuli that can serve as inputs to the autocorrelation processor and two photographs of the computer plot of their discrete autocorrelated outputs are shown in Fig. 4. The first plate in this figure shows a straight dotted line stimulus and its autocorrelation. The second plate shows the same dotted line embedded in random noise dots. In the second plate, the peaks in the autocorrelation space most closely associated with the straight line of dots are higher than the other peaks. This is a clue of how this mechanism might be used to discriminate a periodic line of dots from random noise dots—form has been converted into amplitude and the highest peaks are associated with the original form. Of course, it is not this simple for other nonlinear forms, but similar relative amplitude transformational cues may also apply in such cases.

The autocorrelational space is made up of a number of peaks distributed in the $\Delta x, \Delta y$ space. By applying the following empirical expression:

$$F_m = \frac{\sum_{n=1}^{N} \sum_{i=1}^{I} (A_n \cdot A_i)/D}{N} ; (n \neq i) \qquad \text{(Eq. 2)}$$

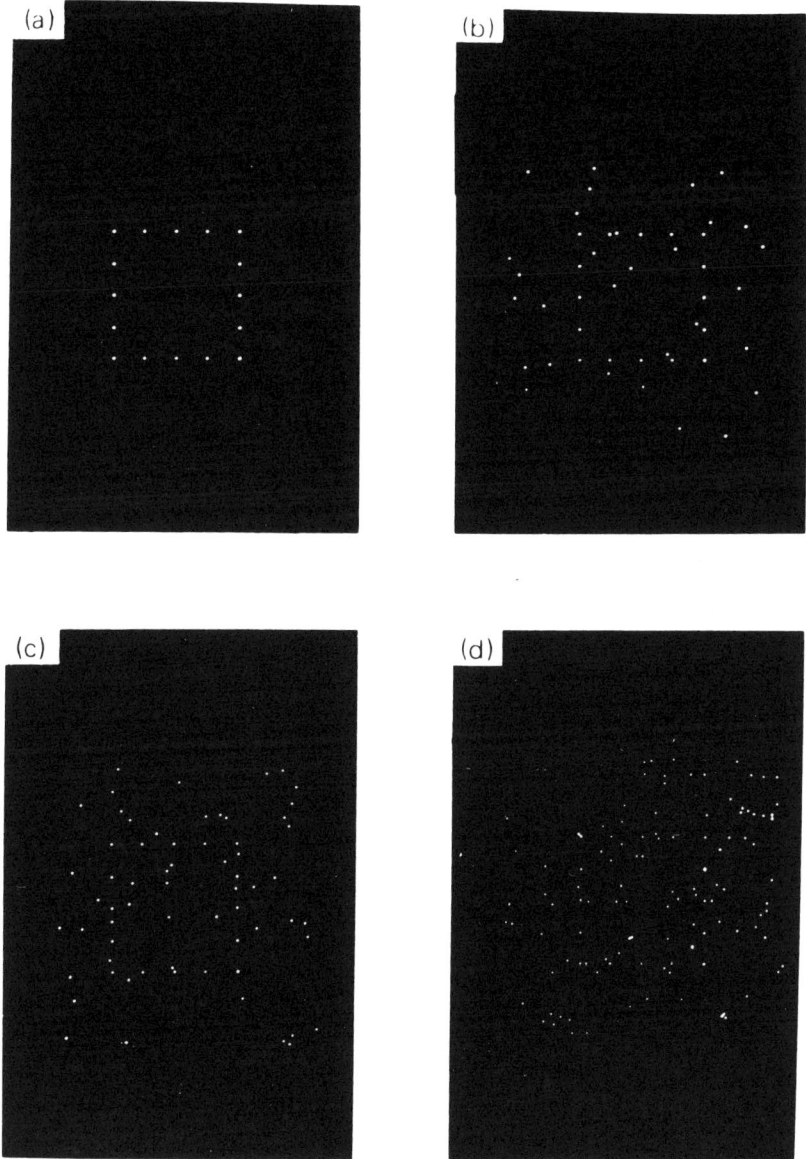

FIG. 3. A dotted square presented in four different levels of random dotted noise. Stimulus displays had the appearance of one of these in each presentation in the earlier two dimensional studies: (a) no masking dots, (b) 30 masking dots, (c) 50 masking dots, and (d) 100 masking dots. Note the progressive decline in the detectability of the target square as the number of masking dots increases. (From Uttal, 1975.)

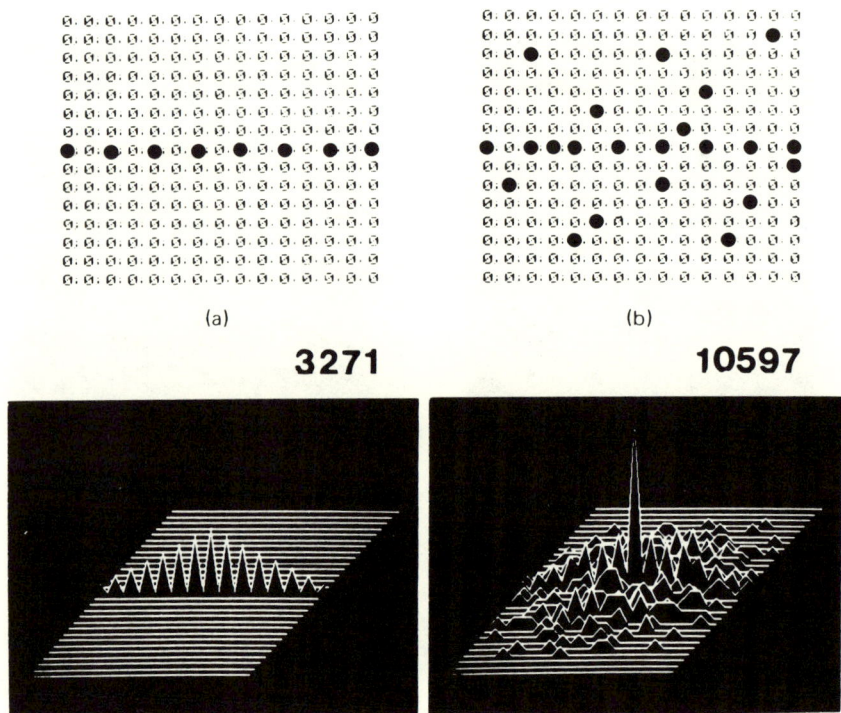

FIG. 4. Sample autocorrelation plots showing (a) the autocorrelation of an eight-dot straight line, and (b) the autocorrelation of an eight-dot straight line mixed with 14 masking dots. Each autocorrelation plot is composed of three items: the simulated stimulus pattern, the graphic display of the autocorrelation space, and a number. The number is a figure of merit calculated as described in the text. Note that in (b) the peaks that are mainly the result of autocorrelating the straight line of dots are higher than the peaks that are mainly the result of random noise. This suggests a means by which regular patterns can be extracted from noisy backgrounds based on the amplitude discrimination of autocorrelogram peaks. (From Uttal, 1975.)

a single numerical "figure of merit" (F_m) had been generated for each autocorrelated stimulus pattern. In this expression A_i and A_n are the amplitudes of peaks taken pairwise, D is the pythagorean distance in the $\Delta x, \Delta y$ space between the two peaks, and N is the number of peaks. This purely arbitrary and ad hoc figure of merit turned out to be closely associated with the relative psychophysical detectability of the stimulus form.

The effect of variation of a number of different attributes of stimulus forms were evaluated in these two dimensional psychophysical experiments. Specifically, I considered the effects of each of the following attributes and found the results indicated for the following list of dimensions:

1. Dot numerosity—more dots, more detectable.
2. Line orientation—no effect.
3. Deformation of straight lines into curves and angles—more deformation, less detectable.
4. Colinear dot-spacing irregularity—more irregular, less detectable.
5. Transverse dot-spacing irregularity—more irregular, less detectable.
6. Missing parts in triangles—sides were more important than corners.
7. Polygonal orientation—no effect.
8. Distortions of squares into parallelograms—more distortion, less detectable.
9. Organized straight line patterns versus "pick up stix" patterns composed of the same lines—more organized, more detectable.
10. Distortions of squares and triangles by misplacing one or more corners—more distortion, less detectable.
11. Figural goodness—no effect.

The order of detectability of the forms in each of the psychophysical experiments was compared with the order of the figures of merit from the autocorrelation evaluation of the simulation. In almost every case, the two rank orders were in agreement. There were, however, some discrepancies between the two rankings. Some forms producing differences in the figure of merit in the simulation had no comparable differences in psychophysical performance. Furthermore, while the figure of merit for forms that varied in "figural goodness" were in substantial agreement with the psychophysical data, there were some particular cases in which reversals of order appeared. These discrepancies seemed to be mainly due to a lack of sensitivity on the part of the autocorrelation model to forms that possessed preponderantly diagonal arrangements of the constituent dots. All of these discrepancies between theory and psychophysical findings are believed to be due to deficiencies in the formulation of the empirical figure of merit expression.

This then is the work which led to the present study. However, this new line of research did not spring into being de novo. Therefore, I now review the history of research and thought on form perception to more realistically embed this work among its intellectual precursors.

A BRIEF HISTORY

Visual form perception has been of interest to philosophers, natural philosophers, and modern scientists in turn for millenia. The history of speculation about the visual processing of form dates back to the very beginnings of classical Greek, Egyptian, and Chinese thought. Sometimes, the problem of perception was considered to be merely a minor waystation on the road to understanding optical (i.e., physical) phenomena, but more often than not interest in optics was itself generated by a desire to understand the fundamental nature of visual phenomena or to achieve the practical goal of treating eye diseases. The Egyptians were practical visual scientists prescribing cures for ophthalmological problems perhaps as long ago as 2000 B.C. Copies of early dynasty papyri prescribing treatments for eye diseases were already antiquities by the 18th Dynasty (c. 1500 B.C.).

Ophthalmological practice in Egypt preceded concern with visual theory, however, by over a millenium, and the Greeks, as they were in so many other instances, were probably the first to speculate about the psychological aspects of the visual process itself. Plato (428?–347 B.C.) believed that the eye projected a "fiery emanation" out to external objects. There the "fire" of the stimulus form and that of the eye "coallesced" and "sensations were thus conveyed to the mind." Though such a theory may sound quaint to us these days with our current knowledge of the physics of light, in fact the "fire" from the eye (obviously reflected light) was (and is) an observable datum and thus Plato's approach was not inconsistent with the limited knowledge of the visual process available during his time.

It remained for Aristotle (384–322 B.C.), as in so many other important instances, to provide the antithesis of the Platonic theory of ocular emanations. Aristotle was probably the first to suggest the rudiments of what we now believe to be the case, namely that vision resulted when something emanated *from* an object and was transmitted to and then absorbed by the eye. No matter that Aristotle also believed that the transmission of light took no appreciable time (until the last few years, this discrepancy with modern physical knowledge made little difference); no matter that he believed that light was transmitted along a transparent medium or ether (it took more than two thousand years to get this idea out of our scientific systems); and no matter that he believed that the mental experience—the sensation itself— was localized in the eye (an error that sometimes seems to be implicitly made by many modern day perceptual theoreticians in a much less forgivable manner). No matter, indeed! Aristotle still laid the foundation of all modern theories of vision and spelled out the details of visual science in a way that ultimately allowed specific ideas and hypotheses to be tested and criticized.

In spite of subsequent backsliding by later Arabic and Greek visual scientists to Platonic emanations, the idea of transmission of something to the eye from an object (rather than the reverse) is the basis of the modern concept of the visual process. It should be noted that Aristotle's ideas, however, did not immediately become the accepted theory. Indeed, for almost a thousand more years the Platonic idea of ocular emanations dominated thinking with great debates occurring between different versions of this fundamentally incorrect theory rather than between the Aristotelian and Platonic hypotheses.

It was neither Plato nor Aristotle, however, who linked vision and geometry, but rather Euclid, the great mathematician, in a book entitled *Optica,* less well known work than his *Elements,* but also dated about 300 B.C. If the study of form in the modern sense had any single starting point, this was it. Euclid was a Platonist with regard to the emanations of light from the eye, but the seven postulates on which this work is based are not only the foundation of geometrical optics but of form perception per se. For example, one of his postulates asserts what we would now refer to as the law of the visual angle or of retinal size (As quoted in Lindberg, 1976). "The things seen under a larger angle appear larger, those under a smaller angle appear smaller, and those under equal angle appear equal. (p. 12)"

The important point in the present context is that this postulate is an expression of *appearances.* It is a psychophysical statement and although we now know that it is not totally accurate (size constancy can make things look much more alike than Euclid implies in this strict geometrical rule) it is a fair generalization of one aspect of form perception. If we modern form perceptionists are to look for our most ancient intellectual roots, we might well find them in Euclid's *Optica.*

In spite of his enormous contribution linking vision and geometry, Euclid's postulates still include a conceptual obstacle to progress—Platonic emanation theory. It was not until about 1000 A.D. that empirical data and an emerging appreciation of the true physics of light began to overcome the popularity of the ocular emanation theories and the Aristotelian concept of signals moving to the eye from the object became widely accepted. It was the medieval Arab scientist Alhazen (965–1039) who was the spearhead of the revival of a neoaristotelian theory of vision.

The list of distinguished philosophers and scientists involved in theorizing about the visual process prior to the renaissance includes some notable personalities: In addition to Plato, Aristotle, Euclid, and Alhazen, we encounter such luminaries as Alcmaeon (500?–450? B.C.), Democritus (460–370 B.C.), Empedocles (?–444 B.C.), Lucretius (99–55 B.C.), Galen (129–1198), Pliny (23–79), Al-Kindi (?–870), Hunanin (?–877), Avicenna (980–1037), Averroes (1126–1198), Roger Bacon (1214?–1292) and Robert Grosseteste (1168–1253). These are only a few of the names that make the list of prerenaissance visual theoreticians almost synonymous with that era's great intellects. The reader interested in a more detailed history of early visual theory can be directed to no more thoughtful and comprehensive source than David Lindberg's (1976) fine book, my guide for the preceding discussion.

About 1000 A.D. the main stream of inquiry into visual theory changed direction. Prior to the medieval times, as I have noted, the great issue had been the battle between the Aristotelian concept that something made its way from the object to the eye and the ocular emanation theories championed by Plato, Euclid, and Galen among others. With the ascendency of the Aristotelian model, under the intellectual leadership of the Arab scholars Alhazen and Avicenna in particular, visual scientists began to express interest in two quite different visual issues. First, there was a great increase in anatomical studies, particularly in Arab lands where scholarship and science were preserved during the dark years of late medieval Europe. Second, there was a flourishing of Euclid's perceptual and geometric synthesis. The geometrical optics of image formation in the eye merged with the new appreciation of perspective in art to define a field of research and scholarship that would have been incomprehensible to the prerenaissance visual scientists. Tricks of form perception based on the new ideas of perspective proposed by Leon Battista Alberti (1404–72) formed the basis of new art forms, the trompe l'oeil paintings, and even more interesting the wood inlays or "Intarsia" recently described by Tormey and Tormey (1982). Near the turn of the 17th century the great astronomer Johann Kepler (1571–1630) essentially solved the general problem of the optics of the retinal image for all times. Of course not all the details of his model were correct, but the major foundations of modern geometrical optical theory were established and Platonic emanations permanently laid to rest.

The important fact in the context of the present discussion is that the relative contributions to perception of the optics of space and the eye, on the one hand, and the neural system, on the other, were becoming apparent. Some distortions in form were due to optics! Some were due to the transformation carried out by the nervous system! What we see, it was becoming appreciated, is a joint function of physics and biology!

However, at this time something else was stirring that was to be of at least equivalent importance for visual perception research. Among the other great intellectual revolutions of the 15th century, scholars were beginning to consider the human being from quite a different point of view than had their predecessors. The day of scholastic theology based on Augustinian ideas placing "rightness of will" and "divine grace" ahead of "intellectualism" and "experimentation" was waning. Both Thomas Hobbes (1588–1679) and René Descartes (1596–1650), enlightened by advances in commerce, industry, technology, and science, were championing an idea that had been neglected for a millenium and a half—the mind (read that word as soul, if you wish) of man was a legitimate target for scientific inquiry!

Modern psychology, visual and otherwise, dates from this time—the 17th century—more than any other. Despite the residual theology in Descartes' concept of mind, his theories are essentially naturalistic and biological. They invoke supernatural entities only in passing. Though a mind-body dualist, Descartes did accept the notion that the problems of vision could be examined scientifically. Descartes spoke of the anatomy and the physiology of the eye in a way that is totally compatible with the thoughts of modern scholars in the field. If one substitutes the words perceptual awareness, mind, attention, or cognition for soul—and ignores the pineal gland, Descartes' putative seat of interaction between the mind and the body—one is left with a centralist theory of sensation asserting that seeing occurs as a result of brain (as opposed to receptor) activity that is not too distant in its fundamental concepts from current theory. The essential core of a philosophy invoking some kind of representational coding of visual images in a materialistic substrate is just as evident in Descartes' writing as in any contemporary work. Descartes distinguished between phenomenal and physical space in a manner that led easily to the idea of psychoneural equivalence (a monistic idea) even though he was not willing to accept such a solution to the mind-body problem himself.

The role of visual perception in mental processes was also a predominant topic of concern among the British empiricists. All knowledge, said John Locke (1632–1704), Hume (1711–1776), and others of their genre, is gained through the senses. Thus the centerpiece of what was at the time the closest approximation to modern theoretical psychology was none other than a set of facts and theories of visual information processing. Many of the issues of what those philosophers called *epistemology* turn out to be nothing less than meagerly disguised queries concerning the visual process. How do we perceive shapes? How do we determine size? How do we determine magnitude? Is space directly or indirectly perceived? Is vision innate or learned? During these rich years these predominantly visual questions were the foundation themes of the empiricists' philosophical inquiry and the crux of their differences with the rationalists. So many of the fundamental issues—the mind-body problem, the nature of external reality, and the general epistemological issue of how we gain knowledge—all converged onto questions dealing with the visual processes. One question in particular—How do we see forms?—was formulated then, and obviously still interests many of us today.

The culmination of the empiricist line of inquiry may be considered to be Bishop George Berkeley's (1685–1783) "*Essay Towards A New Theory of Vision*" (Berkeley, 1709). Berkeley emphasized one issue in particular, that if not entirely novel, was clearly new in attracting so much attention, and that remains of interest up to the present time. Berkeley distinguished between *mediate* visual stimuli (such as the perception of depth) that he believed required some indirect evaluation to be perceived and those that seemed to be *immediate* and innate (such as the width or color of an object). But this is an often misunderstood part of his theory. "Immediate" and "mediate" are attributes of the stimulus and Berkeley asserted that there is no difference in the manner in which they are perceptually processed. Both had to be interpreted to be perceived according to his theoretical orientation.

So far so good, nothing yet said differs greatly from modern thinking on the matter. However, Berkeley went on to assert further that both kinds of attributes of the stimulus (mediate and immediate) are actually defined in terms of the perceiving process and cannot exist without the perceiver. It is this immaterialist or idealist philosophy that is generally not acceptable to modern science, and that has distracted us from appreciating the many fundamental truths in Berkeley's philosophy of vision. My point is that indirect (mediate) and direct (immediate) dimensions of perception can be just as realistic and materialistic (in a process sense) as are physical objects themselves.

Berkeley went on to propose specifically that we must *learn* to see the mediated percepts, and in the case of depth, visual experience has to be linked with tactual experience for a coherent perception to occur. It is this hypothesis, that we must *learn* to see some things, that has led to much recent research in developmental perceptual psychology. This epistemological speculation also underlies the continued interest in the famous inverted vision experiments of Stratton (1896, 1897), Köhler (1951), and Snyder and Pronko (1952) and the fortuitous studies of individuals who regained their sight after prolonged blindness in their youth. Similarly, Berkeley's distinction between mediate and immediate stimulus dimensions permeates much of our thinking about the perception of visual space. Many contemporary visual scientists still seem to believe that depth is different in some fundamental way than width or height. I believe this is an erroneous extrapolation of Berkeley's work, but it does illustrate the persistence of his teaching even in the light of contradictory evidence.

Debates concerning the differences between sensation and perception, immediate and mediate dimensions, the possibility that some visual skills have to be learned while some are innate, and the distinction between depth (Z) and the other two dimensions (X, Y) are thus still active today. As we shall see, the idea that some dimensions are more direct than others is not supported by the findings I report in this volume. All dimensions of visual experience seem to be extracted from transformational invariances and constructed according to certain symbolic rules regardless of whether they are coincidentally isomorphic to retinal maps or not. According to the data I shall report later in this book nothing is immediate. As I have noted, this conclusion is consistent with Berkeley's ideas that both immediate and mediate stimulus dimension have to be similarly processed to be perceived but, of course, from a materialist's rather than an immaterialist's point of view.

Another aberrant idea that has persisted in visual theory involves the role of eye movements in the perception of visual form. From the time of Etienne de Condillac (1715–1780) to the recent past (as evidenced by Donald Hebb's theory) it has been suggested that we see forms as a result of successive fixations on the component features of stimulus. There is no question that complex stimuli are examined by moving the eyes from point to point with great vigor. However, there is also no question that form recognition is no less than superb even in stroboscopic or tachistoscopic illuminations far too brief to allow the involvement of eye movements. Because of this definitive disproof of any significant role of eye movement in form perception, I shall say no more of this archaic, though persistent, theoretical fallacy.

A critically important step in the history of modern theories of form vision occurred when experimental neurophysiology came into its own. Knowledge of the anatomy and physiology of the larger chunks of the brain became increasingly available in the eighteenth century. The *fact* that physical signals of some kind (representing or encoding the shape as well as the quality of stimuli) are conveyed from the receptors to the brain became universally accepted. Johannes Müller's (1801–1858) theory (Müller, 1848) of sensations was couched specifically in terms of the neural conduction of information from the retina to the brain. From this point in history on, visual theory was predominantly materialistic, monistic, and realistic, and Bishop Berkeley's earlier immaterialism was mainly relegated to the history books except in a few aberrant minority views. The issue of whether the material substrate of the perceiving mind is extended throughout the nervous system or localized in a particular nucleus, though still controversial, is a question framed in quite a different context than the one in which the debate between the materialists and the immaterialists of the preceding centuries was embedded.

Müller and his contemporaries placed vision once and for all among the other brain processes. The idea that the activity of neurons in particular places might be selectively representative of particular percepts was an important new concatenation of ideas. By the time of Ernst Mach (1838-1916) visual perception was being analyzed in terms of *neural networks* in a way that hardly differs from the tone of today's theorizing. The controversies between the "feature creatures" and the "spatial frequency freaks" (two facetious terms I shall subsequently define) in perceptual psychobiology fall well within this materialist-reductionistic rubric.

Another important concept concerning form perception that persists in today's thinking was introduced by Thomas Reid (1710–1796), Christian von Ehrenfels (1859–1932), Ernst Mach (1838–1916), and their successors, the Gestalt psychologists. All of these scholars emphasized the global organization of the patterns, an approach in sharp opposition to the elementalism expressed by the Empiricists Locke, Hume, Berkeley, and the Mills. For reasons to which I have already alluded, the founding Gestaltists, Max Wertheimer (1880–1943), Kurt Koffka (1886–1941), and Wolfgang Köhler (1887–1967), concentrated their empirical efforts on a set of demonstrations rather than a series of systematic parametric experiments. Nevertheless, they were able to show that some forms were "seen" better than others and to emphasize the fact that how forms are perceived depends more on the organization of the form than it did on the parts of which it is constructed. Despite the failure of their theoretical explanations, this is a conclusion towards which my data have also inexorably driven me.

Of course, the wholistic Gestalt approach has had its ups and downs. The dominant theme of elementalism in current thinking has been stimulated by neurophysiological and computer technologies. But, it is clear that despite these powerful conceptual forces, a new interpretation of wholism is resurgent. Consider, for example, the strongly Gestaltist tone of the recent work of W. R. Garner (e.g., Garner, 1974; Garner & Clement, 1963), or of J. R. Pomerantz (e.g., Pomerantz, 1977). Obviously the wholistic idea is still with us in spite of the compelling intellectual force exerted by the discovery of feature detecting neurons and the development of equally elementalistic computer instructions. Indeed, I find this neogestaltist approach far more congenial than I would have thought 20 years ago and believe the content of the research I present here is a supportive argument for the very important role played by wholistic perceptual processing.

It must be acknowledged, however, that in spite of these outposts of wholism, recent theories of form perception have in the main tended to be elementalistic and neuroreductionistic in both concept and language. They speak either of single cells that are selectively sensitive to local trigger features (i.e., certain spatial-temporal attributes) of a stimulus form (the belief structure of the "feature creatures") or, even more recently, of channels selectively sensitive to the spatial Fourier components of two dimensional stimulus forms (the belief structure of the "spatial frequency freaks").

Briefly, let's now review the mathematical aspects, as opposed to the anatomical ones, of spatial frequency channel theories of form perception. Stripped of it's excess physiological assumptions, the important contribution made by Campbell and Robson (1968) with their introduction of Fourier-type ideas into visual science cannot be denied and should not be underestimated. Fourier analysis is a superb way of describing stimuli and responses in a quantitative manner. Nevertheless, one must not overlook the fact that the neural and mathematical premises are separable and that the analytical mathematics may be valid and useful without validating the neurophysiological assumptions. Fourier's theorem, it must be remembered, asserts that *any* form can be mathematically analyzed into a series of orthogonal functions whether or not that form originally was created by a mechanism implementing those functions. Thus, even though the anatomical channels may be nonexistent, analysis of stimuli, processing mechanisms, or responses utilizing a two dimensional spatial frequency has been, and undoubtedly will continue to be, as useful as in other areas.

Closely associated (in fact in some instances intertransformable) with Fourier analyses are some correlational methods that also model visual perception in one way or another. These methods are collectively specified by the term *convolution integrals* and are expressed as the integral of the product of the observed function and some standard function such as pulse, a sine wave, or even a delayed version of the observed function itself. In other terms a convolution ($f_1 * f_2$) is represented by the expression:

$$f_1 * f_2 = \iint f_1(u,v) f_2(x-u, y-v) \, du \, dv \qquad \text{(Eq. 3)}$$

where f_1 is the observed function and f_2 is the standard function. If f_2 is a repetitive pulse, this expression defines averaging; if f_2 is a series of sinusoids, this expression defines Fourier analysis; if f_2 is a shifted version of f_1, this expression defines autocorrelation; if f_2 is any other function, this expression defines cross correlation. Terry Caelli provides a useful service in a recent book (Caelli, 1981) by comprehensively reviewing this kind of mathematical modeling.

The main point I wish to make here is the conceptual similarity of what may seem initially quite distinct approaches. The convolution rubric includes autocorrelation, cross correlation, averaging, power spectrum, and Fourier analyses. Indeed many of these methods turn out to be formally equivalent to each other. The different methods do, however, imply different physical implementations within the nervous system and it is in this regard that my theoretical orientation mainly differs from that of the "spatial frequency freaks."

The other main contemporary approach tackles the problem of modeling visual form perception in terms of *networks* of discrete neurons. This approach is quite distinct both from the convolutional mathematics (a form of analysis that is fundamentally conceptualized in terms of continuous components) and the single cell theories. The network approach, like the single cell theory, deals with discrete and discontinuous entitites but emphasizes their interaction rather than their individual function. The classic network theory stressing lateral inhibitory interaction was made famous by Hartline, Ratliff, and their coworkers (e.g., Hartline & Ratliff, 1957; 1958) and exemplified more recently by the work of Grossberg (1978) and Anderson, Silverstein, Ritz, and Jones (1977). The statistics of discrete cellular functions and intercellular interactions are the processes stressed by these theoreticians.

I have criticized these single cell, local feature, Fourier channel, and network neuroreductionist approaches to the problems of form recognition elsewhere (Uttal, 1981) and I shall not clutter this small volume by repeating those arguments here. It is sufficient for me to note that an increasingly large number of perceptual scientists are coming to appreciate that the logical foundations of both the Fourier channel and the single cell theories of molar form perception leave much to be desired. To this bald assertion I would only add that the data obtained in cellular physiology experiments interacted (and continues to interact) synergistically with the existing nonphysiological, but equally elementialistic, tradition in psychology (as well as with the emerging appreciation of the logical nature of modern digital computers) to produce a continuing theoretical bias towards local features rather than global form. Jim Pomerantz (1978) has criticized this point of view in a way with which I completely agree.

> The principal difficulty of feature-analytic theories of perception, which the Gestalt psychologists repeatedly emphasized, remains: namely, a pattern is more than a listing of its component parts. A complex stimulus is not simply a collection of angles any more than it is merely a collection of lines. Rather, the structural relations among these angles can be critical in differentiating between different shapes, and the human visual system is clearly sensitive to these relations. [p. 227]

Where does one turn then for insight and understanding of how we see forms if the neuroreductionistic and their local-feature-theory fellow travellers are deemed to be inadequate? I believe that descriptive mathematical models, stripped of their excess and separable neurophysiological baggage, provide the best chance of progress in this field. However, it must be understood that the autocorrelational approach I am championing here is not a discrete neuronal network model in the tradition pioneered by Pitts and McCulloch (1947) and Rosenblatt (1963). The neural networks involved in the processes of interest in this context are much too complicated for that approach to succeed. Indeed, I have argued elsewhere (Uttal, 1981) that most interesting perceptual phenomena are far beyond any conceivable elementalistic neuroreductionism of that genre. Rather, the kind of model that I feel is most likely to be fertile and valid in the future is one in which the functional, operational, and procedural aspects of the *process* (as opposed to the neuron or neuron net) are modeled and evaluated. The alternative reductionistic approach emphasizing realistic neuron-like elements, more often than not, turns out to be based on nothing more than a facile metaphor arising from a loose analogy between electrophysiological findings and the phenomenology of the perceptual process itself.

Process models exist today, but their functional premises are often unnecessarily confounded with extraneous neurophysiological premises. In fact, the neurophysiological or implementation premises are nearly always independent of the process in any perceptual theory and can usually be filtered out without damage to the essence of the model. As one especially important example, consider Hoffman's (1966, 1978) mathematically elegant theory based on the mathematical entity known as the *Lie group*. The Lie group is a formal means of dealing with vector fields and their transformations. Lie was a Norwegian mathematician who discovered a criterion indicating whether or not a differential equation was solvable. That criterion was the invariance of a solution of the differential equation when it (the solution) was transformed in certain ways. Lie pointed out that one need not be able to produce the solution to determine if it is so invariant. The criterion set of invariant transformations constitutes a group under certain conditions. For example, if two successive rotations produce a form that is the same as that produced by a single rotation of the form, then the two transformations are invariant and belong to a Lie group.

I cannot go any deeper into the obstruse mathematics of Lie groups, but the point made by Hoffman is that this type of analysis can be used to examine the effects of the transformations imposed by the nervous system on stimulus information. In particular, the spatial pattern defined by the distal stimulus can be treated as a vector field in the same manner as the field of flow in a sheet of fluid. Using this model Hoffman has attempted to model visual constancies and form memory (Hoffman, 1978) as well as Piagetian theories of visual development (Hoffman, 1976).

Hoffman also uses modern neurophysiological data (feature selective single cells) as the primitives of his vector field analysis, but as I noted previously, it appears to me that this is both superfluous and unnecessary. The mathematical and neural assumptions are separable. The transformational mathematics stands on its own and could survive even the total negation of the specific physiological premises he invokes. Of course, it is nice if the two domains are consistent; on the other hand, analogic consistency between the neural and vector field models does not validate either one or the other.

The important thing that Hoffman has contributed is a field type theory of visual processes that provides a means by which we can begin to consider how the action of individual elements (whether they be specifically neuronal or any other discrete functions) could be transformed into molar effects. *This still unsolved perplexity—the conversion of the discrete and local into the continuous and global—remains the principal problem in perceptual psychobiology.* It is not too much of an exaggeration to say that it is among the most challenging problems in human intellectual history.

But, it is not the only question—there are others, and this brings me to my next task. I now list what I believe are the major perplexities motivating perceptual research today.

1. What is the relationship between responses in the discrete neuronal substrate and the molar perceptual response?
2. Are visual percepts learned or innate?
3. Are some dimensions of visual stimuli and perception primary and others derived?
4. Do we see in a way that depends on overall forms or do we see by processing local features?
5. Is form perception a pheripherally or centrally mediated process?
6. What are the neural codes used by, and the anatomy of, the visual transmission pathways?
7. How do we differentiate between figures and ground, between signal and noise, or between different areas of a complex scene?
8. What is the geometry of visual as opposed to physical space?
9. What is the adaptive utility of various visual processes?
10. How do we organize stimulus forms that have no unique organization of their own?
11. How do we synthesize percepts from stimuli that only suggest the perceptual outcome?
12. Contrary to 11, how do we analyze complex scenes into perceived components?
13. How are percepts represented internally?
14. And, finally, the specific attribute question—what attributes of a form determine how it will be perceived?

The empirical research that I will present to you during the course of these lectures is intended to attack some of these issues in a manner specific enough to produce empirical rather than only speculative answers. As I discuss the mundane practical details of my experiments and their outcomes, I hope it is not forgotten that my goal is, in fact, to contribute at least a little towards answering these fundamental questions. My coworkers and I are not carrying out experiments for their own sake. We are carrying out these experiments in an attempt to provide concrete answers to some of these persistent questions of visual science. Of course, our work is not germane to all of these issues—I really don't think that these experiments have much to say about the relationship between the brain and the mind. They, like all other psychophysical experiments, are indeterminate with regard to internal neurophysiological mechanisms. Nor do they speak to the degree of innateness of visual perception—we have not made any effort to study the development of those processes. Nevertheless, I believe they do add something to our knowledge about the wholistic-elementalistic dichotomy, to our understanding of the issue of globality versus discreteness, and to the primary versus derived controversies. Of primary interest, however, is what they have to say concerning the specific attribute problem. If a little light is cast on these issues, our efforts will have been satisfactorily spent. So, enough of this history and philosophy, and on to technical detail.

2 The Experimental Paradigm

However important, the ambitious theoretical and epistemological questions described in the previous chapter must be concretized in the form of specific experimental procedures if we are to make any progress towards their solution. The epistemological puzzles "How do we gain knowledge from the external world?" and "How do we see forms?" are necessarily translated in the remainder of this book, therefore, into the very specific question: *What are the effects of various manipulations of visual form on an observer's detection of a dotted signal embedded in dotted noise in three dimensional space?* This prosaic empirical translation of the esoteric questions posed in the previous chapter is not framed in as awesome or as grand a vocabulary, but in fact it is aimed at exactly the same issues as the grand epistemological puzzles. The empirical procedures and results dominating the discussion in this chapter are, however, only vehicles used to approach the grand puzzles; they are themselves not things of great importance, only conveniences and curiosities! The dotted form detection task, in other words, is used in the present studies in the same way as the fruit fly is used in genetics research—as an abstraction, an idealization, a particularization, and a manipulable version of the unmanageable generalization implicit in the broadly and vaguely defined general puzzle. I am, frankly, interested in these data and these experiments only to the extent that they provide information about form perception in general.

The experimental paradigm is also a simplification and abstraction of the total multilevel process that leads to visual perception. I ask—what happens to detectability when you change the spatio-temporal properties of a dotted form? I remind you that this is a Level 3 problem in the jargon of my taxonomy. How exactly we go about asking this question is the topic of this chapter.

GENERAL PROCEDURE

All of the experiments on dotted signal detection I report here are carried out using a two alternative, forced choice, detection paradigm. The percentage of the total number of trials in which the stimulus forms are correctly detected is the dependent measure of performance. Stimulus forms to be detected are constructed of one or more dots and are prearranged by the experimenter into a sequence varying along some more or less well defined dimension. John Brogan, a mathematician-programmer working with me, has developed some extremely powerful automatic aides for preparing files of ordered stimulus forms. Using a graphic input device (a Houston Instrument digitizing pad), we are now able to create prototypical, dotted stimuli (e.g., a single repetitively flashing dot, a sequentially presented series of dots arranged in a straight or curved line, a dot outlined area, or a random array of dots constrained to an area in a plane) in two dimensional space and then transform them into either two or three dimensional forms by means of appropriate programmed algorithms. These transformed stimulus forms are then stored in a disc storage file, to be called later by the main experimental control program for random presentation.

In these experiments, dotted stimulus forms are typically hidden in varying numbers of randomly placed masking dots. These formless constellations are referred to as *visual noise*. The organized stimulus forms are interspersed both temporally and spatially among these random masking dots. The major effect of variations in the number of masking dots is to alter the detectability of the stimulus form; the greater the number of masking dots, the less detectable the stimulus forms. In some of the experiments I describe in these lectures the visual noise dots are distributed throughout an apparent cubical volume, in other experiments, they may be themselves constrained to a single plane.

Fig. 5 shows a dotted line stimulus form—a line consisting of seven dots—typical of those used in this study. This figure presents the form in four sample stereoscopic displays with progressively higher levels of visual noise present in each display. The observer's task is to report which of two sequential, one sec long, stereoscopic presentations contains the stimulus form. Each presentation displays a dichoptic pair of images that, when perceptually fused, creates the impression of a cubical volume in which the dots constituting the stimulus form and the random dotted visual noise appear at various times and positions depending on the design of the experiment. The right and left-eyed images are presented on the right and left halves of a split screen oscilloscope coated with a high speed P-15 phosphor. The observer views the two images through rotating prisms that are individually adjusted at the beginning of each session for comfortable convergence. A septum divides the two halves of the screen so that neither eye sees the field of view of the other eye. The perceptual result is the appearance of a highly realistic cubical volume in which the events and stimuli to be described occur. This cubical volume looks like a perfectly transparent region in space

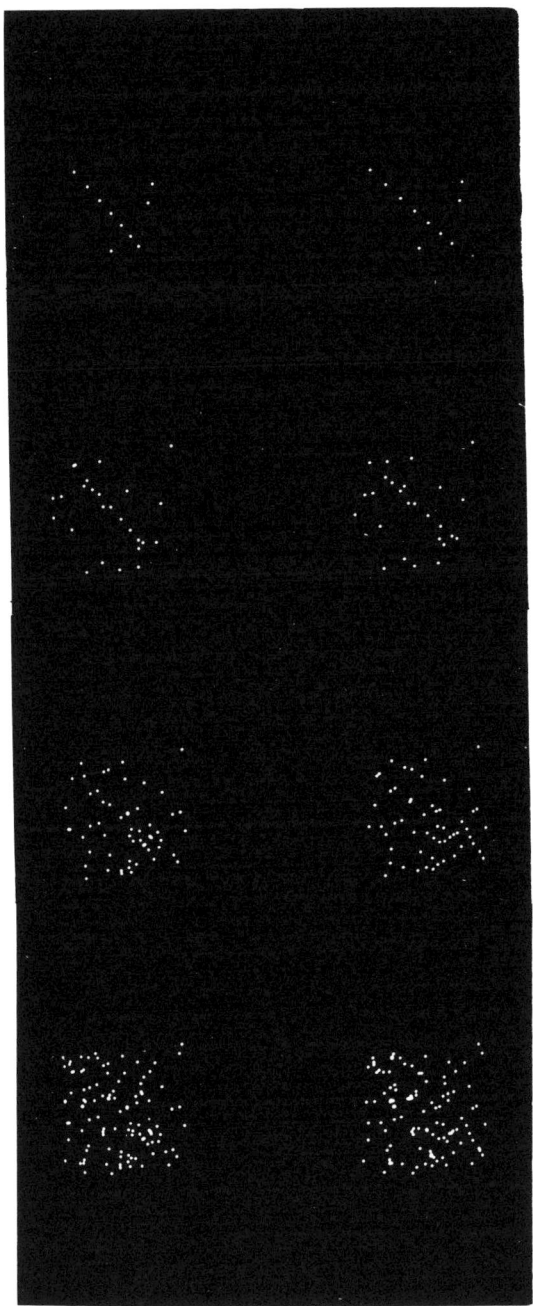

FIG. 5. Four sample stereoscopic dotted line stimulus forms in different levels of dynamic dotted visual noise. (A) 3 noise dots/sec; (B) 20 noise dots/sec; (C) 50 noise dots/sec; (D) 100 noise dots/sec. The noise dots and the stimulus form dots in the actual stimulus display may be distributed anywhere within the one second presentation duration. These still photographs obscure the dynamic quality of the display.

filled at various times with a varying number of point-like lights. In some cases the lights may come on and stay on for a one second epoch and in others they may simply flash once and disappear like briefly illuminated snowflakes. Some of these point-like lights may be arranged in an orderly way; others may be randomly distributed in the cubical volume.

An experimental *trial* consists of two *presentations;* either the first or the second presentation contains a *stimulus form* (e.g., a repetitively flashing dot, a line of seven dots, or a shaped plane of dots) plus dotted *visual noise*. The other presentation contains exactly the same noise pattern, but instead of the stimulus form, an additional number of randomly placed "dummy" dots. The number of dummy dots is equal to the number of dots in the stimulus form, and is limited in spatial extent to the maximum and minimum X, Y, and Z values of the dots of the stimulus form, or some other appropriate region of the apparent cubical space. Dummy dots are presented at the same time as the stimulus form dots would have occurred—timing information being transposed from the file specifying the dots of the stimulus form to the file specifying the dummy dots during the preliminary processing prior to each trial. In this manner, both presentations contain exactly the same number of dots and have exactly the same temporal patterns. In some of the more complex experiments the dummy dots may also have exactly the same X and Y coordinates as those of the stimulus form; the Z axis values alone are randomized. Thus, in this case, what had been dots organized in a plane (the stimulus form) becomes a random collection of the same number of dots (the dummy) in a volume with a cross section shape identical to that of the stimulus form.

The purpose of the dummy dots is to maintain the total number of dots, and thus the luminosity of the display, constant in both presentations. Therefore, the two sequential presentations are alike in all regards except one—the dummy dots do not contain the critical piece of information that is present in the stimulus form, namely organization or arrangement, the attribute that is the main target of these experiments.

It is important to remember, therefore, that spatial arrangement of the stimulus form dots constitutes the sole difference between the two alternative presentations. The observer's task is to specify in which of the two presentations the *organized* stimulus form (as opposed to the disorganized dummy dots) occurred, but there is no other cue available for the solution of this problem other than spatial arrangement itself. Everything else has been controlled and made equal in the two presentations.

It should also be appreciated that in some instances (experiments dealing with single flashing dots or dotted lines), there are monocular cues that allow the task to be performed with only one eye. In such cases, I have compared the detectability of form under monocular (one eye covered with a patch), binocular (both eyes viewing the same nondisparate stimulus), or dichoptic viewing (each eye viewing a stimulus that is disparate with the other eye's view). Differences in detectability between the three viewing conditions, as well as the differences due to form, tell us something about the visual processes involved in detecting forms in space.

The sequence of visible events in each trial is presented in a precise order under the control of a master computer program. First, a single fixation-convergence dot is illuminated for one second at the geometrical and stereoscopic center of the apparent cube. The purpose of this dot is to help the observer align his eyes so that the subsequent stimulus information is properly registered for stereoscopic viewing. The strong perception of a dot filled cube obtained in the various experiments indicates that this is a successful strategy in spite of the very brief exposure of the individual dots (only 50 microseconds elapse before the image fades to less than 1% of its initial luminance on the P15 phosphor used in our display oscilloscopes.)

Immediately following the display of the fixation-convergence dot, the first of the two alternative presentations mentioned above occurs. Each presentation typically lasts for 1 second (although other durations are used in some experiments) during which individual randomly positioned masking noise dots may either be serially presented at equal temporal intervals or repeatedly intensified to produce a stable (in time) array of randomly positioned dots for the entire second. Because of the persistence of the visual system's response, in the former condition the apparent cubical space appears to be dynamically filled with a varying number of twinkling dots in random position. I refer to this as the *dynamic* masking mode. The latter condition produces the snapshotlike appearance of a static array of dots. I refer to this as the *static* masking mode. Which type of visual noise is used is determined by the needs of the specific experiment. Similarly, the particular stimulus form chosen determines when, as well as where, constituent dots are plotted within the static or dynamic masking dots. The stimulus form may be either in the first or second presentation: The dummy dots will be in the other.

The first presentation is then followed by a one second period in which the solitary fixation-convergence dot is again presented. The second of the two presentations then occurs. Following the second presentation the screen remains dark until the observer responds by depressing one of two hand held pushbuttons indicating that he has "seen" a stimulus form in the first or second presentation. At that point, a "plus" or a "minus" indicating either a correct or incorrect choice is briefly flashed on the oscilloscope. The cycle then repeats. The observer is forced to make the choice. He cannot equivocate or qualify his answer. In this manner some control over individual differences in criterion level is achieved.

Given the widespread application of laboratory automation by psychologists, one not so novel aspect of these experiments is that they are all totally run by real time, on line microcomputers. The control program is initially loaded from the computer's disc memory into its working randomly addressable semiconductor memory at the beginning of each day by the experimenter. At this point the parameters for the session are set by the experimenter and the computer carries out certain initialization segments of the control program. Next, the observer signs on at the computer terminal and begins the experimental session by depressing either one of the two response buttons. At the end of fifty minutes the observer terminates the session by typing a code letter into the computer console. His performance is immediately analyzed by the computer and printed out along with identifying and timing information. Pooled data from several observers and/or conditions are subsequently analyzed by another more comprehensive data analysis program.

Use of this dot masking paradigm has certain advantages. First, we have control over the detectability of a form without varying the form or the intensity of its constituent dots. Dots also are roughly independent in their physiological effects on the retina since it is unlikely, even at the high dot densities we use, that a single receptor will be repeatedly stimulated. Since dots are known not to interact through lateral inhibitory interaction mechanisms, this independence is even greater than might have been thought. Most important of all, however, is the fact that dots have minimal attributes of their own. It is only by virtue of their spatiotemporal arrangements that they take on "meaningful" form.

OBSERVERS

In each of the experiments we report here, at least three, usually four, and often eight undergraduate students at the University of Michigan were used as paid observers for one academic term. Each was tested for normal stereoscopic vision with an anaglyphic screening procedure (Figure 8.1–2* from Julesz, 1971) and self reported normal or corrected refraction. From time to time observers, however, have been dissociated from the project after demonstrating adequate stereopsis with anaglyphs, but failing to display an adequate level of discrimination performance in the computer controlled task.[1]

The data reported here are from several groups of observers representing two sets of experiments carried out several years apart. Adequate replication of all of

---

[1]Earlier studies in the ISR Perception Laboratory had suggested that a large proportion of possible observers were stereoanomalous. This anecdotal evidence was supported by Richard's (1970) contention that approximately 30% of the population may be at least some degree deficient in stereoscopic perception. However, a follow-up study, carried out by Millicent Newhouse—an Ann Arbor Pioneer high school student who served as the ONR science apprentice in my laboratory in 1981–1982—has shown (Newhouse & Uttal, 1982) that actually only 1 in 103 randomly sampled Ss was totally stereodeficient when carefully tested with an anaglyphic screening procedure. (Two others who did not have binocular vision were, for obvious reasons, stereoblind.) Only six others displayed persistent one way stereo deficiencies. Patterson and Fox (1981) have also recently reported the same low level of stereoanomaly in the general population.

the older work has been carried out to assure that no significant difference in results occurred as a result of new procedures or equipment. (In the present report I describe only the new version of the instrumentation.) All observers are pretrained with unmasked versions of the stimulus forms for several days prior to the actual data collection sessions of each experiment.

APPARATUS

The stereoscopic stimuli in this experiment are generated by a hybrid computer system consisting of a Cromemco System 3 digital microcomputer and a subsystem of Optical Electronics, Inc. analog computer components. This hybrid computer approach circumvents one of the most difficult problems in the presentation of this kind of haploscopic stimuli. While it is not particularly time consuming to generate the tabular representation for any single dot or group of dots in a digital computer (X, Y, Z, and t coordinates can be generated by simple algorithms or from prestored information), the prompt construction of the actual real time analog signals required to control the split screen oscilloscopic display is a much more difficult programming task. This difficulty is exacerbated in the highly demanding submillisecond real time environment of the present study. The computer generated and stored X, Y, Z and t coordinates specifying the location in space and time in the apparent cubical space for each dot must be transformed into two sets of two-spatial-dimensional coordinates (X_L, Y_L, t for the left eye and X_R, Y_R, t for the right eye) with the proper disparity, perspective, and separation to project a haploscopic pair of images at the proper locations on the oscilloscope for the left and right eye respectively. Each pair of dots in the left-eye and right-eye images must be precisely positioned so that it can be processed by the visual system into the perceptual experience of a three dimensional space.[2] The problem is that the transformation from X, Y, Z, t to X_L, Y_L, t and X_R, Y_R, t involves extensive trigonometric calculations that would quickly overload the capacity of the modest-sized digital microcomputers used in these studies.

The analog subsystem (shown in Fig. 6) provides a means of finessing this digital processing overload difficulty. The trigonometric problem is solved by means of analog circuitry in real time whenever the signal voltages are required to plot a haploscopic pair of dots on the oscilloscope. It is only necessary to provide this subsystem with the three analog voltages representing the three-

---

[2]It is interesting to note that the transformation of the X, Y, Z, t internal representation in the computer to the X_L, Y_L, t and X_R, Y_R, t representation on the face of the oscilloscope is the inverse of what the visual system's conversion of the haploscopic images (X_L, Y_L, t and X_R, Y_R, t) into an illusion of a space filling volume. In neither case does a volume actually exist in physical three-space, however. Certainly in the computer and probably in the "mind," volumes are "represented" in what is best described as a symbolic code.

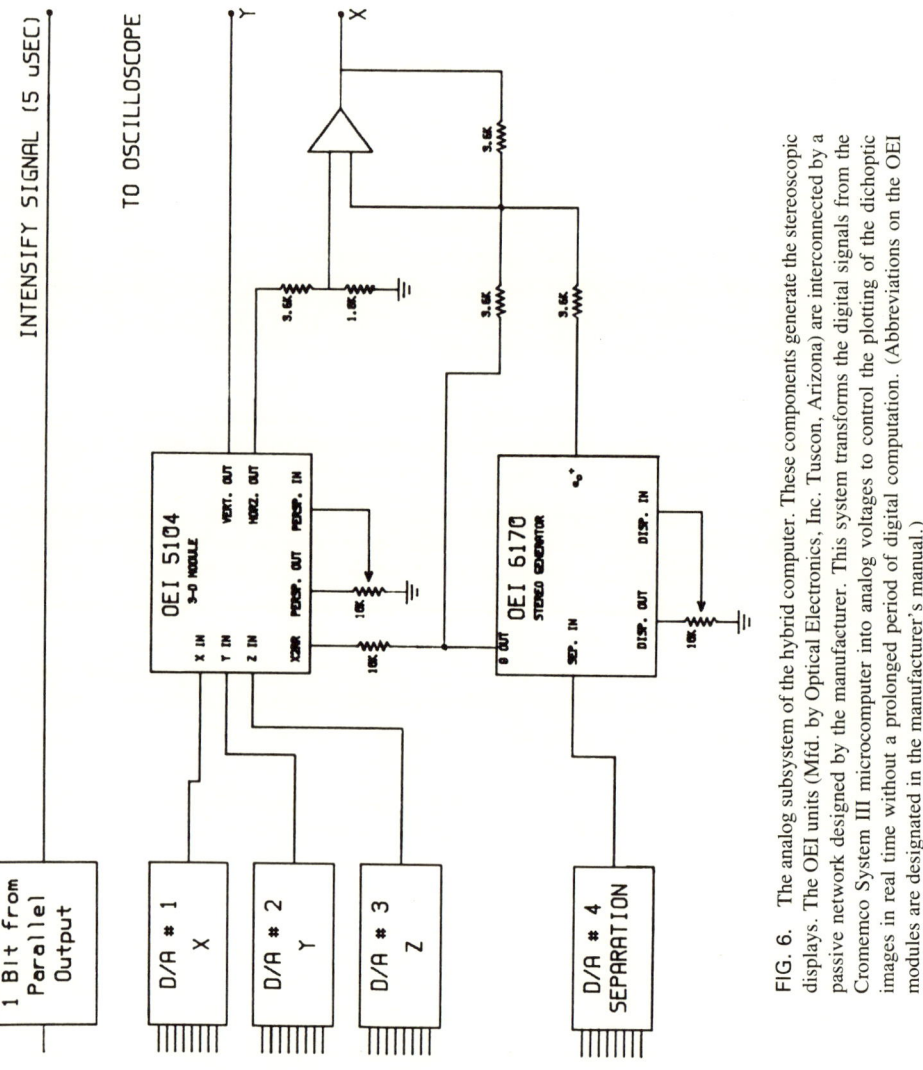

FIG. 6. The analog subsystem of the hybrid computer. These components generate the stereoscopic displays. The OEI units (Mfd. by Optical Electronics, Inc. Tuscon, Arizona) are interconnected by a passive network designed by the manufacturer. This system transforms the digital signals from the Cromemco System III microcomputer into analog voltages to control the plotting of the dichoptic images in real time without a prolonged period of digital computation. (Abbreviations on the OEI modules are designated in the manufacturer's manual.)

space coordinates X, Y, Z at the appropriate time. These three analog voltages are easily and quickly obtained from the internal digital X, Y, Z representation by means of high speed digital to analog converters. In our hybrid computer the digital to analog converter used is the California Data Corporation DA-100, a four channel system. Each channel is capable of converting any single dimension of the digital representation into the equivalent analog voltage in approximately three microseconds.[3] Three channels of the system are used to convert the X, Y, Z dimensions and one is used to regulate the spatial separation between the left and right eye haploscopic images drawn on the oscilloscope. The disparity and perspective of the two images are adjusted with external regulating potentiometers and are kept constant throughout the experiments.

The speed of operation of the analog Optical Electronics Inc. subsystem (it has a band pass of DC to 500 kHz) is fast enough so that the entire set of trigonometric computations is carried out in a few microseconds, a duration comparable to the settling time of the entire electronic and display system used in the study and to one or two average digital computer instruction execution times. One thus has only to wait for a few computer instructions before sending an intensify signal (obtained directly from one bit of a parallel output port of the microcomputer) to the oscilloscope to maintain good dot quality. The Optical Electronics Inc. components are thus so fast that they carry out this conversion in what is easily "real time." The speed of generation of haploscopic pairs of left and right eye images is constrained, therefore, only by the minimal digital computer programming required to read information from an internally stored table of X, Y, Z, t values (all of which are either computed in the intervals between trials or arbitrarily specified by the experimenter prior to the trial) to the digital to analog converters.

As I noted earlier, there are two ways in which the stimulus and noise dots may be presented—the "flurry of snowflakes" dynamic mode and the "snapshot-like" static mode. In the dynamic mode a system of three real time clocks located in the digital computer controls the times at which the dots of the stimulus form and visual noise are displayed in each presentation. The first clock regulates the times at which the dummy dots or the dots comprising the stimulus forms are plotted. Each dot of the stimulus form is represented, as we have noted by four coordinates (X, Y, Z, t). The t value is used to set this first clock so that at the appropriate time the computer will be interrupted from a waiting routine to plot the left and right eye images (X_L, Y_L, and X_R, Y_R) of that particular dot. Those intervals need not be regular and, indeed, are not in some of the experi-

---

[3]To achieve this high speed conversion, however, I had to modify the delivered system by removing capacitors C10, C13, C16, C19 from the four digital to analog converter output stages. These capacitors are identified on the circuit diagrams provided by the manufacturer, California Data Corporation of Newburg Park, California. With the capacitors in place the rise time of the system was seriously degraded.

ments to be described later. The second clock is set to interrupt the computer at regular intervals—defined at load time by the experimenter. This is the interval between the regularly spaced (in time) briefly flashed noise dots. A nonrepeating sequence of these randomly (in space) positioned dots is plotted during the entire period of each stimulus presentation—one second, a duration controlled by the third clock. In this dynamic mode the dots of the stimulus and the dots of the noise are interspersed among each other in time as well as space.

In the static mode, the display remains constant during the entire 1 sec presentation duration (still controlled by the third clock described above). However, the dots of the stimulus and noise are not presented at precisely controlled intervals—the first two clocks are not used. Rather, all of the noise dots are plotted as fast as they can be read out of memory and then all of the dots comprising the stimulus form. A variable interval (specified by the experimenter when the experiment is set up each day) then passes before exactly the same noise and stimulus dots are replotted on the oscilloscope. The variable interval in this case is required to control the apparent brightness of the display. Because of the persistence of vision (and the decision to make the variable interval less than the flicker fusion interval) this static display appears to remain stable, much like a still photograph, during the entire one second presentation duration.

In most of the static and dynamic experiments the noise dots are distributed throughout the perceived cubical space. However in a few experiments (as noted in the appropriate discussion in Chapter 3) the noise itself is restricted to a plane. The subject's task in this case is to discriminate the plane into which the stimulus form dots have been constrained from the plane into which the noise dots have been constrained.

The field of view presented to each eye on the two halves of the CRT is shielded by an opaque screen through which a pair of 5.4 deg × 5.4 deg apertures had been cut for the left and right image respectively. This shielding screen is attached directly to the face of the oscilloscope. The viewing distance from the observer's cornea to the CRT surface is 31.75 cm. The screen is far enough from the observer and the persistence of the oscilloscope is short enough that each dot appeared to be virtually point-like in both time (unless it is refreshed as in the static mode) and space. Luminance is adjusted with a Salford S.E.I. photometer to approximately 0.1 candles/m^2 and kept constant at approximately this level from day to day.[4]

The two pushbuttons used by the observer to respond are connected to Schmitt triggers with capacitive inputs designed to smooth switch contact bounce. The outputs of the Schmitt triggers are fed to two of the bit positions on an eight bit parallel input port of the computer for acquisition and processing.

---

[4]Luminosity, however, does not play an important role in determining the level of detectability. Performance is much more strongly related to the signal (stimulus dot numerosity) to noise (noise dot numerosity) ratio and to the spatio-temporal form of the stimulus dots.

THE PERCEIVED CUBICAL SPACE

Stereoscopic depth is defined by the horizontal disparities between X_L, Y_L and X_R, Y_R for each dot. Horizontal retinal disparity, however, does not define absolute depths but rather cues the observer to relative depths; i.e., a dot is perceived *in front of* or *in back of* the reference depth (the point in depth at which the lines of sight converge and disparity is zero) by a certain amount. In such a system, even if the reference depth is changed, the relative relationships may remain constant. Furthermore, in the hybrid computer system utilized in the present study, the electronic disparity adjustment is uncalibrated and arbitrary. It is, therefore, necessary to calibrate the actual disparity of dot pairs by direct measurements from photographs of special test patterns on the display screen and from measurements of the distance from the observer's eye to the display screen. These angular measurements are then related to the Z axis values stored within the computer. It should be noted that this relationship between disparity and internally represented Z values is accurate only for our system and as it is adjusted for these experiments. Within this constraint, we determined that if the observer fixated on the fixation-convergence dot centered in the apparent cube, then the maximum crossed relative disparity for a dot positioned on the front surface of the apparent cube is 14 min. of visual angle and the maximum uncrossed disparity for a dot positioned on the rear surface of the apparent cube is also 14 min. of visual angle. These maximum crossed and uncrossed disparity values were arbitrarily chosen so that the perceived volume appeared to be as close to a cube as possible. Because of the several stages of transformation involved, all disparity values should be considered to be approximate. Furthermore, in some of the experiments reported here less than this full range of disparity is utilized.

3 Experimental Design and Results

I now present the rationale, design, and results of a series of experiments dealing with the detection of dotted stimulus forms masked by dotted visual noise and presented in stereoscopic space. The experiments to be discussed are categorized in terms of the dimensions of the stimulus form. They include three classes of studies: Those dealing with the detectability of single flashing dots; those dealing with the detectability of lines of dots (timed to appear either as simultaneously flashed lines of dots or moving dots); and those dealing with planes of dots. The first two categories of stimuli are always investigated using the dynamic mode. On the other hand some of the planar studies are carried out in the static mode in which all of the stimulus form and noise dots appeared stationary and constant throughout the one second (or less) presentation period. The random dot steregram techniques I use, of course, are based on Bela Julesz' (1960) pioneering work.

The organizing theme of this program of experimentation is thus the increasing dimensionality of the stimulus forms. That is, I start with dots, stimuli that are themselves spatially nondimensional even though positioned in a three dimensional space. The major parameters in this case are the size and variability of the intervals between succesive presentations of a single dot or the position of the dot in the cubical viewing space. The experiments then go on to explore the detectability of lines of dots, themselves linear (i.e., one dimensional) forms, that are also presented in various orientations in three dimensional space. The major parameter of interest in the linear experiment is the temporal sequence in which the lines are plotted. At some future time it will be necessary to explore the effect of the specific spatial geometry (i.e., the number of and spacing between the dots of a line) of linear and quasilinear forms, but for the present it seems safe to assume that the inferences (see p. 23 in this book) drawn from studies carried out in two dimensions (Uttal, 1975) in this regard are in the main generalizable to the stereoscopic environment of the present experiments. Finally, in a series of experiments on planes the stimulus forms are themselves two dimensional, but also embedded in a three dimensional space. One does not have to stretch one's imagination too far to guess where these experiments are heading in the future. Indeed experiments on nonplanar surfaces are currently underway in my laboratory and some on solids are planned for the future.

It should also be noted that in many of the experiments involving dots and lines, time—a fourth dimension—is also involved. In this sense our experiments are carried out in a four dimension space-time manifold rather than in a purely spatial three dimension one.

Another important point must be made concerning the absolute value of data obtained in these experiments. In fact, *inter*experiment comparisons of absolute values are often not meaningful. Different groups of observers are used in different experiments and individual differences in performance in these tasks are often great. These differences may have profound quantitative effects on the results of experiments involving only a few observers. For example, any eagle-eyed eidetic imagers among my audience will note the great discrepancy exhibited in the results of Experiments 10 and 11 (to be presented shortly.) One curve in both Fig. 36 and Fig. 38 is obtained under identical conditions (viewing duration = 1000 msec and noise dot numerosity = 50). These two curves, however, are from two different groups of observers and are quite different in absolute magnitude, even though identical in trend. A close examination of individual records makes what happened quite clear; different people do different things in unpredictable (at observer selection time) ways! Therefore, when drawing conclusions I have necessarily concentrated on relative *intra*experiment differences (or nondifferences) for which intrinsic controls for all variables exist. As our data indicate clearly, intraexperimental findings are quite regular and consistent.

Similarly, it is often the case that when more than one stimulus dimension or attribute is varied in the same experiment, results are complex and confusing. Tests of the theoretical model in Chapter 4, in some cases, will fall victim to exactly this difficulty.

Finally, I must also warn my audience that, though it is convenient to categorize these experiments in terms of the dimensions of the stimulus forms, studies of dots, lines, and planes all contribute to the solution of the form perception problem in a way that is independent of their dimensionality. In these experiments dots, lines, and planes are all studied to tell us something collectively about the following influences on detectability:

1. The globality of visual spatial interactions
2. The isotropy of visual space

48   3. EXPERIMENTAL DESIGN AND RESULTS

3. The influence of periodicity in time and space
4. The effect of form on detection

among others. The neat little dimensional taxonomy (i.e., dots, lines, and planes) I use here should not be taken too seriously. Indeed, in the concluding discussion, I, too, cast it aside.

With these introductory caveats in hand, let's now consider the design and outcome of the experiments in detail.

DOTS

Experiment 1

Design and rationale. Experiment 1 is the foundation experiment for the study of the detectability of repetitively flashing single dots embedded within a volume of dynamically timed and randomly placed visual noise dots (each of which flashes only once). Three independent variables are manipulated in this experiment—the interval between successive presentations of the stimulus dot, the position of that dot, and the masking noise density. In the following paragraphs, I shall consider each of these variables in detail to set the stage not only for the discussion of this experiment but of others to follow.

With regard to the interval between successive flashes of the stimulus dot, it must be remembered that the stimulus dot is distinguished from any of the random noise dots only by the fact that it (i.e., a dot located at a single position in the apparent cubical volume) is flashed four times rather than only once. In this first experiment the three regular temporal intervals between successive flashes are all set equal to each other at one of four possible values (50, 100, 150, and 200 msec) in each trial. These four interval values are used in random order during each daily session. In each presentation the stimulus dot is always timed such that the stream of repetitive flashes is centered at the temporal midpoint (500 msec) of the one second long presentation. The same interval value is used in the dummy stimulus presentation, but in this case four temporally separated dots are scattered about in four random positions in space. These four dummy dots do not, therefore, meet the criterion of the stimulus dot—repetitive presentation at a single point in space. It is on the basis of this criterion, and this criterion alone, that the observer chooses which presentation contains the stimulus form.

The second independent variable manipulated in Experiment 1 is the position of the stimulus dot. The repetitively flashing dot could occupy any one of the seven possible positions shown in Fig. 7 in any trial. Again, the particular position used in each trial was selected by a random number algorithm. The outer outline cube shown in this drawing delimits the (5.4 deg × 5.4 deg × 28 min disparity) cubical space perceived by the observer. The inner outline cube is an

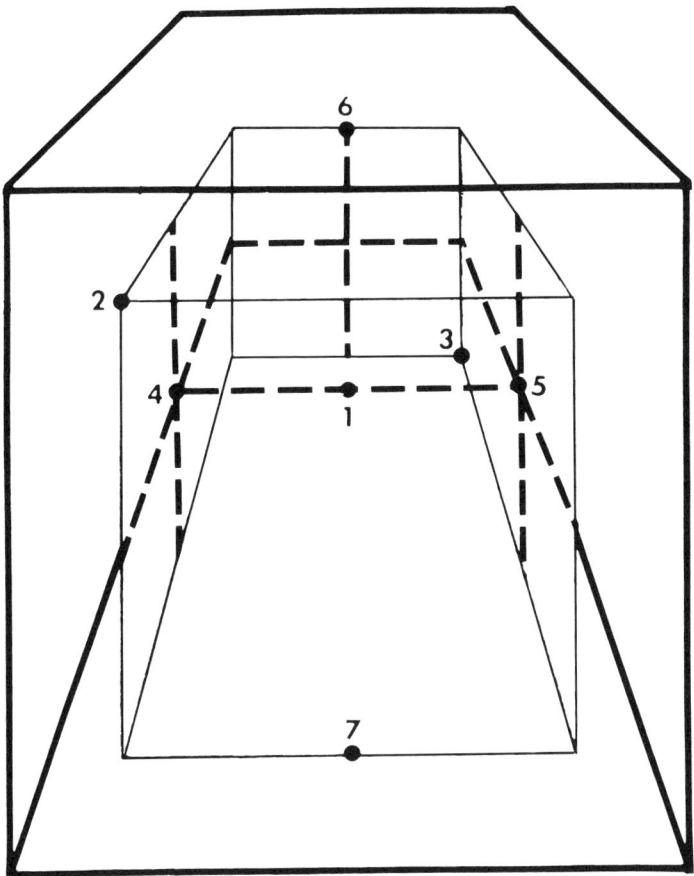

FIG. 7. A graphic depiction of the seven positions in which the flashing dot used in Experiment 1 might be located in any trial. The flashing dot stimulus is placed in only one of these dot positions in each trial. The outlines of the cubical spaces are not visible to the observer: They are presented here only to aid visualization of the stimulus space.

aide to the localization of the seven possible positions of the stimulus dot. (It must be remembered, however, that neither the inner nor the outer outline cube, is visible to the observer.) For example, position 1 is situated at the perceived center of the apparent cube, that is, the location of the fixation-convergence point. Another example is that location 5 is centered on the right hand side of the inner outline cube. Which of the seven positions used is also chosen randomly prior to each trial. For those of you who can free fuse stereoscopic pairs a more realistic display of the stimuli for the experiments is shown in Fig. 8.

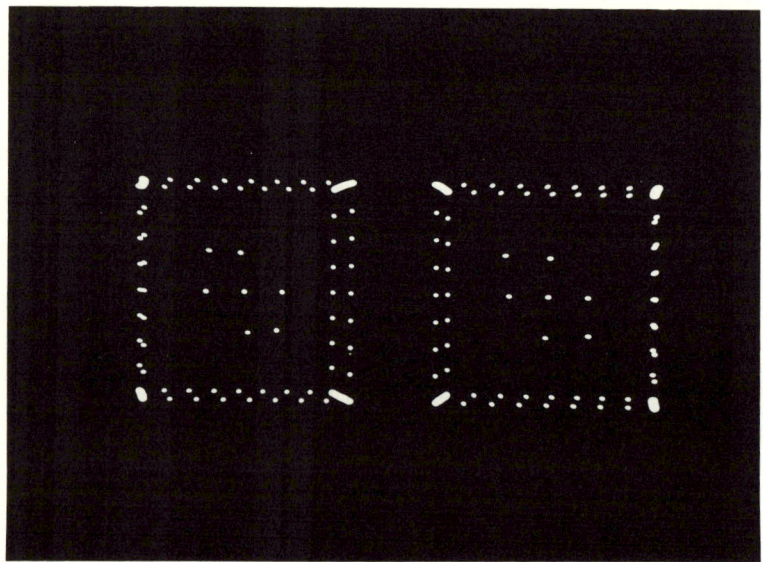

FIG. 8. A stereoscopic display of the same information shown in Fig. 7. Again, the outlines of the cubical space are not present in the actual experiment and only one of the stimulus dots is present in each trial.

The third parameter varied in Experiment 1 is the masking noise density. Densities of 10, 14, 20, 33, and 100 masking dots/sec are utilized. To evaluate the advantage forthcoming from depth, this experiment was run under two viewing conditions; the standard dichoptic one, which allowed stereoscopic perception and a binocular one, in which both of the observer's eyes viewed the left eye image of the stereoscopic pair. In the binocular condition, therefore, no disparity, and thus no perceived depth, is present.

This experiment is designed so that each daily session includes all possible combinations of the seven positions and four flashing rates presented in random order. Viewing condition and noise density are held constant each day. That is, the experiment is performed dichoptically and then binocularly on alternative days. On successive pairs of days, the noise density is varied starting from the minimum value of 10 dots and ending on the 9th and 10th days with the maximum values of 100 dots/sec. The entire experiment is then repeated varying masking noise dot densities in the reverse order. Approximately 500 trials were executed by each observer in each hourly session. Twenty sessions (2 viewing conditions × 5 noise levels × 2 replications) were thus required to complete this experiment.

Results. The results of this foundation experiment for flashing single dots are plotted on three separate graphs. Figure 9 displays the effect of variations in the masking noise density on detection. As expected, there is a progressive decline in detectability of the flashing dot as the noise density increases. Nevertheless, it is somewhat surprising to note that a single dot flashing only 4 times is still partially detectable (i.e, at better than chance levels) even though it is camouflaged by the frenetic twinkling of 100 random dots. The distinct advantage of the stereoscopic view over the binocular is clearly evidenced at all masking dot densities.

The influence of the position of the flashing dot stimulus is plotted in Fig. 10. The only dot position that appears to have any substantial advantage over the others is position 1—the one located at the very center of the inner cube. The only dot that appears to have any substantial disadvantage is position 3—the one located in the bottom rear corner of the inner cube. Other than that, all dot locations appear to have roughly equal probability of detection. The strong advantage of stereoscopic viewing over binocular viewing is also depicted here; only position 4 seems to not display this advantage and I believe this to be a spurious fluctuation rather than a true nondifference.

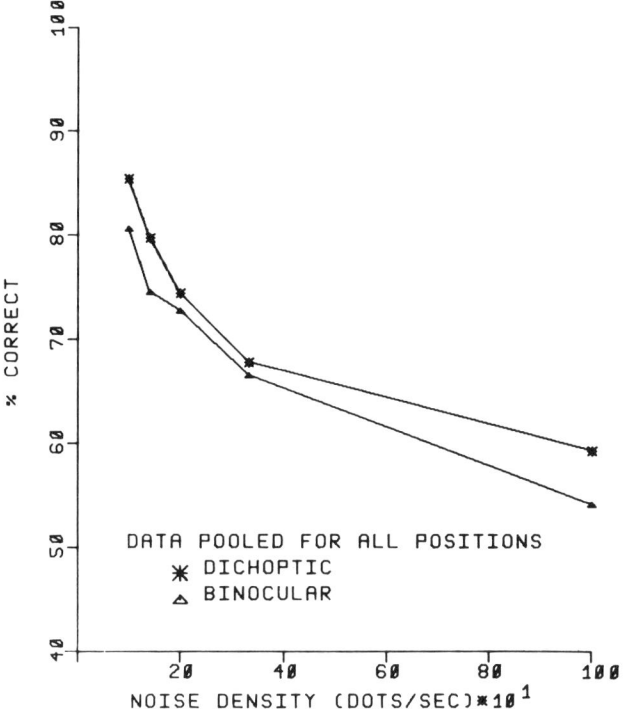

FIG. 9. The results of Experiment 1 plotted as a function of the density of the noise dots. The two curves are for the dichoptic and binocular viewing conditions respectively.

52   3. EXPERIMENTAL DESIGN AND RESULTS

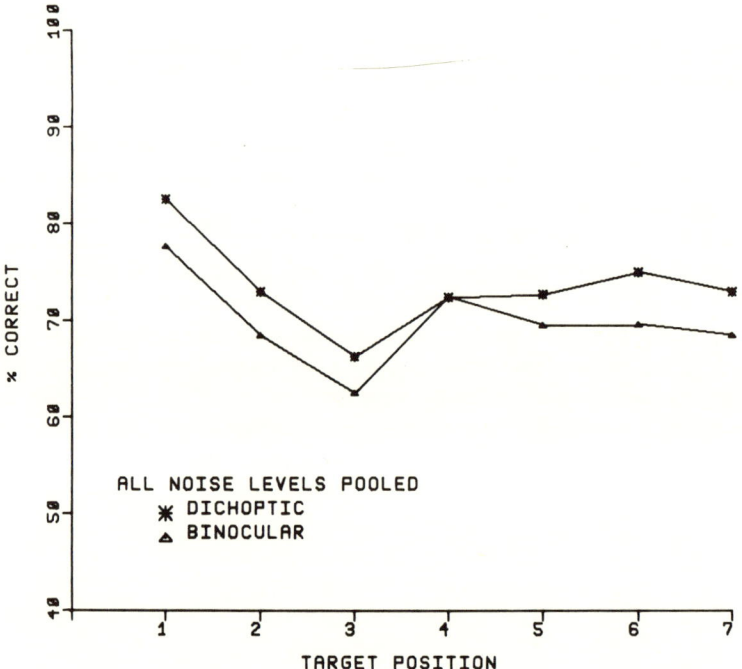

FIG. 10.   The result of Experiment 1 plotted as a function of the position of the flashing dot. The numbers on the horizontal axes are keyed to the positions shown in Fig. 7.

Finally, Fig. 11 plots detectability for all data collected at all noise levels plotted as function of the interflash interval. Most interestingly, the resulting curve is nonmonotonic. Peak detectability occurs at an interval of 100 msec. There is a sharp decline in detectability for longer interflash intervals and a less sharp decline for shorter ones.

Experiment 2

Design and Rational.   Experiment 2 is concerned with the effect of temporal irregularity of the intervals between a repetitively flashing dot on that dot's detectability. The rationale for dealing with these irregular intervals will be explained more fully in the section on line detection that follows. In fact, this experiment was stimulated by that experiment; logic and chronology not being isomorphic in this case. In all regards other than temporal interval irregularities, Experiment 2 is like Experiment 1. The temporal irregularity itself is measured in units of standard deviation about a mean flicker interval that could be set at 50,

100, 150, or 200 msec on separate days. Six values of this variability measure are used including 0, 4.1, 8.2, 12.2, 16.3, 20.4, and 24.5 msec. The actual deviations used here, therefore, are ±0%; ±5%; ±10%; ±15%; ±20%; ±25%; and finally ±30% of the mean flicker interval. For example, to produce an irregular interval sequence with a standard deviation of 16.3 msec from a regular interval series with a mean value of 100 msec, 20% of 100 msec (20 msec) had to be added to one 100 msec interval and 20% of 100 msec (20 msec) had to be subtracted from another. Applying such a procedure in this case would transform a train of four dots separated by three equal 100 msec intervals into a train of dots

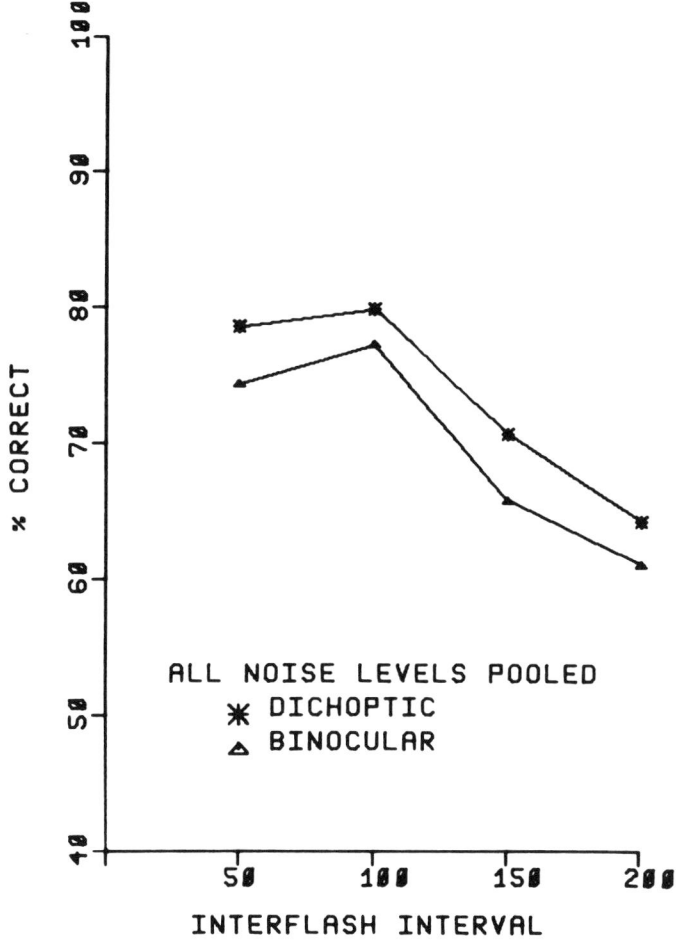

FIG. 11. The results of Experiment 1 plotted as a function of the length of the interval between flashes with data pooled from all noise levels.

separated by 80 msec, 120 msec, and 100 msec. In other trials the sequence might be 120 msec, 100 msec, and 80 msec. However, since either of these two interval patterns has a standard deviation of 16.3 msec both of these irregular intervals would be dealt with identically in the analysis.

The number of dot positions utilized in each daily session in Experiment 2 is limited to four so that all six interval irregularity values could be tested in each session. The four positions utilized are those numbered 1, 4, 5, and 6 in Fig. 7 The masking dot density is kept constant throughout this experiment at 33 dots per sec. Only the stereoscopic viewing condition is used in this experiment. Eight sessions (1 viewing condition × 4 mean intervals × 2 replications) were required to complete this experiment.

Results. Figure 12 displays the results of Experiment 2 segregated by mean interval. The extraordinary result is immediately evident: There is a remarkable

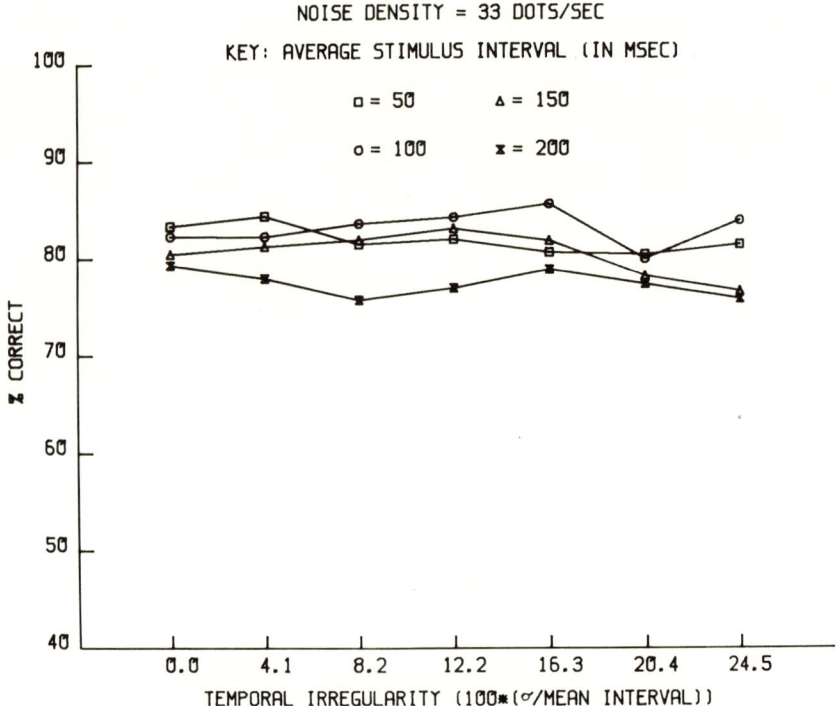

FIG. 12. The results of Experiment 2 displaying the negligible effects of temporal interval irregularity on flashing dot detection. The horizontal axis is a normalized form of the ratio of the standard deviation and the mean of the intervals between the repetitively flashed dot. The four curves vary parametrically with the mean interval.

and surprising insensitivity to wide variations in the regularity of temporal intervals between successive flashes of a repetitively flashed dot. All four curves for all four mean interval values are virtually flat over the full range of interval irregularity values.

Thus, interval irregularity does not seem to play any role over the range of mean interval sizes used here. Beyond this surprising result, it should also be noted that the mean values of the performance scores for these data are substantially higher than for the 33 noise dots/sec condition shown in Fig. 9. This is due to the different sampling of observers used in the two experiments.

LINES

Experiment 3

Design and Rationale. Experiment 3 is the foundation study for all of the experiments involving straight lines that are to be reported here. In particular, this experiment is designed to examine the detection of straight, regularly spaced dotted lines in a visual noise filled stereoscopic space. Regular dotted lines, for the purpose of this experiment, are defined as those in which the dots are separated by equal intervals in both time and space. Figure 13 superimposes the four different diagonally oriented dotted line stimuli used in this experiment onto a single drawing. However, it must be remembered that only one of these lines is used in any one stimulus trial. The stimulus always consists of seven dots in the linear experiments I now report. (In the earlier two dimensional work, Uttal, 1975, it was determined that the number of dots in a line played an important role in its detectability, but the impact of this variable in the three dimensional environment has not yet been explored.) The outer outline cube in Fig. 13 represents the total extent of the volume in which the dotted visual noise dots are randomly distributed. The apparent cubical volume is defined by the 5.4 deg by 5.4 deg areas presented to each eye in the X–Y plane and by disparities ranging from 14 minutes (crossed) to 14 minutes (uncrossed) in front of and in back of the central fixation point. Stimulus lines are presented along the diagonals of the slightly smaller volume indicated by the inner outline cube. The X and Y dimensions of the smaller cube are both limited to 3.25 deg. The apparent depth of the first and last dots of each diagonal line is set by disparity values of 12.25 min uncrossed and 12.25 min crossed respectively. The dots of each stimulus line are sequentially plotted from the back plane of the inner cube to its front plane as indicated by the arrow heads. Neither the inner nor outer outlines of the cubes shown here for diagrammatic purposes are ever visible to the observer. For those of you who are able to free fuse stereoscopic pairs, this same picture is repeated in a more realistic version in Fig. 14. In this case, also, the dotted outline cube is not present in the actual experimental presentation and only one of the four diagonal lines is displayed in each presentation.

56   3. EXPERIMENTAL DESIGN AND RESULTS

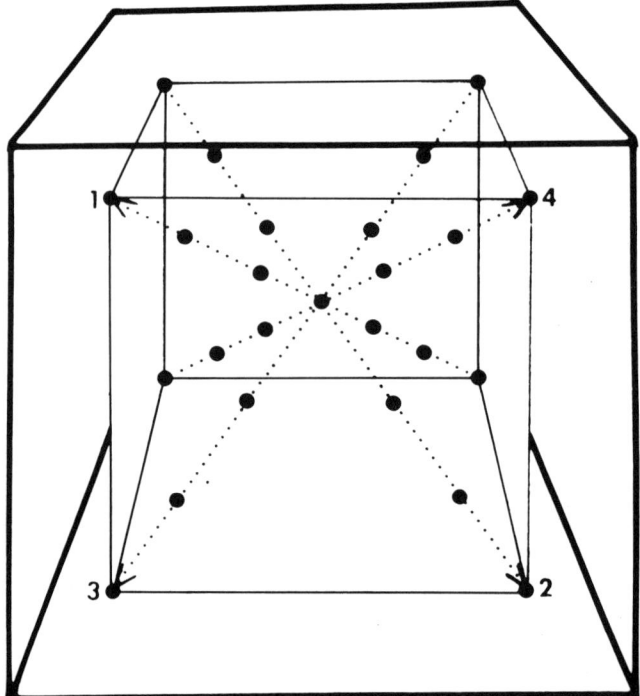

FIG. 13. A graphic depiction of the four diagonal lines of dots used in Experiments 3, 4, 5, and 6. Only one line was presented in each trial. The temporal interval between the dots of each line varied from values so small that the seven dots appeared to be simultaneous to values large enough to give the impression of apparent motion. The outlines of the cubical viewing spaces are not present in the actual stimulus display; they are drawn here as an aid in visualizing the viewing space.

The direction of the dotted stimulus line is one of the parameters manipulated in this experiment. We explored this variable to determine if visual space is isotropic for this kind of visual information processing. Three other parameters influencing line detection, however, were the main targets of our research in this experiment. These three were plotting interval, noise density, and viewing condition. To examine the effect of interval, the seven dots composing each stimulus line are plotted in sequential order with the delays between successive dots varying from trial to trial. The regular and equal interdot intervals used in this experiment include 10, 20, 30, 40, 50, 60, and 70 msec respectively. The middle dot—the fourth—is always plotted at both the spatial midpoint of the cubical volume and at the temporal midpoint (t = 500 msec) of the one sec presentation interval. At the shortest interval, the entire line of dots appears to the observer to

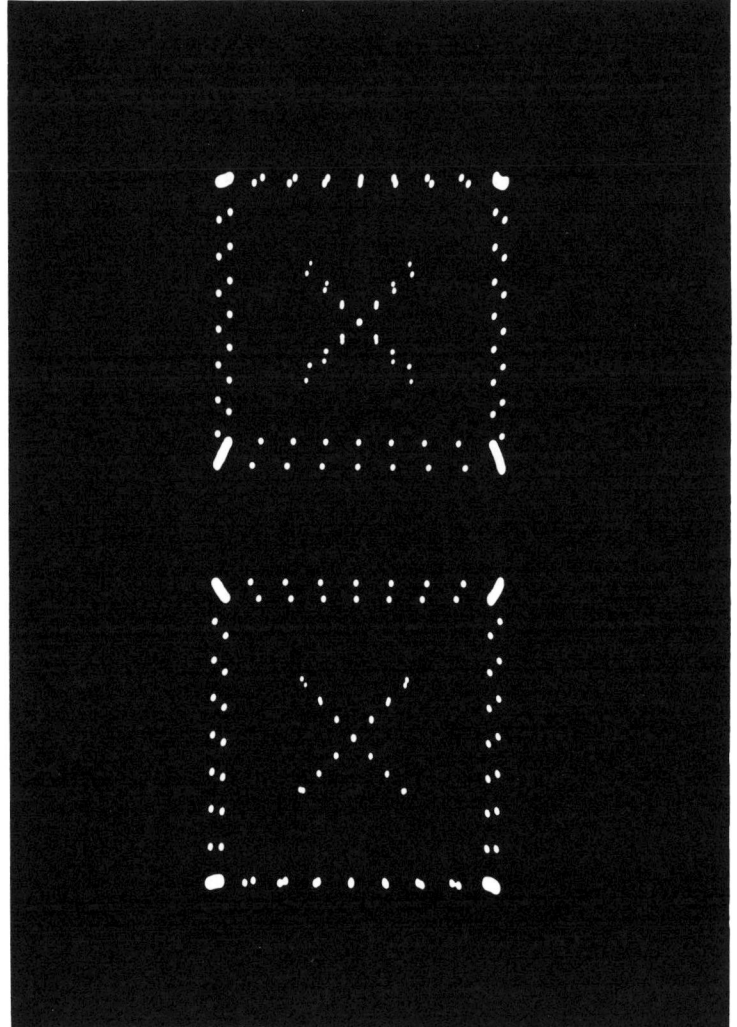

FIG. 14. A stereoscopic picture of the same information shown in Fig. 13.

58   3. EXPERIMENTAL DESIGN AND RESULTS

be plotted simultaneously. At longer intervals, the dots appear to be successively plotted giving rise to an increasingly strong impression of a single dot in apparent movement, but at a progressively slower velocity as the selected interdot interval increases.

A major reason for studying the effects of interval is to compare the results with what a priori might have been hypothesized to be compensatory effects of apparent motion on nonsimultaneous dot plotting. We know from the two dimensional studies that simultaneous appearing lines of dots are easily detected, and it is obvious that there should be some degradation of line detectability at very long intervals. There was, however, the possibility that an increase in apparent motion might compensate for the loss in simultaneity in an intermediate range of intervals. It was not possible, therefore, to predict at the outset of this experiment with any certainty what the overall effect of interval would be.

A further complication is that the greater the interval, the greater the period over which the line of dots is present during the one second long presentation time. Thus, a larger number of masking dots overlaps the stimulus dots in the larger interval conditions than in the shorter interval conditions. At first consideration, therefore, it might be hypothesized that there is, in fact, a real increase in the signal to noise level. However, this analysis is equivocal. The number of noise dots that is simultaneously apparent to the observer is a function of the persistence of the visual system as well as the real time of presentation. At the very least this confounding of the effects of interval per se and of involved noise density must be kept in mind, and not totally excluded.

All of the four directions and the seven intervals used in this experiment are presented in each daily session in randomly selected order. On separate daily sessions, however, the two other parameters—viewing condition and noise density—are varied. To determine the effects of viewing condition, each daily session is repeated six times at each noise density—twice using dichoptic viewing (in which stereopsis was possible) and twice using an eye patch over one eye or the other so that only monocular cues are available. My purpose in using the eye patch was to determine what advantage, if any, is gained from stereopsis by comparing monocular and dichoptic viewing conditions. Five different noise densities were chosen such that the stimulus line is embedded in 125, 166, 250, 500, and 1000 dots per second in this order. Following the descending series, the entire experiment is repeated in reverse order. Thirty sessions (3 viewing conditions $\times$ 5 noise levels $\times$ 2 replications) are thus required for each observer to complete this experiment. Again about 500 trials were executed in each hourly session.

Results.   The major results of Experiment 3 are plotted in Figs. 15, 16, 17, 18, and 19 for masking noise densities of 125, 166, 250, 500, and 1000 dots respectively. On each of these graphs, the abscissa represents the temporal interval between the dots making up the stimulus line. The ordinate represents

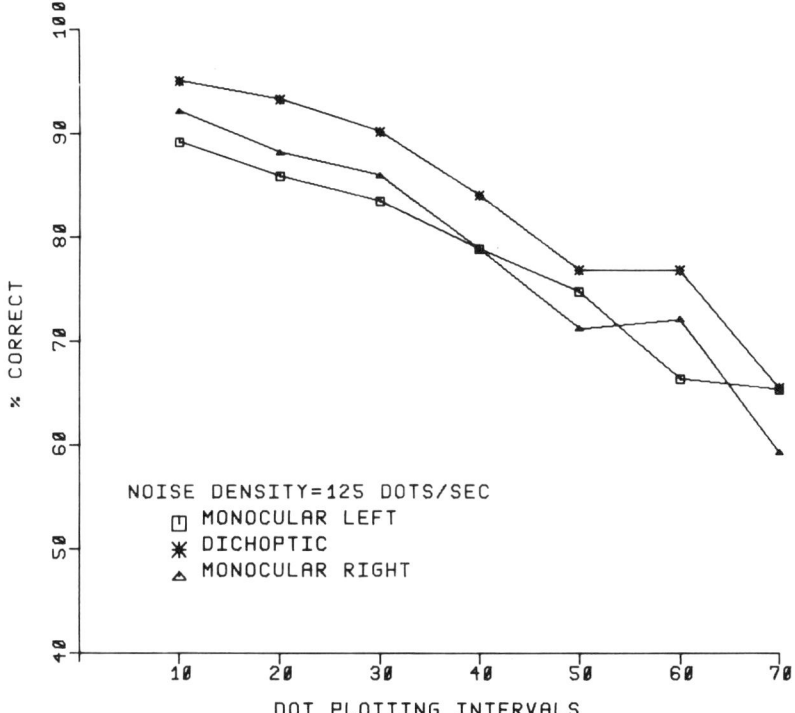

FIG. 15. The results of Experiment 3 for noise densities of 125 dots/sec. The horizontal axis indicates the duration of each of the equal intervals between successive dots. The three curves are for dichoptic, left eye monocular, and right eye monocular viewing respectively. The vertical axis indicates the pooled average of all observers' scores for this condition.

the proportion of trials in which the observer selected the correct presentation; that is, the one in which the stimulus line rather than the substituted dummy noise, was present. The three parametric curves in each of these figures represent the data obtained for the three viewing conditions (dichoptic, left monocular, and right monocular) on three successive days. The data obtained from all four line directions have been pooled to produce these graphs.

Three main results are to be noted in this set of figures. First, the general trend produced by varying noise density is evident. The overall performance of the observers decreases as the noise density increases. Under optimum conditions of minimal noise, dichoptic viewing, and the briefest interdot intervals, (data typified by the left hand portion of Fig. 15) observers perform at the 95% correct detection level, a score that is about the best that can be expected in experiments of this kind. Random errors on the part of the observer always lead to group data being about this much less than 100%. On the other hand, when the visual noise

60   3. EXPERIMENTAL DESIGN AND RESULTS

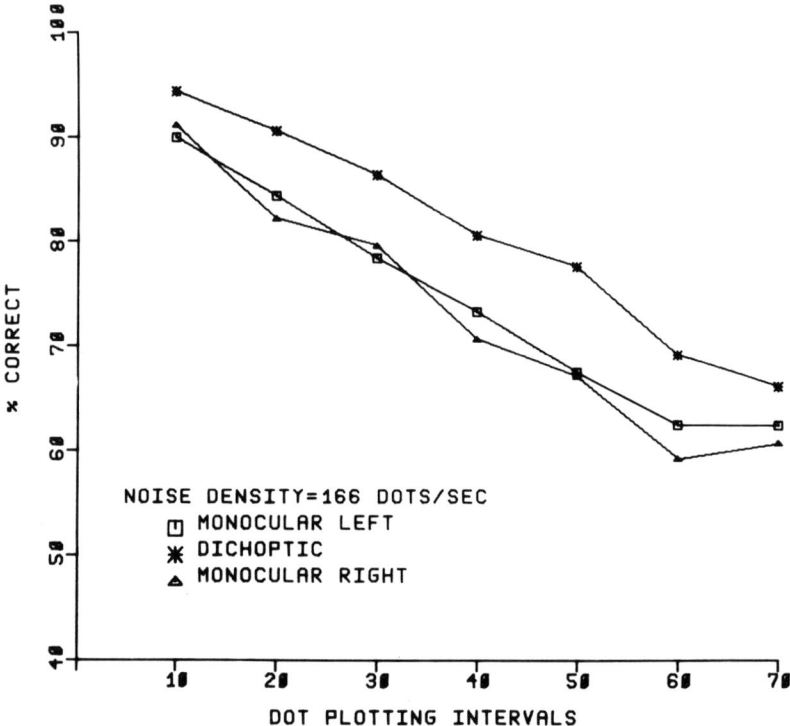

FIG. 16. The result of Experiment 3 for noise densities of 166 dots/sec.

is the densest, the temporal intervals between the dots of the stimulus line are long, and only monocular viewing is allowed (as exemplified by the right hand side of Fig. 19), observers perform at virtually chance levels (50% for the two alternative forced choice design used here).

Second, the effect of viewing condition is also clear. For all noise levels there is a clear advantage obtained when stereoscopic viewing is provided in this detection task. This advantage is reduced by ceiling effects for low noise densities and floor effects for high noise densities, but it is pervasive throughout all five graphs. Indeed, the stereoscopic advantage is substantial: in some conditions it is greater than 12 percentage points, a value which is about a quarter of the total range of responses (50% to 95%) obtainable in this type of experiment. On the other hand, differences between the two monocular viewing conditions are small.

Third, and most important for the purposes of this study, there is also an unequivocal and major effect of dot plotting interval replicated from one noise level to another. The hypothesis that apparent motion might compensate for increased interdot intervals is obviously unsupported. Any such effect is obviously swamped out by the loss of the much stronger influence of simultaneous dot plotting. Dotted stimulus lines become progressively less detectable as the interval between them increases. Indeed, the slope of the function relating detectability and interdot interval is virtually constant. There is not the slightest suggestion of even a slowing of the diminution in detectability at the longer intervals in the series. Such a deceleration would have been expected if apparent motion had *any* significant influence on detectability. Whatever detection mechanism is at work here, it is clear that apparent motion can not substitute for simultaneity, or ameliorate the effect of the effective increase in the number of noise dots due to the longer duration of the line of dots if that is the cause of the decline. (However, as we shall see shortly, stimulus conditions producing apparent motion may have other positive influences. Experiments 4, 5, and 6 indicate that irregularities in time and space do seem to be smoothed over at the longer intervals that produce apparent motion.)

Figure 20 displays the results of the other major parameter of this experiment—track direction. Only data from the 166 noise dot/sec condition have been presented here, but all other dot densities produce similar results. These data

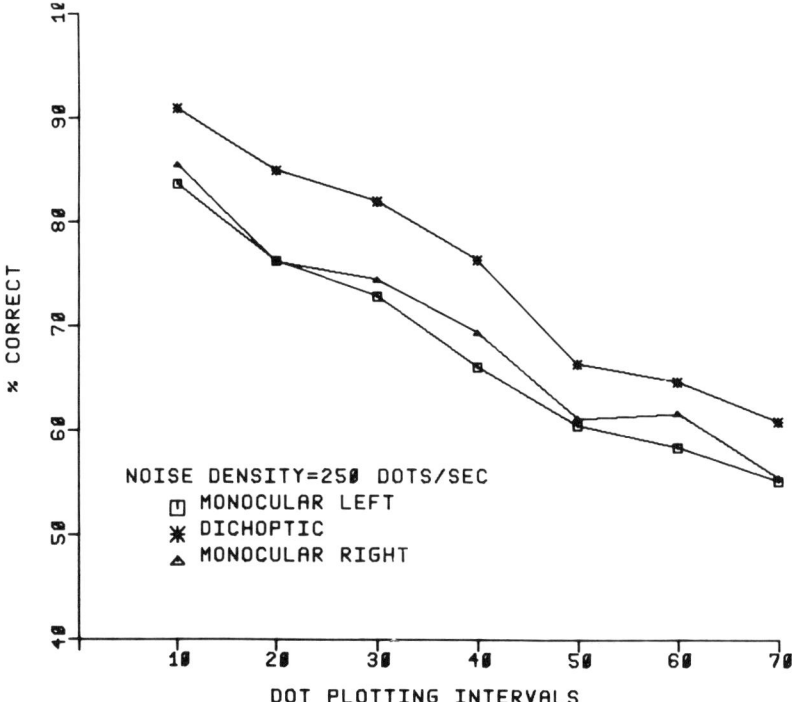

FIG. 17. The results of Experiment 3 for noise densities of 250 dots/sec.

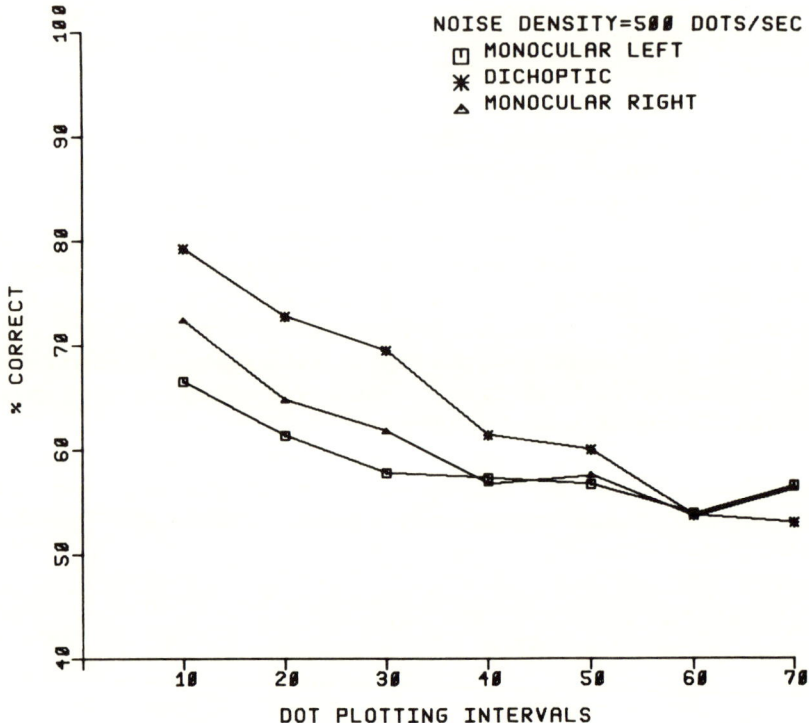

FIG. 18. The results of Experiment 3 for noise densities of 500 dots/sec.

strongly suggest that visual space is isotropic; that is, there is no advantage accruing to any of the four track directions for the perceptual mechanisms underlying this kind of dotted line detection. This insensitivity to orientation and direction in three dimensions is in accord with our earlier findings (Uttal, 1975) indicating the absence of orientation effects for two dimensional stimuli, but quite in contrast to well known orientation effects often demonstrated with continuous line stimuli.

Experiment 4

Design and Rationale. Experiment 4 investigates the effect of temporal irregularity on the detectability of a dotted stimulus line. The main independent variable in this experiment is variability around a mean value of the intervals of time between the successively plotted dots of the line. The mean interval in this experiment could assume any one of the seven values (10, 20, 30, 40, 50, 60, and 70 msec) used in Experiment 3, but is kept constant during each session. Interval irregularity is measured in terms of standard deviation from the mean value. For example, standard deviations of 0, 2.9, 6.45, 10.4, 14.4, 16.8, and 20.4 msec are utilized in the 50 msec mean interval condition. In this case, for example, a standard deviation of 16.8 msec, corresponds to an interval sequence of 75, 35, 25, 50, 65, and 50 msec respectively. To keep the mean interval constant whenever one interval was enlarged by adding a certain number of milliseconds, another interval must be decreased by an equal amount. All other irregularity values were scaled correspondingly. To make the irregularity values comparable for all of the mean interval values, we normalized them by dividing the standard deviation by the mean interval and multiplying by 100. This results in normalized irregularity values of 0, 5.8, 12.9, 20.8, 28.9, 33.7, and 40.8 for all mean intervals.

In sum, these irregularity values are not standard deviations but are normalized numbers representing *proportionately* equal irregularities for all mean intervals. The masking noise density is kept constant throughout Experiment 4 at 250 dots/sec and only the dichoptic viewing condition is used to test the detectability of seven temporally irregular but evenly spaced colinear dots. Each observer was run twice under each of the mean interval conditions for a total of 14 sessions.

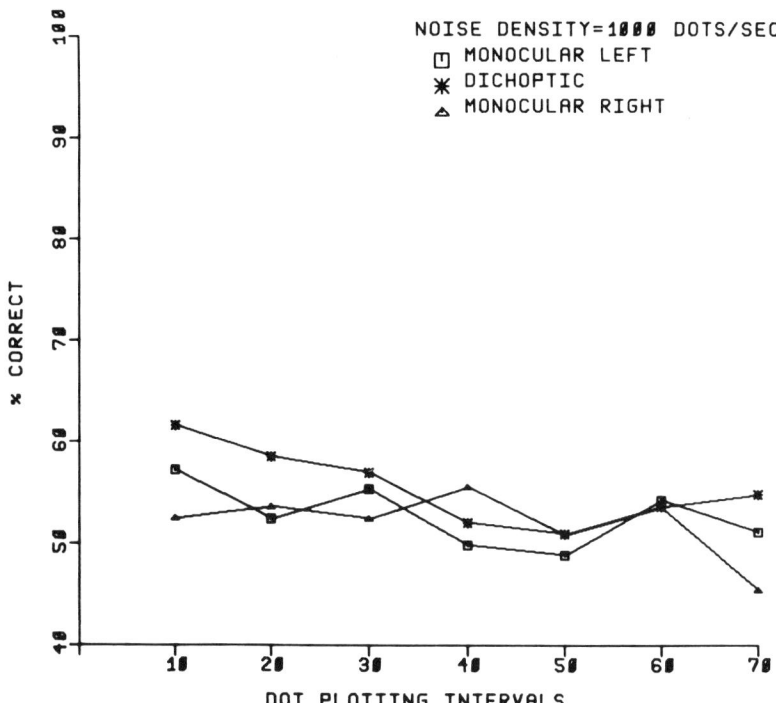

FIG. 19. The results of Experiment 3 for noise densities of 1000 dots/sec.

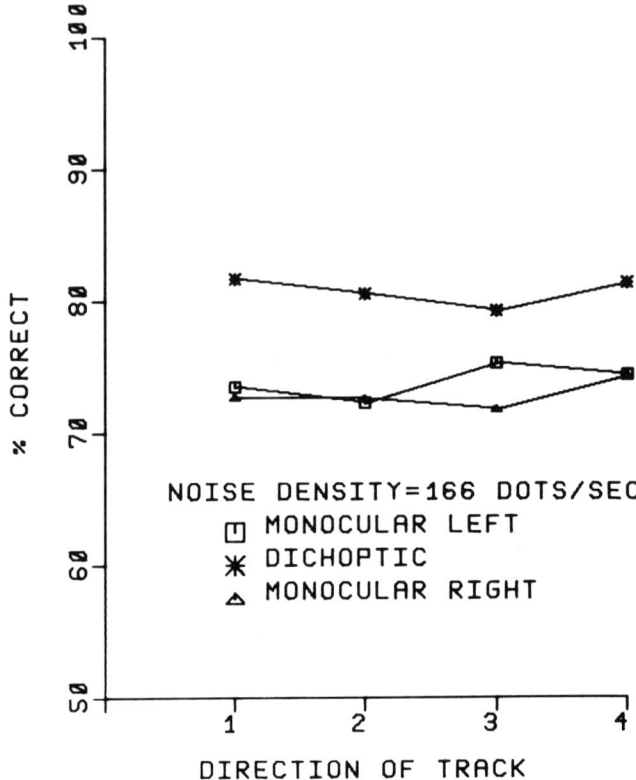

FIG. 20. The results of Experiment 3 (for noise dot densities of 166 dots/sec) reanalyzed to display the negligible effect of track direction. This experiment is, of course, incomplete. Other nondiagonal orientations should also be used.

Resuts. Figure 21 depicts the results of this examination of the effects of temporal interval irregularity on dotted line detection. Surprisingly, there is virtually no observable effect of irregularity measured in this experiment. The extreme flatness of this family of curves (parametric in mean interval) is even more obvious if we pool all the data for the different mean intervals and plot it as shown in Fig. 22. The detection process of the visual system, however sensitive it may be to mean interval, appears to be totally insensitive to even extreme temporal interval irregularities.

Experiment 5

Design and Rationale. In my earlier work (Uttal, 1975) spatial irregularity had been shown to be a powerful determinant of the detectability of straight lines in two dimensional space. I had initially assumed, therefore, that spatial irregularity would also be a powerful influence on the detectability of stimulus forms in three dimensional space and had not planned to confirm this presupposition. However, the surprising results of Experiment 4 suggested that this hypothesis should indeed be tested.

Therefore, to determine if there is any effect of spacing irregularity on detection Experiment 5 utilizes dotted line stimuli consisting of seven dots with regular temporal intervals, but irregular dot spacing. In this experiment, the irregularity of the *spacing* (as opposed to temporal interval in Experiment 4) is used as the independent variable; specifically, the spatial coordinates of an evenly spaced dotted line are transformed to create irregular spacing similar to the way in which temporal irregularity was manipulated in Experiment 4. For example, a 10% change in two spatial separations is made in one case—one spatial separation being enlarged and the other being reduced by that amount. In this manner the overall length of the line remains constant.

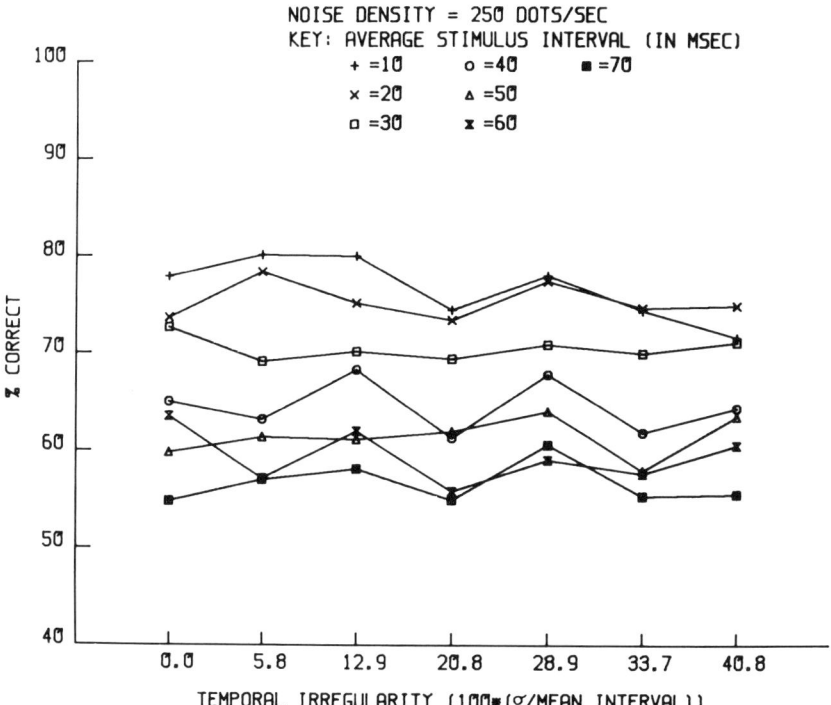

FIG. 21. The results of Experiment 4 displaying the negligible effect of temporal interval irregularity on the detectability of a straight dotted line. The horizontal axis is a normalized form of the ratio of the standard deviations and the means of the temporal intervals between the evenly spaced dots of a straight line. These seven curves vary parametrically with the mean temporal interval between dots.

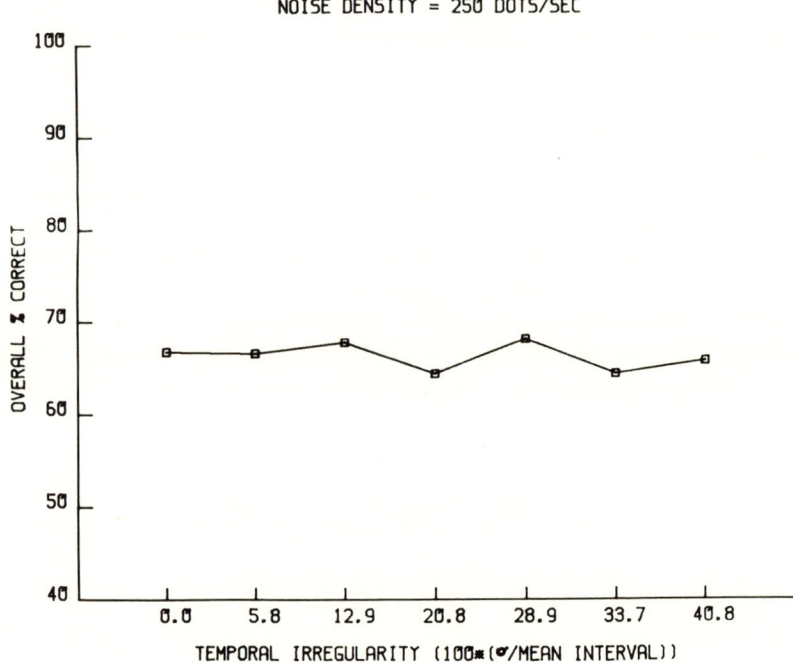

FIG. 22. The data shown in Fig. 21 has been pooled across all mean intervals to emphasize the small effect of temporal irregularity on line detectability.

Seven combinations of spatial separation changes are used in this experiment defining progressively increasing spatial irregularity values. These combinations are ±0; ±10%; ±10% and ±20%; ±20% and ±30%; ±50%; ±30% and ±50%; and finally, ±50% and ±50%. Because of the arbitrary nature of the Z-axis, no particular units can be associated with the actual Euclidean distances corresponding to these irregularity values (i.e., to add degrees of visual angle subtended in the X-Y plane to seconds of stereodisparity would be meaningless.) Therefore, I have simply designated the seven states of increasing spatial irregularity as 0, 1, 2, 3, 4, 5, and 6.

Mean temporal interval values of 10, 20, 30, 40, 50, 60 and 70 msec are used in separate sessions. A single noise level of 250 dots/sec is used throughout this experiment. Only the dichoptic viewing condition is used and each of four observers is run twice under each of the seven mean interval conditions for a total of 14 daily sessions.

Results. The results of Experiment 5 are plotted in Fig. 23 segregated on the basis of mean interval. This graph suggests that there are two groups with different properties—mean intervals of 10, 20, and 30 msec in one group and 40,

50, 60 and 70 msec in a second group. To make this point clearer, the data for the two groups have been pooled and replotted in Fig. 24. The curve for the first group shows a modest decline in performance (from about 83% to 77%) while the curve for the second group is virtually flat at about 70% over the full range of spatial irregularity values used. The upper curve, representing the pooled results for the 10, 20, and 30 msec mean interval conditions, incorporates the short interval conditions that produce the closest approximations to the appearance of simultaneity. The lower curve, representing the pooled results for the 40, 50, 60, and 70 msec mean interval conditions, incorporates those conditions most likely to produce the experience of either sequentiality or apparent motion.

I believe these data indicate that there is virtually no effect of spacing irregularity when the dots in the line are separated by a period of time (i.e., 40, 50, 60, or 70 msec) that is long enough to produce sequentiality or apparent motion!

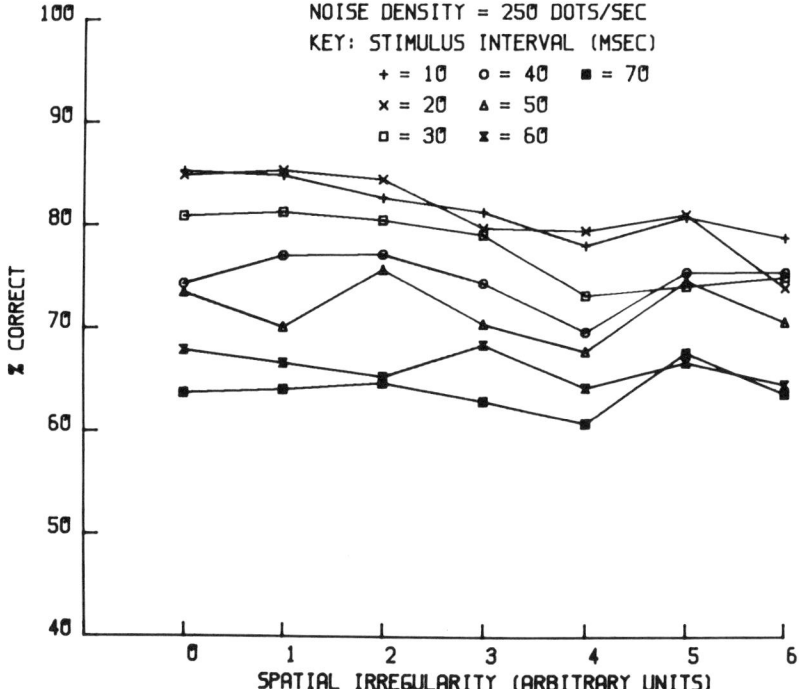

FIG. 23. The results of Experiment 5 displaying the negligible effect of spatial interval irregularity on the detectability of a straight dotted line. The horizontal axis is scaled as an arbitrary series of increasingly irregular spacing, but since minutes of disparity must be added to degrees of visual angle, the scale is not an equal interval one. The seven curves vary parametrically with the mean temporal interval between dots.

68 3. EXPERIMENTAL DESIGN AND RESULTS

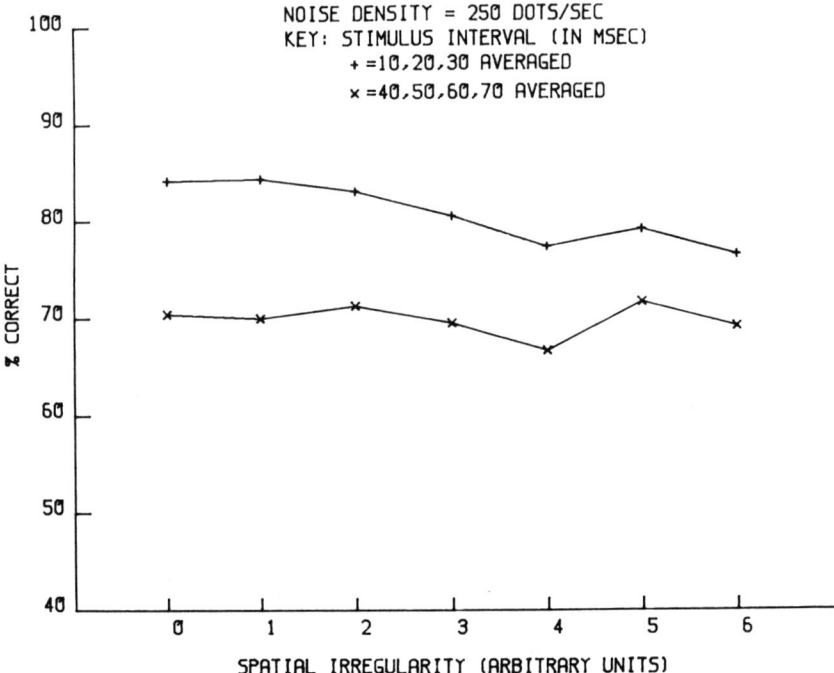

FIG. 24. The data of Experiment 5 displaying the negligible effect of spatial irregularity pooled into two curves; one for 10, 20, and 30 msec intervals and one for 40, 50, 60, and 70 msec intervals. A slight difference between the two pooled data sets can be observed. The effect of spatial irregularity is somewhat greater, though still small, for the 10, 20, and 30 msec intervals.

This is a remarkable outcome in light of the fact that the detectability of dotted lines in both the two and three dimensional cases in which all of the dots are presented rapidly enough to appear to be simultaneous does display significant sensitivity to spacing irregularity.

Experiment 6

Design and Rationale. Having found that neither temporal nor spatial irregularity produced significant deficits in the detection task when the duration of the interval between successive dots is relatively long, it became a challenge to determine just how far the stimulus form could be distorted before performance on the detection task would, in fact, deteriorate. The next logical step was to prepare a set of stimuli in which the order of presentation is nonsequential. That is, if the dots in a line are numbered 1, 2, 3, 4, 5, 6, and 7 in order of position from the start of the line to the end, I asked—What happens if they are plotted out of this normal positional order? To answer this question the experiment presents stimulus lines in seven increasing degrees of disorder. The least disordered line, of course, was the one produced by plotting the spatially numbered dots of the line in the "correct" sequence; that is, 1, 2, 3, 4, 5, 6, and finally 7. The most disordered line used in this experiment is produced by plotting the dots in the temporal order 1, 6, 4, 5, 3, 2, and finally 7.

Table 2 lists the seven arbitrarily disordered patterns that were used in this experiment. The degree of disorder has been roughly quantified by establishing a "disorder score" equal to the sum of the displacement scores of all dots that are moved from their nominally "correct" sequence. The displacement score for each dot is the number of sequential steps it is moved. For example, if the dot in position 6 is actually presented second in temporal order, its displacement score is 4. The disorder score for the line is the sum of the displacement scores for all of the dots in the line. The disorder score for each line is also indicated in Table 2.

It is possible to speculate that if the temporal interval between successive dots is very small (10 msec) then the effect of order should be minimal. The persistance of the visual system and the short intervals should make the dots, despite all of the degrees of disorder, appear to be presented simultaneously. On the other hand, as the interdot interval becomes longer, the detection scores for the

TABLE 2
The Presentation Orders of the Dots in a Straight Line Used in Experiment 6.

Dot Positions in Temporal Sequence							Number of Displacements in Dot Order
1	2	3	4	5	6	7	0
1	2	4	3	5	6	7	1
1	3	2	5	4	6	7	2
1	2	5	3	6	4	7	6
1	4	3	6	2	5	7	8
1	4	6	2	5	3	7	10
1	6	4	5	3	2	7	12

3. EXPERIMENTAL DESIGN AND RESULTS

more irregular dot sequences should fall off. To test this admittedly hesitant prediction (given the surprises of experiments 2, 4, and 5) the regular temporal intervals between the plotting of the sequential dots are varied from day to day. On seven sequential days interdot intervals of 10, 20, 30, 40, 50, 60, and 70 msec are used. The experiment is then run in the reverse order for a total of 14 days. A single noise density of 250 dots per second is used throughout the experiment; and only the dichoptic viewing condition is used.

Results. The results of this experiment are shown in Fig. 25. These data indicate that there is a systematic, though modest, effect of disorder. All data have been pooled and replotted in Fig. 26 to show the general trend of this effect. I appreciate that it is not too meaningful to simply assert that this effect is relatively "small" or "large," but in this case I feel compelled to note that these data, especially at the longer durations where disorder should be very disruptive, reflect

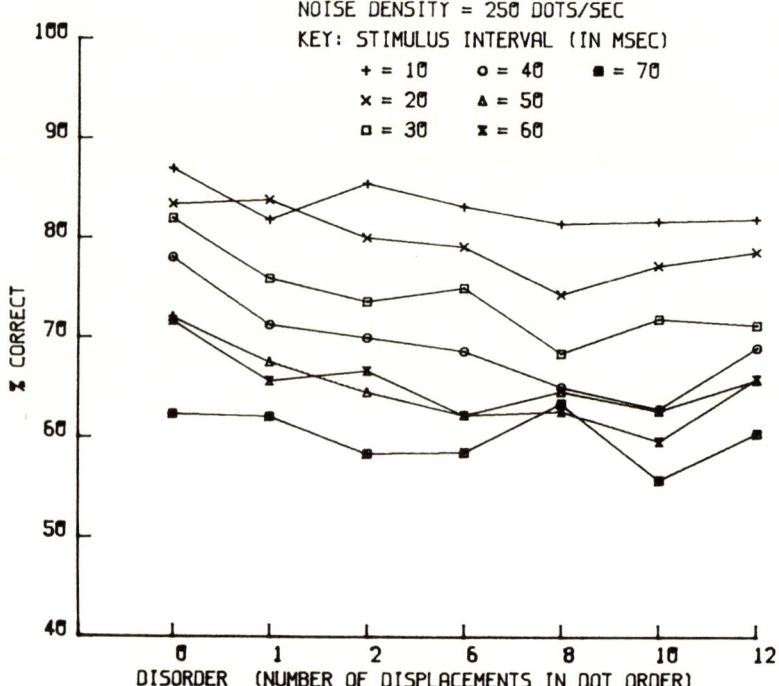

FIG. 25. The results of Experiment 6 showing the effect of disorder on the detectability of a straight dotted line. The horizontal axis is sealed in terms of the sum of the individual dot displacements; individual dot displacements being defined in terms of the number of "out of order" positions that dot has been shifted as shown in Table 2. The seven curves vary parametrically with the (regular) stimulus interval.

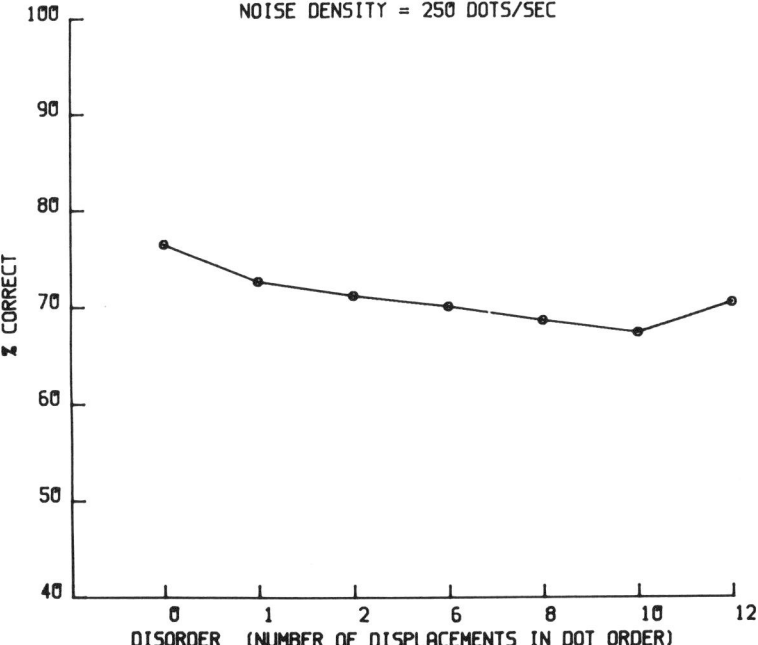

FIG. 26. In this figure the data displayed in Fig. 25 are pooled for all temporal interval values to show the overall trend of the disorder effect. This single curve shows a small but consistent effect of disorder.

an astonishingly weak effect of order. (The reason for the elevation of the scores for disorder score "12" is not known but is believed to be spurious.) Except for the fact that the dots are colinear, their temporal pattern should make them look like so many random dots. How the visual system accomplishes this fact is yet to be explained. The simple fact is that even in this extremely irregular situation, the visual system responds better than I for one could have imagined.

PLANES

Experiment 7[5]

Design and Rationale. Experiment 7, the first experiment on plane detection is designed to determine the effect of viewing duration and disparity on stereoscopic depth discrimination. To provide the basic parametric data concern-

---

[5]This experiment has been published separately (Uttal, Fitzgerald, & Eskin, 1975a). It is presented here in a much reduced and heavily edited version to make this lecture series self-contained.

72   3. EXPERIMENTAL DESIGN AND RESULTS

ing stereopsis this foundation experiment for planes uses a different paradigm than that used in Experiments 1 through 6 as do Experiments 8 and 9. Rather than having the observer detect a stimulus form hidden in randomly positioned masking dots, the observer is required to report in which of two sequential trials there is a depth difference between two planes each of which is defined by random (in X and Y) arrangements of dots. The positive stimulus for this experiment consists of two steroscopic planes plotted perpendicularly to the observer's line of sight at different depths as shown in Fig. 27. (It must be kept in mind that the outlines in this figure are not seen by the observer—only the arrays of random dots defining the two planes.) One, a reference plane, extends over the full range

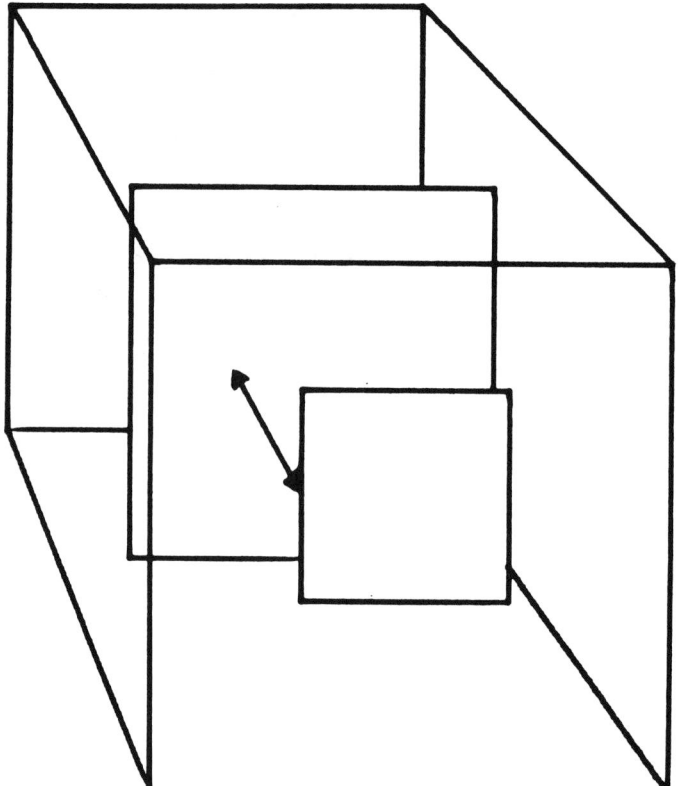

FIG. 27.   A graphic depiction of the two plane discrimination methods used in Experiments 7 and 8. The large reference plane is placed at the fixation point (zero disparity). The smaller test plane varies in its depth relative to the reference plane as well as in such other properties as dot density. Neither the outline of the cube nor the outline of the two planes are seen by the observer. The planes are defined by the positions of random arrays of dots.

of a 5.6 deg × 5.6 deg viewing field for each eye. The observer converges his lines of sight on dots at the apparent depth of this plane. This disparity value thus defines the reference depth—a depth that appears to be at the center of the perceived cubical space. The other, a test plane, extends over a smaller field subtending 2.8 deg × 2.8 deg. The test plane always contains ¼ of the number of dots in the reference plane on the closest approximation possible. The Z axis (i.e., the disparity) of the test plane could be specified to locate it either in front or in back of the reference plane by crossing (converging) or uncrossing (diverging) the disparity. The negative stimulus presentation consists of a single planar array of random dots in which no depth difference had been programmed. The viewing time and the number of dots in both stimuli are also independent variables manipulated in this experiment.

In both this experiment and Experiment 9, therefore, the two sequential presentations in each trial have the same dot density and distribution in the X, Y plane. To achieve this equality of numerosity an additional group of random dots, equivalent in number and X, Y plane extent to those in the test plane, is added to the reference plane dots. These additional dots are located at the same zero-disparity Z-axis depth as the reference plane to negate any secondary cues of density or pattern in the experimental task. Depth difference is the only cue to the discrimination of the test plane from the reference plane.

Experiment 7 is run in three parts. The first part, explores the effect of disparity and dot numerosity at an exposure duration of 500 msec. Reference plane dot numerosities of 4, 10, 30, 50, 100, 200, 300 and 377 are used in this part of the experiment. The numbers of dots in the test planes are, therefore, equal to 1, 3, 8, 12, 25, 50, 75, and 94 respectively. Eleven steps of disparity are used varying from 5.60 min (crossed) to 5.60 min (uncrossed) in 1.12 min steps. No vergence aid other than the plus or minus feedback signal and the stimuli themselves is used in this part of the experiment.

In the second part of Experiment 7, stimuli are exposed for only 5 msec. The same disparities are used as in the first part, but only reference plane dot numerosities of 50, 30, 10, and 4 could be tested because of the shortened display time. Test plane numerosities of 12, 7, 3, and 1 respectively, therefore, are used. In this part, a pair of vergence adjusting fixation-convergence dots is displayed during the intervals between the feedback signal and the stimulus presentations and between the first and second stimuli in order to eliminate the possibility that vergence drifts would interfere with the perception of these brief stimuli.

The third part of the Experiment 7 provides the link between the first two parts by determining the specific effect of exposure duration on stereoscopic depth. This part of the experiment always uses stimuli that contain 100 dots in the reference plane and 25 in the test plane. The same disparity schecule is used as in the first part of the experiment, but scanned the exposure duration dimension. Durations of 500, 400, 200, 200, 50, 40 and 20 msec are used. No vergence adjusting point is used in this part of the experiment.

74   3. EXPERIMENTAL DESIGN AND RESULTS

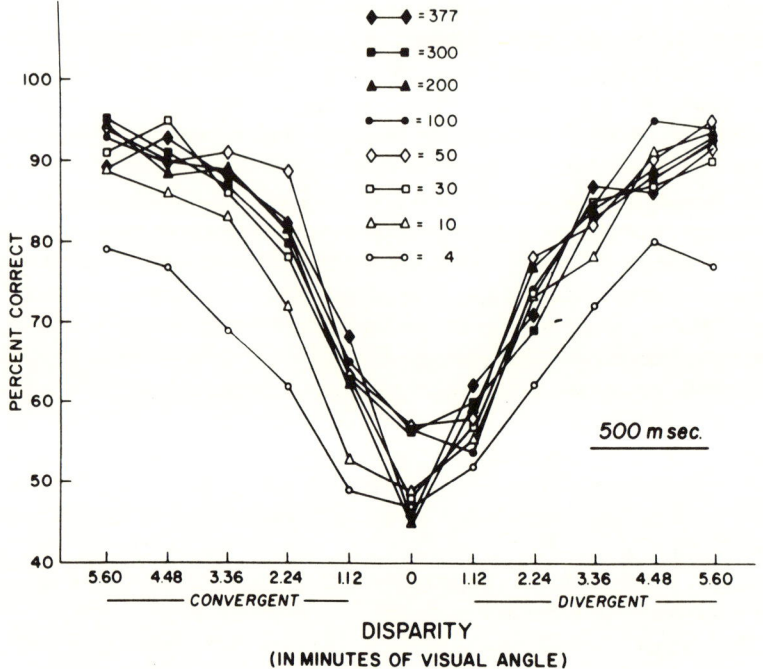

FIG. 28. The results of the first part of Experiment 7. At the prolonged exposure duration used (500 msec), there is little effect of dot numerosity on two plane discrimination except at the lowest value; however, the effect of disparity is strong. Observers continuously and symmetrically improve their performance with increases in both convergent and divergent disparity. The family of curves is parametric with the number of dots in the reference plane. This part of the experiment did not use a convergence aid.

Results. Figs. 28, 29, and 30 display the results of the three parts of Experiment 7. Fig. 28 shows the effects of both disparity and dot numerosity on the stereoscopic perception of two planes exposed for 500 msec. As the more or less symmetrical limbs of the curve indicate for crossed and uncrossed disparities, respectively, there is a gradual decline in the ability of the observer to discriminate between a reference and a test plane as the disparity decreases from a maximally crossed disparity of 5.60 min to zero disparity, and then a gradual increase in the discriminability as the disparity once again increases to the maximum uncrossed value of 5.60 min. Although it is not possible to assert the following generalization for all parametric curves, it is clear that there is a reliable difference in the detection scores for zero disparity and the next smallest value (1.12 min) for at least some of the dot numerosity situations mentioned here. Thus, in some instances employing this task and instrumentation, stereoscopic discrimination appears to be effective for disparities of approximately this value. This value may be considered an estimate of the stereoscopic threshold as measured with the present experimental task and with this type of instrumentation.

The effect of dot numerosity, on the other hand, is small. With the exception of the two lowest values (4 and 10 dots in the reference plane and 1 and 3 dots in the test plane), all of the other curves representing the discriminability of the more densely dotted test and reference planes seem to lie superimposed on top of another. The 10-dot condition has a slightly lower value than the others only for the crossed disparity condition, while the 4-dot condition averages about 15% lower than the cluster of other curves for both crossed and uncrossed conditions. The best performance level obtained with maximum values of both disparity and dot numerosity is 95% for this relatively long exposure duration of 500 msec.

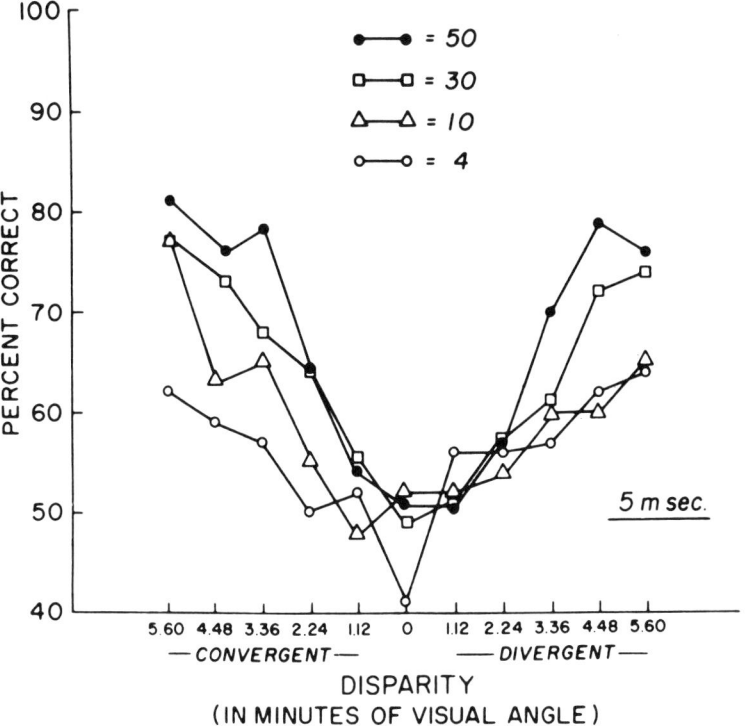

FIG. 29. The results of the second part of Experiment 7. At this brief exposure duration (5 msec) the effect of dot numerosity is greater than in Fig. 28, but the same continuous and symmetrical increase in sensitivity with increases in disparity is observed. Because of the brief exposure duration, this part of the experiment used a convergence aid. The family of curves is parametric with the number of dots in the reference plane.

76   3. EXPERIMENTAL DESIGN AND RESULTS

Figure 29 presents the results of the second part of Experiment 7 in which the exposure duration is only 5 msec. In this case, the best performance level is about 80%—indicating a considerable deficit solely as a function of the exposure duration. This occurred in spite of the fact that a vergence-aiding dot is used in this brief exposure condition. Furthermore, there appears to be a somewhat larger differential effect of dot numerosity for this shorter exposure duration. The typical difference between the corresponding scores for the 50-dot condition and for the 4-dot condition is about 20% with these brief exposures, compared to 10% for the longer durations used in the first part of this experiment.

The results of the third part of Experiment 7 are shown in Fig. 30. In this case, the disparity curves have been presented parametrically as a function of exposure duration. Clearly, the effect of reducing exposure duration is abrupt and occurs at one step between .4 and .2 sec. This suggests that a very brief stimulus (.020 sec) is nearly as effective as one ten times long (.2 sec). This is probably attributable to simple persistence of the visual image. The absolute values of the lower curves (100 dots at 40 and 20 msec) in this figure are lower than those of the curve for 50 dots at 5 msec in Fig. 29, indicating that the convergence

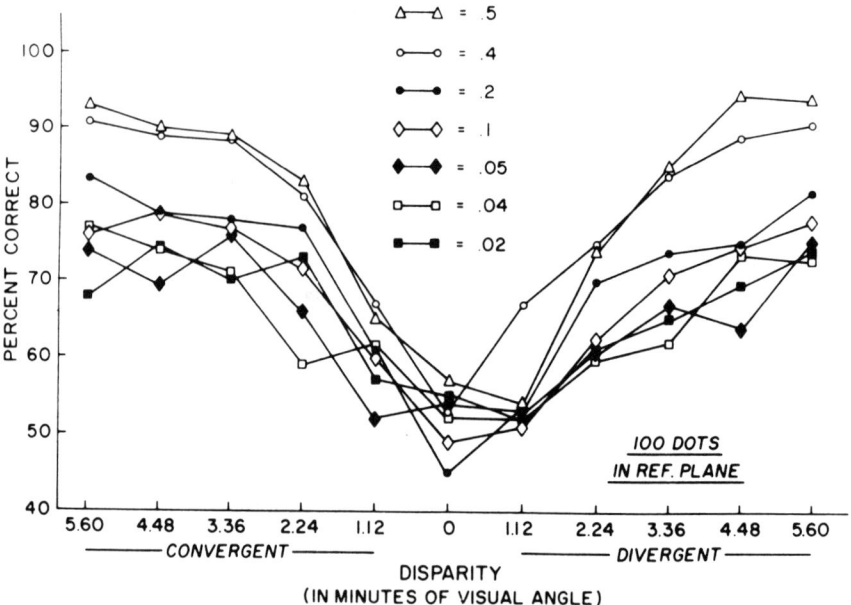

FIG. 30. The results of the third part of Experiment 7. The effect of reducing the viewing duration is seen to progressively reduce the performance level. Nevertheless, the same pattern of symmetrical and continuous increase in performance as either convergent or divergent disparity is increased is seen at all durations. The family of curves is parametric with the viewing duration measured in seconds.

adjustment point substantially helped the observer to process the available stereoscopic cues.

Experiment 8[5]

Design and Rationale. Experiment 8 is identical in procedure to Experiment 7 with the exception that, as in Julesz' (1964) experiment, a masking burst of 250 random dots follows the display of the two planes at a variable interval. By means of this procedure, I hoped both to substantiate the estimate of stereoscopic time obtained by Julesz and to determine the function relating performance and interval between the offset of the test plane and the onset of the masking burst over a more complete range than he had examined. Because of visual persistence, processing time is not adequately measured by the method used in Experiment 7. The purpose of this experiment is to counteract that persistence.

A single numerosity condition is used for this experiment: stimuli consist of 100 dots in the test plane presented against a reference plane consisting of 250 dots. The masking burst of 250 dots, distributed throughout the apparent cubical volume, is plotted as rapidly as possible at intervals of 1, 10, 20, 30, 40, 100, 150 and 200 msec following the test and reference planes. Only one interval between the stimulus and blanking mask is used each day, but disparities are varied from trial to trial by randomly selecting among values between 5.60 min (crossed) and 5.60 min (uncrossed) in 1.12 min steps. Two values of exposure duration—40 and 20 msec— are used in this experiment.

Results. This attempt to determine the amount of time required for stereoscopic information processing by varying the interval between the stereo test and reference fields and a masking stimulus composed of randomly distributed (in the three-dimensional viewing space) dots results in a function exhibiting a marked discontinuity at about 50 msec as shown in Fig. 31. These main results of this experiment are plotted as a function of the interval between the stimulus planes and the masking burst with all disparity and both exposure duration conditions pooled. At the moderate masking densities used in this experiment, only one of the three Ss is completely reduced to chance levels of performance at the shortest masking intervals. In fact, the average performance level is 59% when only a 1-msec interval exists between the stereoscopic test planes and the mask. As the separation increases, there is only a slight (if any) increase in performance until the interval of 50 msec is reached. At that point, an abrupt increase to a 68% performance level is observed. For intervals greater than 50 msec there is again little improvement. The fact that there is sharp discontinuity at 50 msec suggests that approximately this amount of time is necessary for the establishment of the perception of depth. This finding is in agreement with the estimate of stereoscopic perception time made by Julesz (1964).

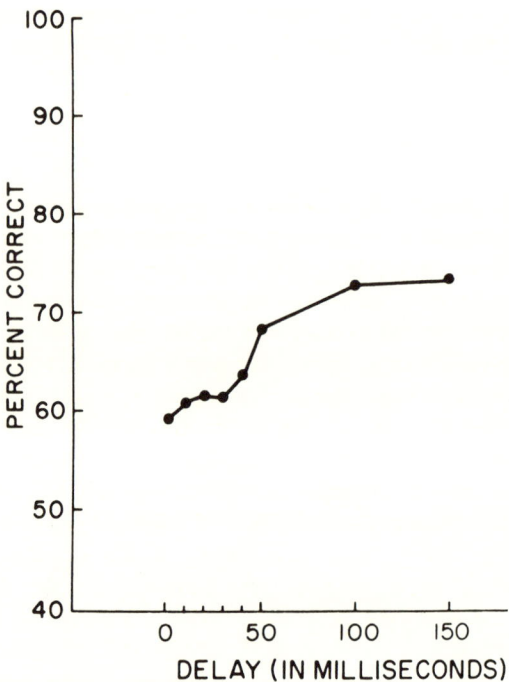

FIG. 31. The results of Experiment 8 in which a blanking field made up of an array of dots randomly distributed throughout the viewing space is used to interfere with the processing of the stereoscopic percept. Data from both parts of the experiment have been pooled in plotting this figure. There is a discontinuity at about 50 msec but no great increase in performance at shorter or longer stimulus-mask intervals. This discontinuity suggests that, as suggested by Julesz (1964), a 50 msec processing period is required for stereoscopic perception.

This finding is quite dissimilar to the function obtained for backward masking of two-dimensional stimuli. In that case, there is a continual increase after a 10-msec initial plateau (Uttal, 1973) confirming the original suggestion by Sperling (1963) that only 10 msec is required for the processing of simple two-dimensional stimuli.

The data obtained in this experiment have been segregated in Fig. 32 and Fig. 33 for the two exposure durations. Fig. 32 shows the results for the 40-msec exposure duration. The curves have been plotted as a function of disparity with the interval between presentation of the two stimulus planes and the masking burst as a parameter. The decline in the performance with both decreasing disparity and decreasing interval is clearly evident. Figure 33 presents similar data for the 20-msec viewing condition. In this case, the performance scores at the shorter durations are more depressed than are those for the 40 msec durations.

PLANES   79

Figures 32 and 33 both exhibit an asymmetry between the performance levels of the convergent and divergent disparity conditions. Convergent values less than 50-msec display a shallower slope than the divergent values.

Experiment 9[5]

Design and Rationale. In Experiment 9, all of the stereoscopic parameters of a plane—numerosity, exposure duration, and disparity conditions—are reduced to minimum levels. Only two dots are used in each stimulus presentation; the S is required to specify which of two sequentially presented, side by side, pairs of dots differ in depth. (The other pair of dots is located at a common central depth.) The purpose of this experiment is to determine stereoscopic discriminability as a function of disparity under these severely reduced conditions. Prior to the first presentation, as well as between the two presentations, a dichoptic fixation-convergence pattern composed of the four corners of the viewing field is displayed so that vergence will be stable and the images fused when

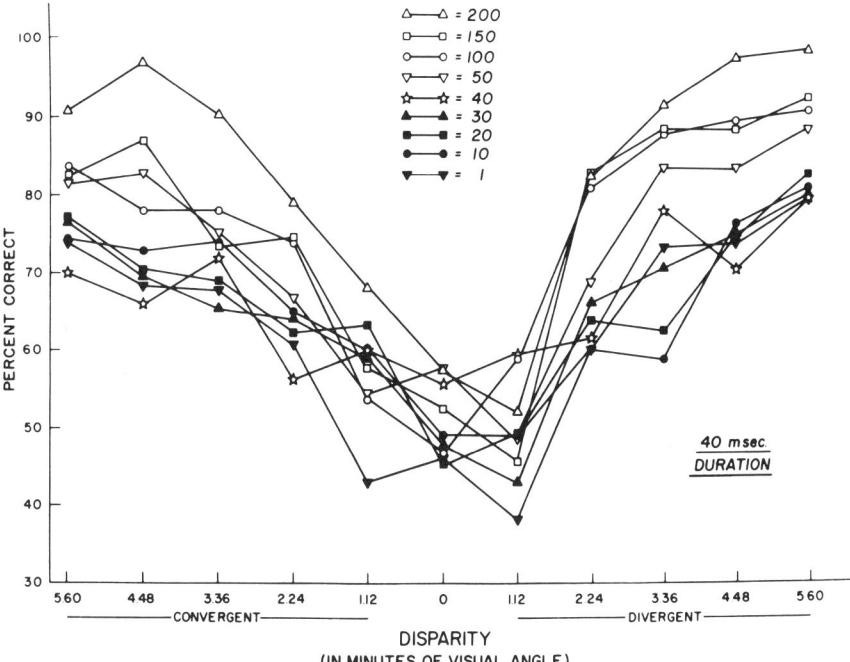

FIG. 32. The data for exposure durations of 40 msec that were pooled in Fig. 31 are presented separately in this figure. The family of curves is parametric with the interval between the stimulus and the mask measured in msec.

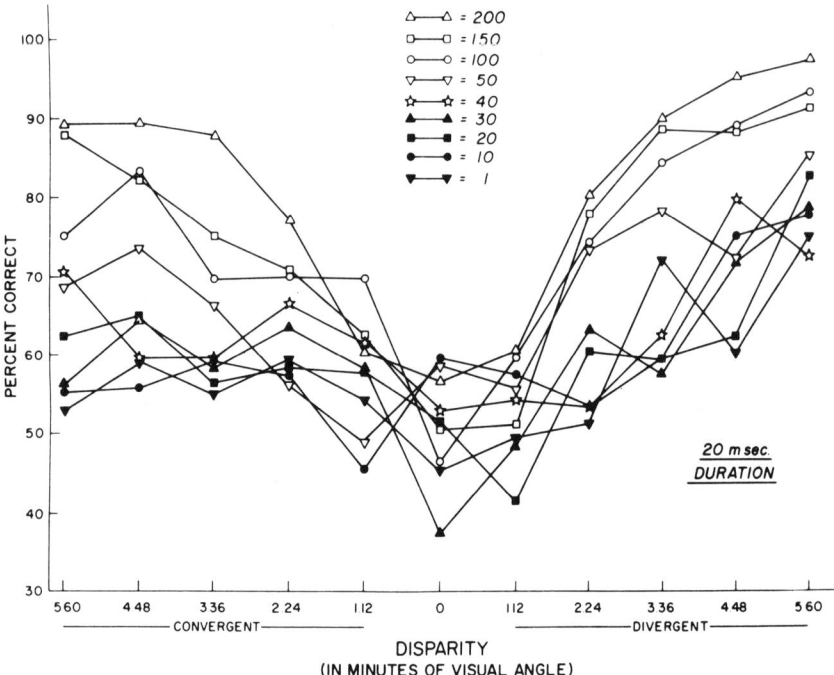

FIG. 33. The data for exposure durations of 20 msec that are pooled in Fig. 31 are presented separately in this figure. The family of curves is parametric with the interval between the stimulus and the mask measured in msec.

the single pair of stimulus dots is so briefly flashed. The dot stimuli are intensified only once and the exposure duration is, therefore, equivalent to the decay time of the phosphor (50 usec). The major independent variable in this experiment is disparity ranging from 5.6 min (crossed) to 5.6 min (uncrossed) in approximately 0.50 min steps.

Results. In spite of the fact that all stimulus conditions are reduced to their minimums, observers in this experiment are still able to perform at a creditable performance level as shown in Fig 34. Performance levels range from 80% at the greatest disparities down to chance levels when the disparity was zero. Both crossed and uncrossed disparities seem to produce comparable results with the function being nearly symmetrical around the zero disparity condition.

In Experiments 7, 8, and 9 the stimuli presented to the observer consist of two planes or two dots; the task in these cases is to specify in which of the two presentations the planes or dots were at different depths. In the following experiments, I return to the form detection paradigm used in Experiments 1–6 in which the stimulus form is hidden in an array of masking dots dispersed throughout the apparent cubical volume. In some of the experiments, the planar stimulus forms are hidden by dynamic random visual noise. In other instances, they are hidden in a static pattern that is stably and continuously exposed.

Experiment 10

Design and Rationale. Experiment 10 builds on the fundamental data obtained in Experiments 7, 8, and 9 to further delineate the basic perceptual processes involved in plane detection in stereoscopic space. The main goal of this experiment is to determine the effect, if any, of global shape on detectability. A secondary goal is to determine the effect of variations in the number of noise and stimulus dots on the detectability of a plane. This experiment is particularly relevant to the overall purpose of this study because it is the first to specifically

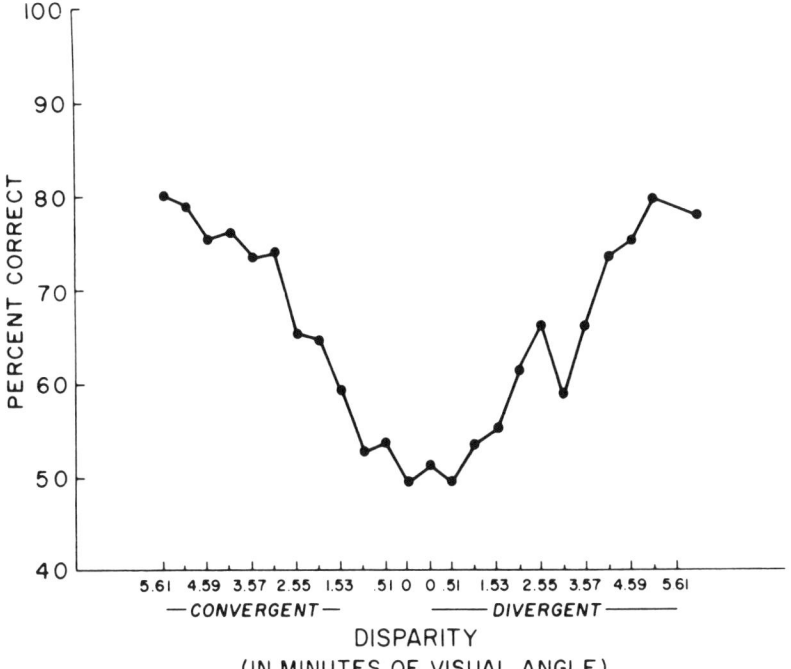

FIG. 34. The results of experiment 9 for a severely reduced stimulus consisting only of two dots presented at the briefest possible durations. Disparity sensitivity remains high and continuously and symmetrically improves with increases in either convergent or divergent disparity. The minimum detectable disparity remains less than 1 min of visual angle—even with this impoverished stimulus. Values for zero disparity were collected twice and not pooled in this figure.

82   3. EXPERIMENTAL DESIGN AND RESULTS

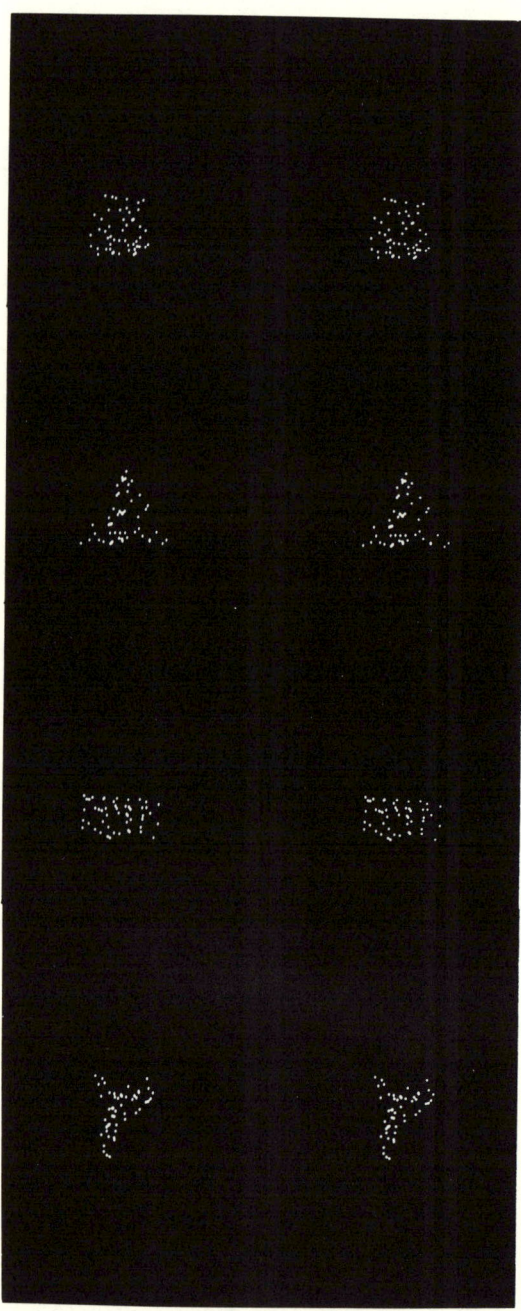

FIG. 35.   Samples of the stimuli used in Experiment 10. The four different planar stimulus shapes are formed by random arrays of dots all located at the same depths in stereoscopic space.

study the effects of the shape of planar stimuli on performance in the three dimensional detection task.

For use in this experiment, sets of stimulus forms of different shapes are generated by the special program utilizing the Houston Instrument Hipad graphic input digitizer. The program allows the user to generate polygonal regions filled with a specified number of randomly positioned dots and to store the locating coordinates of these dots in a disc file capable of being called by the stimulus control program in random order. In particular, the four stimulus forms used in this initial experiment on planar forms are a square, a rectangle, a triangle, and an irregular polygon formed by the rearrangement of the segments of the square. All four forms are equal in area and centered in the 5.4 deg by 5.4 deg presentation region. Each subtends exactly one quarter of the presentation region, although in a manner contingent upon the shape of each form.

Figure 35 shows a high density (50 dots) version of each of these four stimuli. Note that there is no explicit outline or contour; the shape is subjective in the same way as is the Kaniza triangle (Kaniza, 1976) and is defined by the distribution of the contained dots. Obviously, the polygonal form of each stimulus becomes more and more fully apparent as the number of dots increases. The dummy, or control stimulus in this case is an array of dots with the same X and Y coordinate values as the dots in the stimulus form, but with randomized Z coordinate values. Rather than having its constituent dots arranged in a plane, the dummy stimulus, therefore, contains the same number of dots distributed in a solid with the same frontal area as the plane. It is on this difference alone—the distribution in depth of the dummy and stimulus dots—that the observer must make his decision in this experiment.

The number of constituent dots in each of the four forms is varied in this experiment; each form could contain 5, 8, 10, 20, 30, 40, or 50 dots. The four stimulus patterns and the seven dot numerosities thus define 28 different stimuli, any one of which could be presented in any trial. On four sequential days, these stimulus forms are presented in progressively denser random noise consisting of 10, 25, 50, and 75 noise dots. The cycle of four days was then repeated in reverse order for a total of eight daily sessions. The stimulus and noise dots are presented in this experiment in a static mode with the entire array of noise and form dots being continuously refreshed on the oscilloscope for a period of one second. Only the dichoptic viewing condition producing stereoscopic depth is used in this experiment.

Results. Figure 36 shows the results of Experiment 10. In this figure, the scores for all stimulus forms have been pooled to emphasize the effect of noise dot and stimulus dot densities. The results concerning noise and stimulus form dot density are in accord with our previous results and are presented to simply calibrate the nature of the masking effect for this type of stimulus. As expected, increasing the number of visual noise dots, the parameter distinguising the several curves in this figure from each other decreases the detectability of the stimulus forms. Equally unsurprising is the fact that increases in the number of dots in each of the stimulus form increases the likelihood of any form being discriminated from among the visual noise dots.

Figure 37 plots the same data, but in this case the scores have been pooled for all stimulus dot densities. This figure is also, therefore, parametric in noise dot density but plots detection as a function of the stimulus form. It can be seen that there is no reliable or substantial difference in the detectability of the four forms across all noise dot densities. At the higher masking dot densities, triangles and the irregular polygon do appear to be slightly less well detected than are the

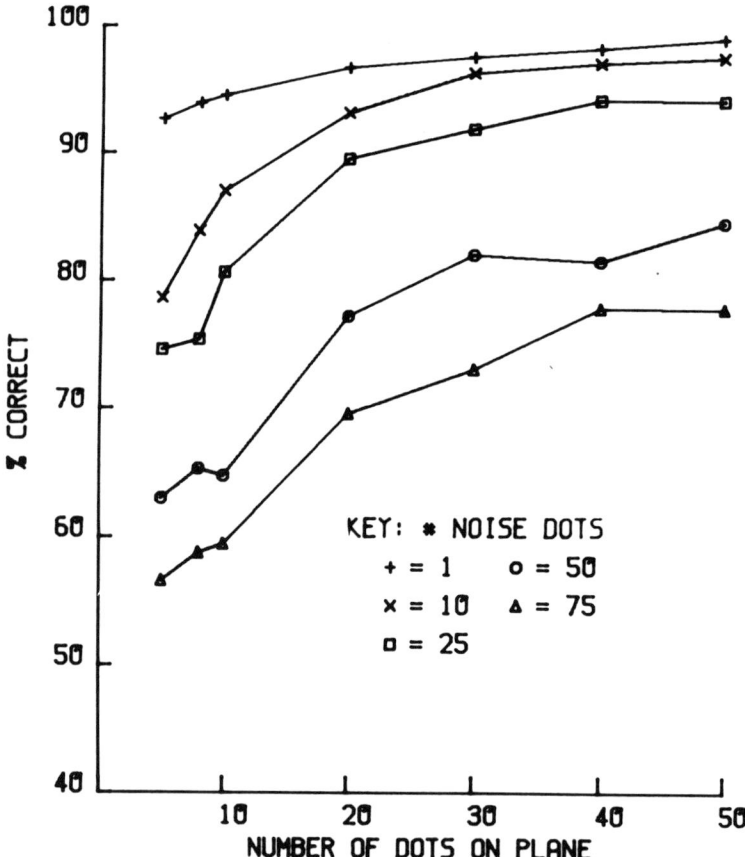

FIG. 36. The results of Experiment 10 showing the strong effect of the number of dots in the stimulus plane on its detectability. The curves in this figure are parametric with the number of noise dots. Presentation duration is kept constant at one sec.

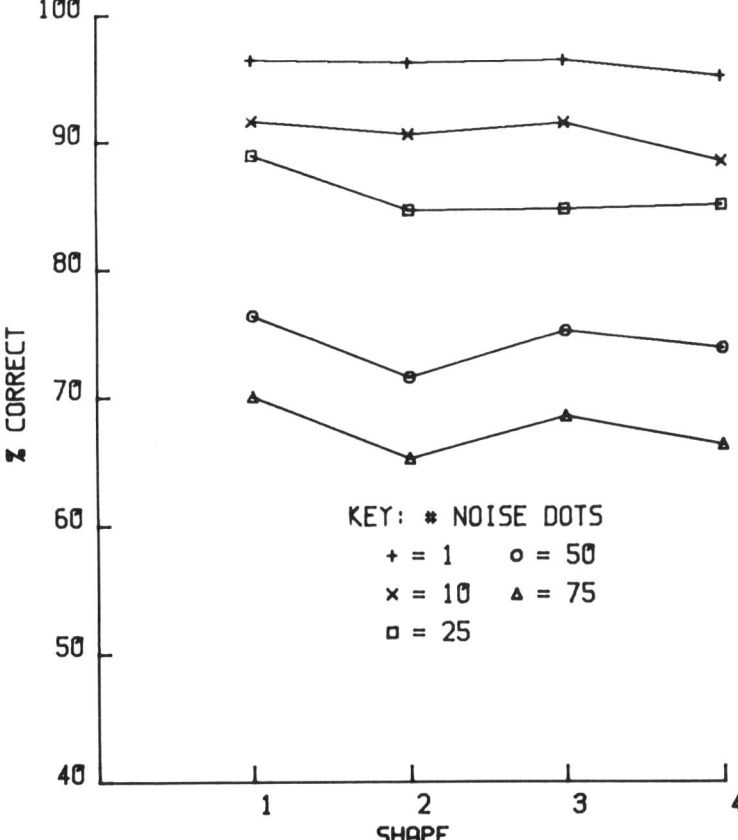

FIG. 37. The results of Experiment 10 reanalyzed to display the negligible effect of stimulus shape on the detectability of the stimuli. The curves in this figure are parametric with the number of noise dots. The presentation duration is kept constant at one sec.

square and rectangle, but the effect is small compared to other differences I have measured. I conclude, therefore, that these data suggest at best a weak global form effect and it is necessary to probe deeper to determine if a real form effect exists. This is the purpose of Experiments 11 and 12.

Experiment 11

Design and Rationale. Because the effect of stimulus form is so small, an attempt is made in Experiment 10 to further impoverish the stimulus by reducing the viewing time of each presentation. In this manner, it was hoped to enhance any form effect. The rationale for this approach is that the very long exposure duration (one sec) used in Experiment 10 may have swamped out any subtle effect of form in that experiment. To achieve the goal of stimulus impoverishment, a modification of Experiment 10 is, therefore, carried out. Experiment 11 utilizes only a single masking noise density—50 dots—a value at which the form had been detected at an intermediate performance level. The number of stimulus dots varies as in Experiment 10. On successive days, however, stimulus viewing durations of 500, 250, 100, and 50 msec are used. Once again, only the dichoptic viewing condition capable of producing stereoscopic depth is used. Experiment

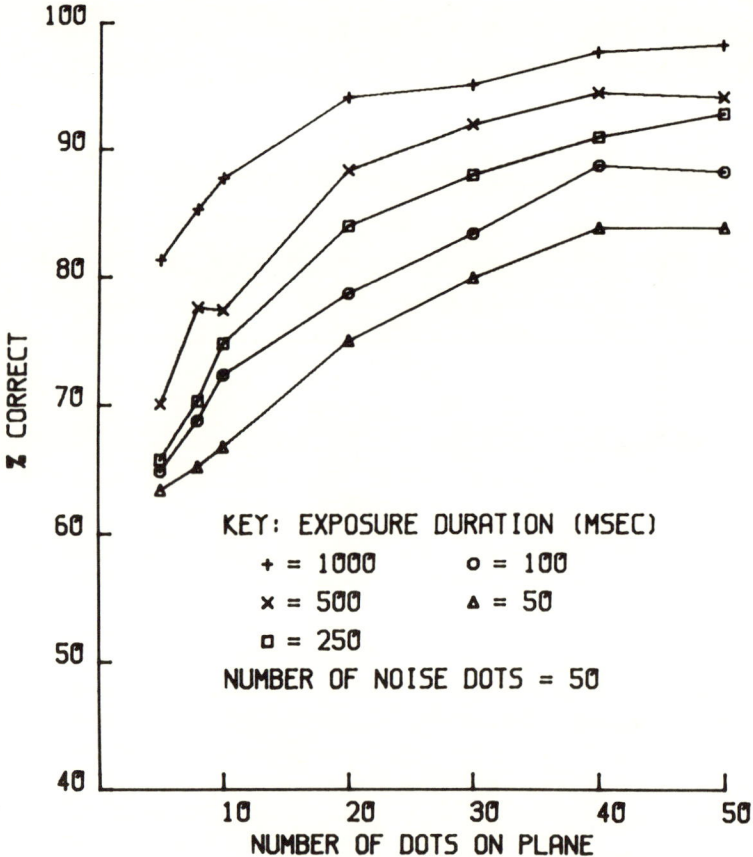

FIG. 38. The results of Experiment 11 in which the presentation duration has been varied to examine the effects of form under this kind of stimulus degradation. The results are plotted as a family of curves parametric with the presentation duration. Each curve shows the results at one duration as a function of the number of dots in the plane. The number of dots in the noise has been kept constant at 50.

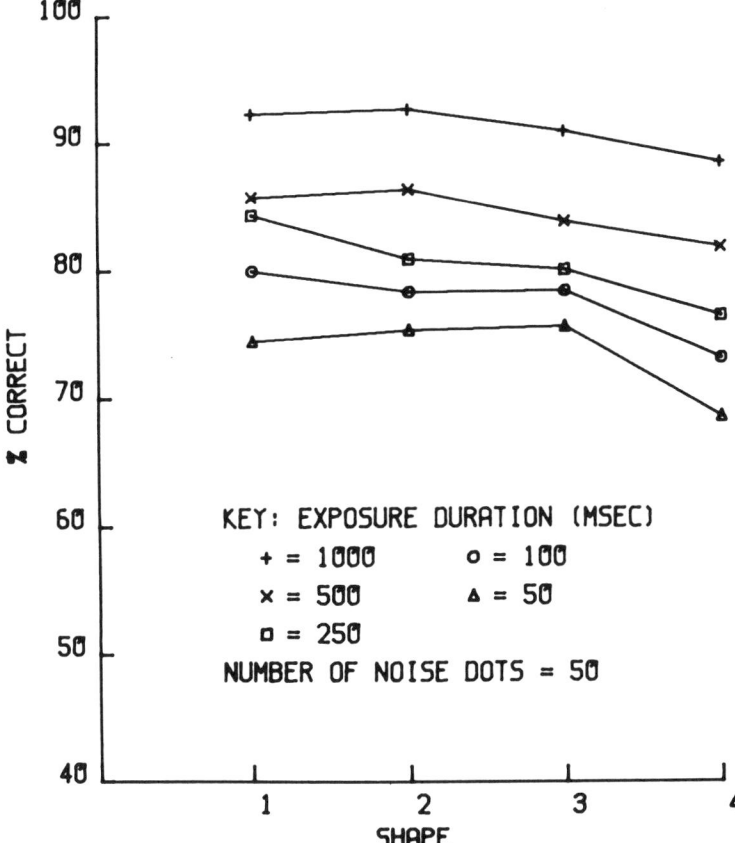

FIG. 39. The results of Experiment 11 reanalyzed to display the negligible effects of shape even when the presentation duration is reduced. Noise dot density has been kept constant at 50.

11 required 8 sessions to complete, with the experiment being repeated in increasing order of duration upon completion of the decreasing duration series.

Results. The results of Experiment 11 are shown in Fig. 38 and Fig. 39. Figure 38 presents the results of this experiment with data pooled across the four stimulus forms to emphasize the effect of exposure duration. Figure 39 presents the data pooled across all stimulus form dot densities to emphasize the effect of form. Both figures are parametric in the exposure duration of each presentation.

Once again, the effects of exposure duration and stimulus dot numerosity are as anticipated. Decreasing exposure duration decreases performance levels as does decreasing the number of dots in the form. The effects of form on detec-

88 3. EXPERIMENTAL DESIGN AND RESULTS

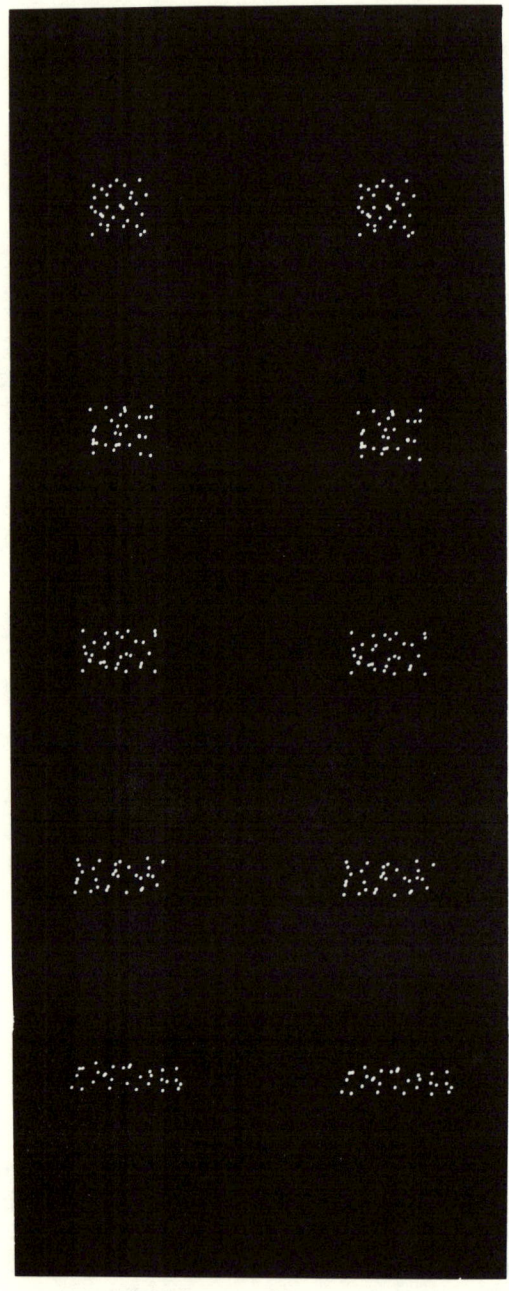

FIG. 40. The five stereoscopic stimulus forms used in Experiment 12.

tability, however, remain equivocal. The weak pattern of effects obtained in Experiment 10 is replicated. Triangles seem no less well detected in this case than squares. If anything, the irregular form only is detected systematically less well than the others.

In general, it appears that this attempt to impoverish the stimulus, while successful in reducing performance levels, is not any more successful in eliciting any strong effect of form than Experiment 10. Experiment 12, therefore, is carried out to pursue the elusive form effect further into its lair.

Experiment 12

Design and Rationale. The negligible effects of form obtained in Experiments 10 and 11 are disappointing and surprising. In many of my earlier experiments in two dimensions (Uttal, 1975) effects of global form had been obtained. In most of those situations, however, there had been a continuous change in some single attribute of the form. Experiment 12 is carried out to more closely approximate those conditions. In this experiment a series of five different forms, starting with a prototypical square, is progressively transformed into four more and more oblong and rectangular dot arrays. These stimuli are shown in Fig. 40. These stimulus forms, like those in the two previous experiments, consist of random arrays of dots constrained to the desired square or rectangular planar area. The number of dots used in each of these stimulus forms is held constant at 30. In separate trials and in random order the stimuli are rotated about the Z axis to any of five orientations (0, 22, 45, 67, and 90 degrees) in order to introduce some positional uncertainty.

On a series of four days, the stimuli are presented in a variable amount of dotted visual noise; the noise is distributed throughout the stereoscopic cubical volume. The observer's task is as usual: Which of two sequential presentations contains the plane as opposed to the volume of random dummy dots? The noise levels utilized are 150, 200, 225, and 250 dots and are presented employing the static method. Viewing is always dichoptic and six observers are used.

Results. Figure 41 depicts the results of Experiment 12 plotted as a function of the five stimulus forms. All of the data from all noise levels and orientations are pooled to depict the average detectability scores. Because of the use of six objects and the high level of pooling each data point represents the outcome of an unusually high number of trials—approximately four thousand.

Obviously there is very little difference between the scores obtained for the square and the two least oblong rectangles. The fourth and fifth stimulus forms, the two most oblong rectangles, however, are detected slightly less well; a 4% drop and a 6% drop from the 90% score of the other three stimulus forms, respectively, are measured for these two most oblong rectangular arrays of dots.

90   3. EXPERIMENTAL DESIGN AND RESULTS

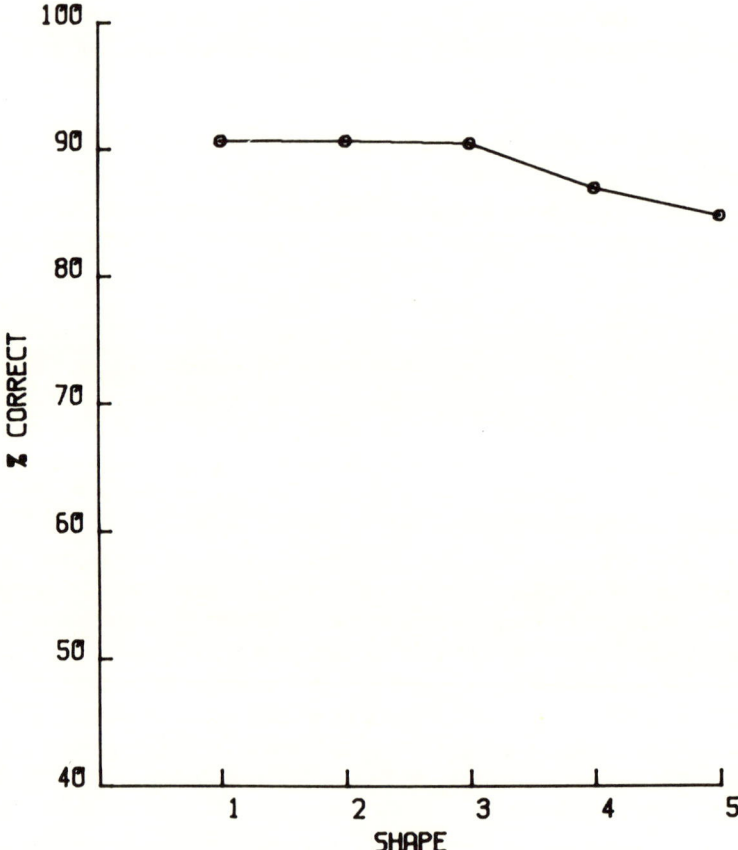

FIG. 41. The results of Experiment 12 analyzed to show the effect of shape. All data for all noise levels are pooled to emphasize the relatively small influence of the shape of a random array of dots on its detectability. The numbers on the horizontal axis indicate shapes varying from a square (1) to the most extreme rectangle (5).

This is a relatively modest decline and may possibly be due to the reduction in the number of dots in what engineers would call the "quality area"—that is the central region in which the dots are most strongly contributing to the detection of the plane. However, comparable experiments carried out in two dimensions with dotted outline forms (see Uttal, 1975, pp. 67–68), in which the visual angle of deformed stimuli (squares distorted to parallelograms) was not enlarged as profoundly as in this present case, showed performance decrements of from 15–20% as opposed to the 4% and 6% decrements observed here. In short, it appears that any effect of global form in this experiment is quite small compared to that observed in comparable experiments using forms created from dotted

PLANES 91

outlines. In my discussion of the formal model I will present a supplementary experiment that will make this point even more emphatically.

Finally, Fig. 42 shows the results of the experiment plotted as a function of the orientation of the forms. These data were obtained by pooling across all noise levels and all shapes. Needless to say, this figure makes it clear that there is no orientation effect present with these dotted arrays.

Experiment 13[6]

Design and Rationale. The effect on detectability of rotational orientation about the vertical axis (i.e., the Y axis passing through the center of the cubical space) is now examined in a two-part experiment. The stimulus situation is diagrammatically depicted in Fig. 43. The stimulus form in this experiment is a square plane subtending 4.4 deg by 4.4 deg when placed in a frontoparallel orientation (i.e., vertical and perpendicular to the line of sight). In separate trials, this plane can be rotated about the Y axis in 10 deg steps to any one of 18 angles that vary from 0 deg (perpendicular to the line of sight) to 89 deg (nearly parallel to the line of sight) and then back to 170 deg, an angle at which the plane once again is nearly in a frontoparallel orientation. An 89 deg value is used, rather than 90 deg, to avoid an end-on alignment of the dots in the plane; a situation in which there would be no physical difference between the stimulus form and dummy dots. As we shall see in Experiment 15 the choice of 89 deg was a lucky guess—there is a surprisingly sharp gradient of detectability associated with these nearly oblique angles.

In the first part of this experiment, stimuli positioned in any one of these 18 steps of angular rotation about the Y axis are randomly presented in sequential trials during each daily session. From day to day the number of dots contained in the stimulus plane is varied in order to scan the effects of the signal-to-noise ratio, while the number of masking dots defining the cubical space is kept constant at 100. On seven sequential days, the number of dots contained in the target plane is 50, 40, 30, 25, 15 or 10 in descending order; this series is then repeated in ascending order. Data from the two series are then pooled to give an estimate of the effect of rotational position and of the signal to noise ratio with constant noise.

In the second part of this experiment, the number of masking dots included within the cubical space is varied and the number of dots in the stimulus plane is kept constant. Values of 25, 50, 75, 100, 125 and 150 masking dots are used in ascending and then in descending order on twelve successive days in order to

---

[6]This experiment has been published separately (Uttal, Fitzgerald, & Eskin, 1975b). It is presented here in a much reduced and heavily edited version to make this lecture series self-contained.

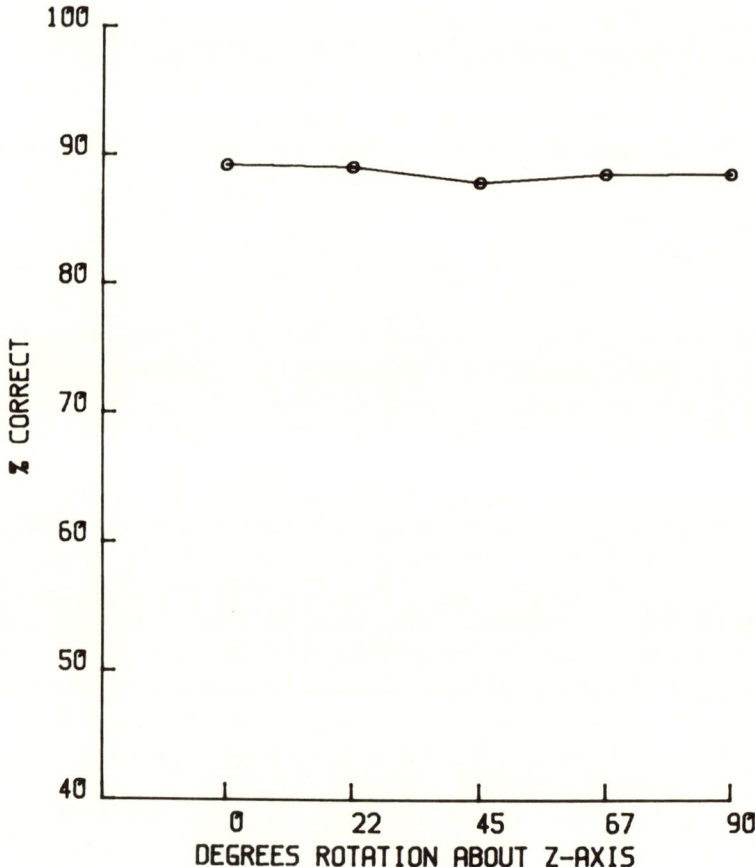

FIG. 42. The results of Experiment 12 analyzed to show the effect of orientation about the Z axis. All data from all noise levels have been pooled to emphasize the minimal effect of orientation of these randomly arrayed areas.

determine the signal-to-noise ratio effects when the masking dot density is varied and the stimulus plane constantly contains 15 dots.

The dummy stimulus in both parts of the experiment consists of the same number of masking dots as used in the stimulus presentation, plus an additional number of randomly positioned dummy dots equal to the number in the stimulus plane, in order to control for density or luminosity cues. However, this latter group of dummy dots is distributed at random *only* throughout the portion of the volume that is limited by the *frontal projection* of the stimulus plane *as it is rotated for each trial*. This projection varies, it must be noted, according to the orientation of the plane in each trial. Regardless of the orientation, therefore, the subject is always comparing two arrays of dots—an array randomly distributed in space and an array in which the dots are coplanar. In each case the projection of these two sets of dots on the front of the oscilloscope is equal; it is the spatial organizational difference between the two arrays that provides the only cue for the correct discriminative choice. The experiment is carried out in the static mode in which the display is repetitively refreshed for a viewing duration of one second.

Results. Figures 44 and 45 display the results of the two parts of Experiment 13. Figure 44 shows the effects of the rotation of the stimulus plane about the Y axis on a family of curves plotted parametrically as a function of the density of the stimulus plane but with masking dot density held constant at 100 dots. Two results are clearly apparent. First, there is no appreciable effect due to the angle of the target plane until the nearly edge-on 89 deg orientation is reached at all

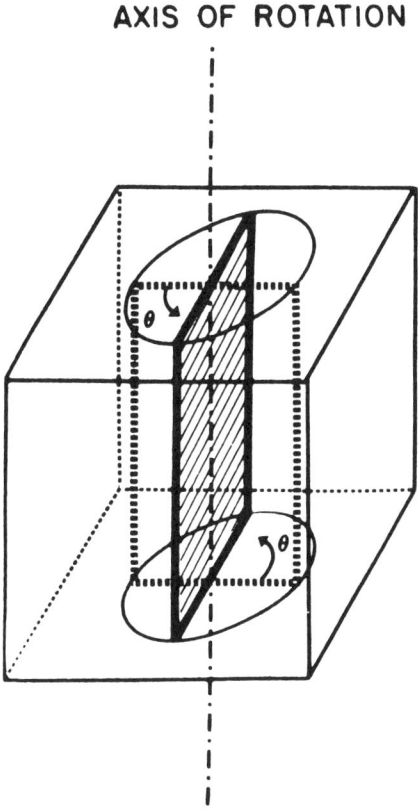

FIG. 43. Diagram of the stimulus used in Experiment 13. The plane could be rotated to any one of 18 angular positions for presentation in any trial. The outline cube defines the extent of the randomly distributed masking dots.

94   3. EXPERIMENTAL DESIGN AND RESULTS

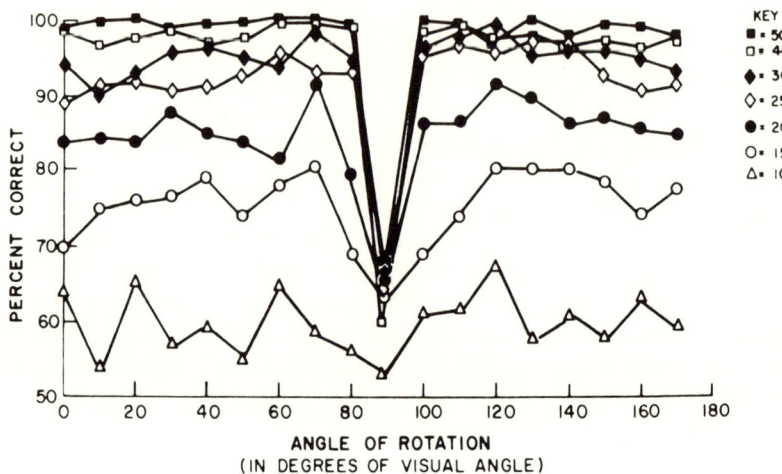

FIG. 44. The results of the first part of Experiment 13. Except for the 89 deg orientations there is no effect of orientation of the plane at any masking dot density, but there is a strong effect of target plane dot density. The family of curves is parametric with the number of dots in the target planes. Masking dot density is held constant at 100.

stimulus plane densities. Although some increase in the "noisiness" of the curves appears as the stimulus plane dot density decreases, the plane is detected equally well at all orientations for a given dot density. In the case of the nearly head-on 89 deg orientation—the one with the least frontal projection area—the dummy stimulus and the stimulus plane are, in fact, very nearly physically indistinguishable from each other, since the dummy dots themselves have been compressed into a vanishingly small volume, that is nearly into a vertical plane.

Second, as would have been expected, in this case where so many dots are randomly distributed throughout space (unlike Experiments 7 or 8 where the dots are restricted to only two planes) the dot density of the target plane has a very strong effect on detectability. The fewer dots in the target plane, the less well the observers are able to distinguish it from the randomly spaced dots defining the cubical space. However, the decline in performance is not linear. Whereas little change is discernible above a stimulus plane dot density of 30, the differential effect on performance increases as the dot density decreases. At a stimulus plane dot density of 10, some of our observers are performing at chance levels; therefore, no attempt was made to pursue this variable to even lower values.

Figure 45 depicts the findings from the second part of Experiment 13, in which the signal-to-noise relations are manipulated by varying the density of the masking dots while holding the number of dots in the stimulus plane constant at 15. This value produced an intermediate score in the first part of the experiment. Figure 45 shows further that there is, as expected, a gradual decline in the performance of the observer as the masking noise density increases. However, the effect of varying the masking dot density appears to be nearly linear as its range is scanned. Once again, no appreciable effect on performance of the angle of rotation of the plane in the cubical viewing space is observed in these data except at an orientation of 89 deg.

The results of both parts of Experiment 13 indicate that observers effectively compensate for the angle of rotation by trading off increases and decreases in the apparent depth of various parts of the plane, as it is rotated, for increases in dot density in the X, Y projected plane. Since it is known from our earlier works (Uttal, 1975) that dot densities are strong determinants of figural detection in two dimensions, it is interesting to expand that conclusion to the concept that masking dot density, as exemplified in the present case, appears to be processed in a three-dimensional manner. Of this, I shall have much more to say in the discussion.

Experiment 14

Design and Rationale. The limited effects produced by rotating a plane around a single axis in Experiment 13 became the incentive for the execution of Experiment 14. Given this insensitivity to rotations around the Y axis, one is immediately led to ask—What effect, if any, is produced by rotations about other

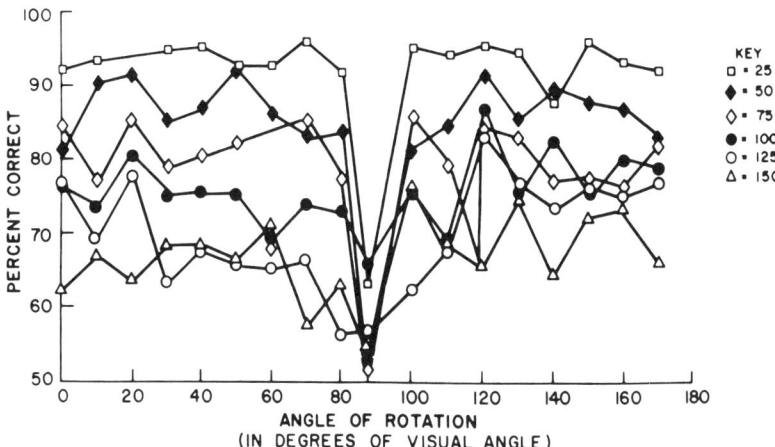

FIG. 45. The results of the second part of Experiment 13. There is, once again, no effect of target plane orientation but increasing masking dot density progressively reduces the detectability of the plane. The family of curves is parametric with the number of masking dots used to define the cube. Target plane dot density was held constant at 15.

axes, either singly or in combination? The purpose of Experiment 14, therefore, is to answer this question. To achieve this purpose, the observer is once again asked to discriminate between a masked planar stimulus and a cuboidal volume filled with the same number of dots and with the same frontoparallel projection area. The planar stimuli used in this experiment are, as in Experiment 13, square when in their frontoparallel projection, and always consist of 20 dots. The prototypical frontoparallel square rotates about a point at the middle of the cubical viewing space (i.e., at a disparity value at the same location as the convergence-fixation point) notwithstanding about which axes it is rotated. The prototype form is rotated into other stimulus forms by means of subroutines appended to the Hipad Digitizer control program. A file of 29 stimulus forms is thus created.

These 29 rotated patterns are designated by the magnitude of the rotational transformations applied to them about the X, Y and Z axes. For example, a stimulus form produced by first rotating the prototype frontoparallel plane 45 deg about the X axis, then 45 deg about the Y axis, and finally 45 deg about the Z axis, would be designated, 45, 45, 45. The order of rotation is very important. Different rotational orders, it should be noted, do not always produce identical patterns even if the magnitude of the rotations about each axis is exactly the same. Rotational transformations, to put it formally, are not commutative. For this reason the order as well as the magnitude of the rotations must be precisely specified. It should also be appreciated that however precise the specification of the rotation, that precision does not necessarily quantify the "complexity" of the resulting stimulus form. Some rotational patterns produce simple transformations, others more complex ones. Indeed the "complexity" of the rotational pattern is primarily a subjective phenomenon. It is only empirically that we can determine how well observers will detect these tridimensionally rotated planes.

Table 3 designates the 29 stimulus forms in terms of the X, Y, Z rotation order described above. These stimulus forms are presented in random order in six sequential daily sessions using the static noise mode with a noise dot density of 100, 125, and 150 dots respectively, once in ascending and once in descending order. A constant viewing time of one sec is used throughout this experiment; only the dichoptic viewing condition is used. Since absolute levels are not germane to the purposes of this experiment, the data from all three noise levels are pooled to show the effect of the various rotations.

Results. Figure 46 depicts the results of Experiment 14. The overall impression that one obtains from an examination of these data is that, once again, there is very little difference between the detectability scores of any of the rotated planes with the exception of the three rotational sequences numbered 5, 17, and 25. Otherwise there is little effect of either the magnitude or the specific combination of axes about which the pattern is rotated. Thus the minimal effect

TABLE 3
The 29 Patterns of Rotation Used in Experiment 14. Rotations Follow a Right Hand Rule in Determining the Positive Angle of Rotation.

Pattern Number	Degrees Rotation About		
	X	Y	Z
1	0	0	0
2	22	0	0
3	44	0	0
4	66	0	0
5	88	0	0
6	0	22	0
7	0	44	0
8	0	66	0
9	0	88	0
10	0	0	22
11	0	0	44
12	0	0	66
13	0	0	88
14	22	22	0
15	44	44	0
16	66	66	0
17	88	88	0
18	22	0	22
19	44	0	44
20	66	0	66
21	88	0	88
22	0	22	22
23	0	44	44
24	0	66	66
25	0	88	88
26	22	22	22
27	44	44	44
28	66	66	66
29	88	88	88

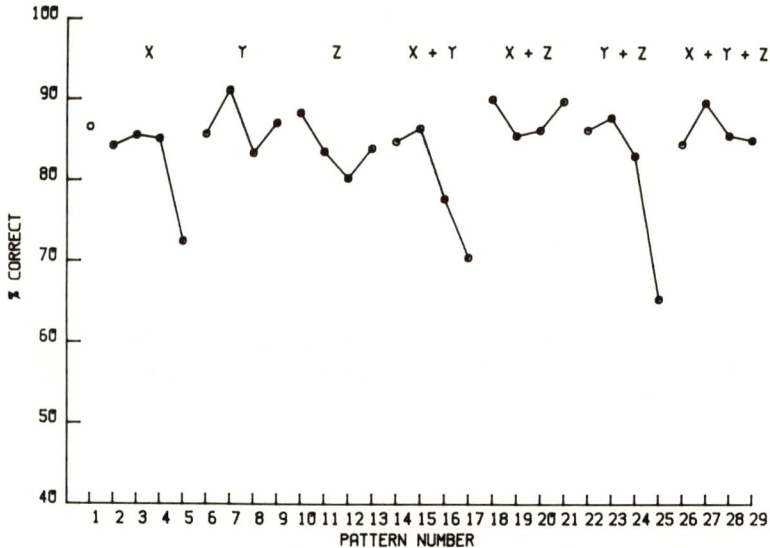

FIG. 46. The results of Experiment 14. Even though stimulus planes are rotated about the X, Y, or Z; X and Y; X and Z; Y and Z; or even the X, Y, and Z axes simultaneously, there is little effect on detectability except for the stimuli numbered 5, 17, and 25 (see Table 3 to decode the pattern numbers). These three conditions correspond to rotations resulting in nearly horizontal planes in which the association of the corresponding dots of the left and right eye images is physically confused.

previously observed for rotation about the Y axes seems to hold both for other axes individually and in combination.

Those three rotation sequences that do show a decrement in performance (5, 17, and 25) all resulted in a plane oriented such that it lay nearly horizontally in the X, Z plane. In such an orientation, the stimulus form appears to be almost a horizontal straight line. Recalling that the cue for stereopsis is horizontal disparity, it becomes obvious why these patterns should result in lower than normal scores. A little thought indicates that the reason is artifactual and unrelated to the design of this experiment. In these conditions, horizontally disparate dots are irregularly superimposed on top of each other. There is a great deal of confusion and ambiguity concerning which dots correspond to which others. In other words, the cues for registration on corresponding points have themselves been masked. This, of course, is not a difficulty for the rotated forms that are oriented vertically. In that case, there is little confusion among the horizontally disparate dots and whatever vertical disparity confusion exists is inconsequential. This is so even at the most oblique angles used in this experiment—88 deg.

One other discrepancy exists, therefore, that must be resolved. The astute reader may have noticed that the maximum angular rotation value used in this experiment is 88 deg while the maximum value used in Experiment 13 is 89 deg. (It is amusing to note that this difference, which turned out to highlight an important point, was originally due to an unintended typographical error.) There is, therefore, a discrepancy between the results of the two experiments for the extreme values used in each even when rotations about the Y axis alone are considered. Stimuli oriented at 88 deg in this experiment are seen as well as those in any other orientation while those oriented at 89 deg in Experiment 13 are much less well discriminated from the dummy stimulus. The small difference in angular orientation produces what seems to be an inordinately large difference. Experiment 15 is designed to resolve this discrepancy.

Experiment 15

Design and Rationale. Experiment 15 is designed to resolve the apparent discrepancy between Experiment 13 and 14. To reiterate, the results of Experiment 14 displayed a severe diminution in performance for planes rotated to an orientation of 89 deg compared to other lesser rotations about the Y axis. Experiment 14, on the other hand, shows no such effect when the plane is rotated to an orientation of 88 deg about this same axis.

Two hypothetical explanations exist that might account for this difference. One is that there is a serious experimental artifact in the design of one or both of these experiments that produces spurious results. The alternative explanation, however, is both more benign and more interesting. It suggests that, in fact, the gradient for discrimination of the stimulus plane from the dummy dots as a function of orientation angle is very steep. In other words, there is no discrepancy; this hypothesis suggests that, however surprising, the psychobiological fact is that one is easily able to discriminate a plane rotated to 88 deg from the dummy stimulus, but is not as easily able to discriminate a plane rotated to the 89 deg orientation.

To test which of these two alternative hypothetical explanations is the correct one, a brief experiment was carried out. The stimuli in this experiment consist of only five types; each is a plane consisting of 30 dots rotated about the Y axis from a frontoparallel orientation to either an 88, 89, 90, 91, and 92 deg orientation. All five of these orientations make the stimuli appear to be an increasingly narrow, vertically oriented line, although only in the 90 deg orientation, of course, are the dots perfectly colinear. The experiment is run with one level of noise (25 dots) in the dichoptic presentation. The static mode of masking is used and each observer participates in only one session.

Results. The results of Experiment 15 are shown in Fig. 47. Clearly the hypothetical explanation that asserts that there is a very steep gradient of discrimination as a function of the orientation of the plane is the correct one. Perfor-

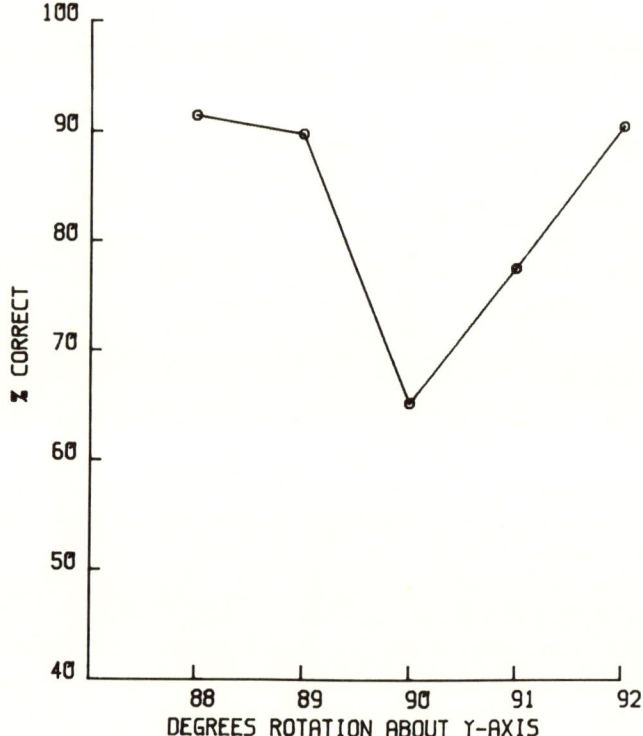

FIG. 47. The results of Experiment 15 displaying the very steep gradient of the drop off of detectability as a function of large angles of rotation around the Y axis.

mance falls off drastically as the angle is rotated from 88 deg to 90 deg and picks up as steeply as it is further rotated only one or two degrees to 91 deg and 92 deg. There is, therefore, no discrepancy between Experiments 13 and 14, but a real difference of substantial magnitude for slight angular differences.[7]

Experiment 16[6]

Design and Rationale. Next, we examined the effect on detectability of varying the apparent depth (disparity) of a frontoparallel oriented stimulus plane within the apparent cubical space. In this experiment, the stimulus plane (sub-

---

[7]The nonchance performance level at the 90° orientation is due to one observer who for reasons that still remain obscure is able to discriminate between the stimulus plane and the dummy dots at this angle. We believe this to be due to his knowledge of the particular patterns used in this experiment: He is our computer programmer.

tending a visual angle of 4.4 deg × 4.4 deg), is randomly translated from trial to trial to positions varying from an apparent position at the extreme back of the cubical space (in this case defined by 5.6 min of uncrossed disparity) to an apparent position at the extreme front of the cube (in this case defined by 5.6 min of crossed disparity). The noise dots are distributed throughout the cubical viewing space in this experiment. Figure 48 is a schematic presentation of the appearance of this type of stimulus showing the range of positions in which it could be placed. (Of course in this case also, the various lines are not seen by the observer.) Eleven disparities ranging between these two extreme values in 1.12 min steps are used in successive trials. On 14 successive days, stimulus plane densities of 50, 40, 30, 25, 20, 15 and 10 dots are used, once in descending, and

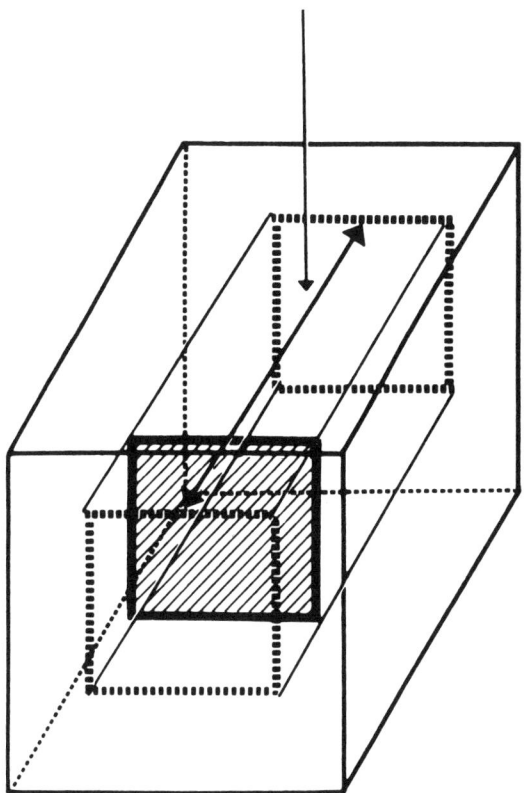

FIG. 48. Diagram of the stimulus configurations used in Experiment 16. The plane could be translated to any one of 11 depth positions for presentation in any trial. The outlines and other guidelines depict the extent of the randomly distributed masking dots but are not seen in the actual experiment.

once in ascending sequence. Noise density is kept constant at 100 dots throughout the experiment. The experiment is carried out in the static mode in which the display is repetitively refreshed for a period of one second.

The stimulus presentation that does not contain the plane does contain extra dots, equal in number to the dots in the stimulus plane, but randomly distributed throughout the portion of the volume that is delimited by the frontal projection area of the target plane. In other words, the dummy dots are distributed in a volume within the cross section of the plane and the depth of the apparent cube. These dummy dots are in addition to the 100 noise dots defining the cubical space and masking the stimulus plane.

Results. Experiment 16, as noted, is designed to measure the effect on stereoscopic detection performance of translations induced by changes in the disparity assigned to a frontoparallel plane. The phenomenological result of this transformation is to make the stimulus plane appear to be located at different depths in the cubical space. Figure 49 shows the results of this experiment. Data are plotted as a function of the 11 disparity settings that are utilized, and as a family of curves parametric with the number of dots in the stimulus plane. It is clear from this figure that in this case the density of dots in the stimulus plane is a

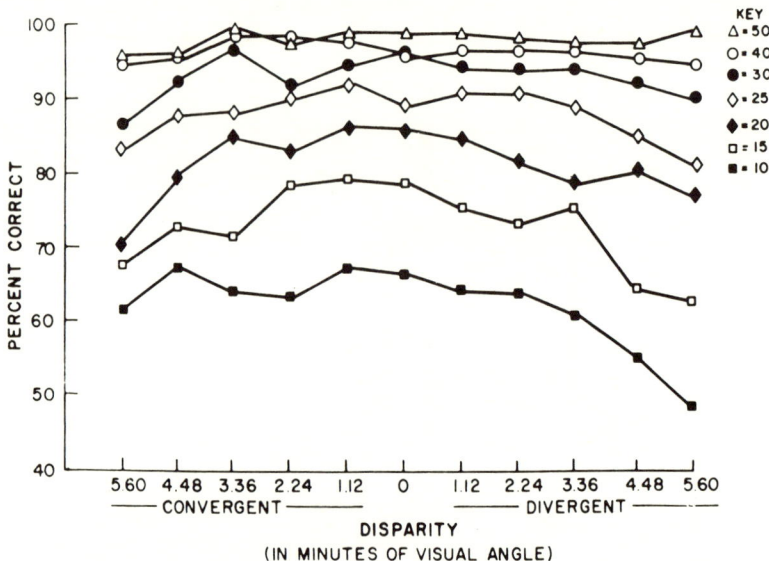

FIG. 49. The results of Experiment 16 with data unpooled. The family of curves is parametric with the number of dots in the target plane. As target plane dot density is decreased the performance level progressively decreases. There is also a progressive decrement in performance observed as either the crossed or uncrossed disparity increases. Masking dot density is held constant at 100.

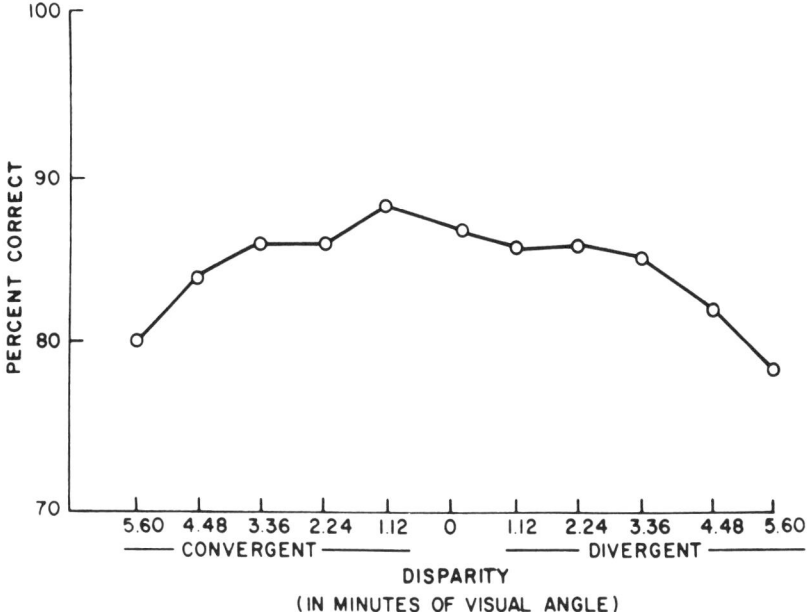

FIG. 50. The results of Experiment 16 with all data pooled to emphasize the effect of disparity. (Note that the vertical axis has been expanded relative to Fig. 49.)

strong determinant of the ability of the observer to discriminate dots arranged in a plane from a random distribution of the same number of masking dots. This is in contrast to the results of Experiments 7 and 8 in which two planes must be discriminated from each other.

A second major effect is also apparent in the results of this experiment. Except for those densities of the stimulus plane so easily detected that disparity does not matter (a ceiling effect), there is a considerable decline in performance associated with shifts of the apparent depth of the plane away from the point of fixation at the center of the cubical space. This is in sharp contrast to the excellent ability, demonstrated in Experiments 13, 14, and 15, to compensate for rotations of the plane in all three dimensions about the center point of the cubical space.

The general nature of this translation-in-depth effect is displayed more clearly by pooling data for all of the noise levels and replotting these pooled values in Fig. 50. Here the range of the vertical axis (% correct) is expanded in order to emphasize the effect. This figure demonstrates that the effect of disparity on performance is symmetrical around a maximum performance score achieved at the center of the dot-filled cube. Performance declines monotonically as the disparity is increased in either the crossed or uncrossed vergence direction. This decline occurs in spite of the fact that the masking effect of the dots surrounding the plane might have been expected, a priori, to be greater when it was centered than when it was at the front or back of the cube. (At extreme disparities the plane is masked only from dots positioned at greater or lesser depths, whereas, at the center, it is masked from both.) Obviously, there is a greater penalty paid for increasing disparity than there is for reducing the number of surrounding noise dots.

Now that the ponderous, but necessary, presentation of the empirical "facts" has been completed, I can turn to the much more enjoyable task of describing what I believe they mean.

4 Discussion

I would like to begin my discussion of the data obtained so far by briefly reviewing my main goals in pursuing this research. Mainly, I want to remind my readers that the purpose of this study is to answer two principal questions. It is all too easy to lose sight of these long range goals in the tangle of experimental detail, especially since many pages have been turned since I last reminded you of them. In brief, my first goal is to determine the nature of the perceptual effects of various spatial and temporal organizational attributes of form by studying the relatively restricted universe of perceptual processes assayed by the dotted form detection paradigm. My second goal is to determine something about the nature of the perceived three dimensional space that is created by the neural processing of disparate dichoptic two dimensional images.

My approach to answering these two questions has been up to this point an empirical one. Specific experiments have been designed and carried out resulting in data that provide varying degrees of illumination of these two issues. Each experiment is designed to contribute in some manner to the development of a point of view or an intuition, if not a complete quantitative and reductive answer. It is my opinion, nevertheless, that the synthetic and integrative interpretation of what these results collectively mean is far more important than the specific outcome of any of the individual experiments. Dots, frankly, are but a vehicle, a means conveying us towards a meta-theory of visual perception. They are an abstraction of visual reality and, though useful, cannot fully enlighten us about all aspects of form perception. In the same vein, the detection paradigm itself is also an abstraction and I do not pretend that it is a totally satisfactory means of explicating all of vision.[8]

How far, then, can we extrapolate from these data to an overall perspective of how we see forms in space? How can these data be modeled by a formal mathematical system in a way that both *describes* the outcome of the experiments and *synthesizes* these data into a meaningful overall point of view? Answering these questions is the purpose of the next two sections of these lectures.

Perhaps the best way to develop such an integrative overview is to consider exactly what I have so far determined in the laboratory concerning the detection of forms in space and the nature of that space. Stripped of technical detail, and in brief, the main empirical facts are:

1. As an unmitigated generality, increasing the number of masking dots monotonically reduces the detectability of a dotted stimulus form if all other variables are held constant. In other words, the raw signal (stimulus dot numerosity) to noise (masking dot numerosity) ratio is a powerful determinant of dotted form detection. Given the main goals of this research, this outcome is neither surprising nor particularly exciting although it is an important cross referencing parameter in this study and of interest in its own right.

2. The position of a repetitive flashing dot in the apparent cubical space exerts only a minor effect on its detectability. A dot placed far off in the rear, lower, right hand corner is seen less well than those at other positions and one centered in space is seen slightly better. Although I have presented no equivalent data concerning the translations of lines or planes, within similar limits and on the basis of my two dimensional results, I believe this result also holds for these multidimensional stimuli.

3. Repetitively flashed dots with interdot intervals of 100 msec. are seen better than those with shorter or longer intervals. The function relating single dot detectability to interdot interval is thus nonmonotonic and suggests the existence of an optimum interval of about this duration.

4. In dotted form discrimination, there is a substantial advantage gained by using a dichoptic viewing condition that allows the perceptual construction of depth compared to either binocular or monocular viewing conditions in which no disparity cue to depth is present. Somewhat surprisingly, binocular viewing produces higher detection scores than does monocular viewing in spite of the fact that there is no informational difference between the two non-disparity viewing conditions.

---

[8]Of course, any laboratory science falls victim to exactly this same restriction. Each scientist chooses a model preparation that is less than total reality and exploits that abstraction to its limits. The dotted form detection task I use is comparable in intent, if not in accomplishment, to the genetics laboratory's use of the fruit fly or the neurophysiologist's use of the cockroach or leech. Just how successful I will be and how powerful a vehicle dotted form detection will ultimately prove to be in our search for understanding form perception is for the future to decide.

5. Increasing the interdot interval between sequential dots in a plotted straight line of dots leads to a monotonic and nearly linear reduction in the detectability of the line. It is, at this point, unclear whether this is a result of the increase in the interval per se or due to the increased number of noise dots encompassed by the duration of the dot train. What is certain is that apparent movement does not substitute in any way for simultaneity.

6. Very surprisingly, irregularity of the temporal intervals between the plotting of successive dots does not appreciably diminish either repetitive dot or line detection. A high degree of interdot interval irregularity can be tolerated without reduction in detection scores.

7. Spatial irregularity of the dots along a straight line does affect detectability at short interdot intervals (less than or equal to 30 msec.). However, at longer dot intervals these same spatial irregularities exert little influence on detectability. In some manner visual mechanisms seen to compensate for these spatial distortions when sufficient time elapses between dots.

8. An increase in the disorder of the sequence in which a series of regularly spaced (in time and position) lines of dots is plotted produces only a modest, though monotonic, decrease in the detectability of the form. This form of irregularity, so extreme that it violates the spatio-temporal topology of the stimulus form, can still be partially overcome, presumably by the same mechanisms that are capable of "smoothing" temporal and spatial irregularity.

9. Dotted line orientation in space is ineffective in influencing detectability scores. Visual space is isotropic for diagonal lines.

10. When two planes are to be discriminated from each other:

    a. The greater the dichoptic disparity between the two planes, the more easily one is discriminated (in depth) from the other.

    b. The effect of the number of dots in the two planes is relatively small. Indeed, discrimination of a highly reduced stimulus consisting of only two dots is easily accomplished.

    c. A reduction in the viewing time leads to a progressive reduction in the discrimination of the two planes.

    d. When a burst of noise dots follows the presentation of a dichoptic stimulus, stereoscopic performance is especially degraded at intervals less than 50 msec.

11. The form of a planar stimulus composed of a random array of dots has a surprisingly small effect on its detectability given what we learned in the earlier two dimensional studies with dotted outline defined forms. Even as the viewing time is reduced, further impoverishing the dot masked stimulus, form defined in this way remains an ineffective variable and any putative effect of form is not enhanced. Furthermore, even as drastic a manipulation as changing the stimulus form from a square to a rectangle is slight. (As we shall see, however, this conclusion does not hold for forms defined by dotted outlines.)

108   4. DISCUSSION

12. There is virtually no effect on detectability when a planar stimulus form defined by a random array of dots is rotated around the Y axis. When the form is rotated in more complex ways around two or three axes the experimental outcome is equally unaffected. Space is also isotropic for planes of this kind.

13. The gradient of form detectability is very steep between 88 and 90 deg of rotation, but virtually flat over the entire range from 0 to 88 deg.

14. When a frontoparallel oriented plane is translated from the front to the back of a noise filled cubical space (in separate trials), it is most easily detected at the center of the cube. Detectability diminishes as the plane is located closer to the front or the back of the cube where disparity is greatest in either the crossed or uncrossed direction.

15. In both the rotation and the translation experiments, in which a random dot array defined plane had to be detected in a random dot filled space, the number of dots in the plane is effective in influencing detectability.

These then are the major findings that have been obtained in this study of the influence of stimulus form on the detectability of dotted forms in stereoscopic space. The discussion now presented is divided into two parts. First I consider the significance of these data in helping to understand the nature of vision—in general and specifically with regard to dotted form detection. Second, I consider how these experiments act as tests of a mathematical model based on an autocorrelational process. In the process of evaluating the model, certain supplemental experiments necessary for the clarification of some residual uncertainties are described and their results reported.

PERCEPTUAL SIGNIFICANCE

The Advantages of Stereopsis

At the outset of this discussion it is important to remind my audience that some of the experiments reported here are confounded by the presence of monocular cues. Both flashing dots and dotted straight lines are detectable to some degree under monocular viewing conditions even though the planar stimuli consisting of arrays of random dots are not. For dots and lines, therefore, one important finding that has emerged from this study is confirmation of earlier work (e.g., Smith, Cole, Merritt, & Pepper, 1976; Pepper, Cole, Merritt, & Smith, 1978) demonstrating that there is a substantial advantage to stereoscopic over binocular/monocular viewing in a variety of tasks involving continuous (as opposed to dotted) stimuli. This result seems to be ubiquitous and uniform within the limits of statistical fluctuation for all of the experiments I have reported to you for which monocular cues exist. One has only to view the last frame of Fig. 5 both dichoptically and monocularly to appreciate the advantage of stereoscopic viewing over monocular viewing for complex stimuli of the kind used in these experiments.

How does one account for the advantage of stereoscopic viewing over binocular/monocular viewing in the dot masking paradigm? The answer to this question is probably closely related to one that may account for the data obtained by Fox and his colleagues (Fox, 1980; 1981; Lehmkuhle & Fox, 1980) for metacontrast and contour interaction, and by Gogle and Mershon (1969) and Mershon (1972) for simultaneous contrast. All of these psychologists determined that the introduction of apparent depth differences reduces the interaction between inducing and induced stimuli. A central idea in conventional neural net theories of these phenomena is that since the two dimensional projection on the retina should allow lateral interactions in either the stereoscopic or binocular/monocular viewing condition, the effects in three dimensions should be the same as in two dimensions. This idea, however, is refuted by the fact that many induction-type interactions such as metacontrast, contour interaction, and simultaneous contrast are diminished when *phenomenological* depth differences between the induced and inducing stimuli exist. Thus any explanation of these phenomena based upon peripheral lateral inhibitory interactions is a priori inadequate.

Let me restate this argument to make its logic clear. Specifically, the two dimensional attributes of the image projected on either retina remain nearly constant as disparity changes; that is, the horizontal spatial separation between the foreground and background elements of the stimuli are nearly the same for all disparities. Thus, any putative peripheral interaction should remain constant. Nevertheless, there is a progressive reduction of the magnitude of both simultaneous and metacontrast as the apparent depth difference increases. The "distance" between the two interacting stimulus elements that is significant, therefore, is not the distance projected onto the physical surface of the retina, but rather the apparent volumetric distance in the mentally constructed X, Y, Z volume, a volume that does not exist in physical or retinotopic reality. Peripheral inhibitory interactions, therefore, cannot account for the associated decline in the interactive effects and, therefore, the responsible process must be a function of higher and more complex levels of neural processing.

The "apparent volumetric distance" explanation also seems to hold for the present results; distributing noise dots in depth also reduces their effect as maskers. That is, the effect of the masking noise is not solely a function of its density on the physically projected two dimensional retinal surface, but also of those stimulus factors (e.g., disparity and perspective) that influence density in the apparent three dimensional space. Therefore, spreading the dots further apart in the perceptually constructed depth dimension is the equivalent of spreading them further apart in the projected plane. Since volumes have more constituent unit elements than planes, the average *density* of the masking noise must decrease when a plane is extruded into a volume even though there is no change in the *number* of visual masking dots present. It is this modulation of the stimulus factors influencing the apparent three dimensional density that I believe accounts for the advantage of stereoscopic over binocular/monocular viewing.[9]

This is an important point. At the very least it means that the related neural inhibitions can not be retinal. At the most it means that simplistic neural interactions at any level of the nervous system can not account for the classic contrast or these new dot masking phenomena. The interactions that matter vary as a function of the central representations of the three dimensions of the stimuli, not of the two dimensions of the retinal projection or the peripheral neural matrix.

The Equivalence of the X, Y, and Z Dimensions

The same logic may also be invoked to understand why there is virtually no effect of rotation in the cubical viewing sphere on the detectability of a plane regardless of the magnitude or complexity of the rotation. The absence of any change in the performance of the observer as the random dot array target planes are rotated to new positions, despite the fact that the frontoparallel projection of the rotated plane increases in density with increasing nonzero angles of rotation, strongly suggests that stimulus dot density, as well as noise dot density itself, is actually processed in a fundamentally three dimensional, rather than a two dimensional, manner by the observer. In other words, dot densities, as defined in the third dimension by the assigned disparity, are perceptually assimilated in accord with their three dimensional characteristics, not in terms of their projected two dimensional properties. The interesting aspect of this outcome is that the three dimensional space no more exists in the brain than it did in the computer: In both cases it is only symbolically represented.

In terms of the concepts of neural coding, this argument makes perfectly good sense (at least to me). There is no physiological reason why the neural representation of the depth dimension should be any less meaningful or handled in any way different than the horizontal and vertical dimensions. In each case a pattern of neural signals is presumably used to represent or encode a physical dimension of the stimulus. The absence of any effect of the angle of rotation in the present experiments supports the idea that the response to these stimuli are only quan-

---

[9]However, it must be remembered that these experiments have also shown that the binocular viewing condition does have a substantial advantage over the monocular one. This may be due to some subtle advantage in central nervous system processing that is gained even when the images from the two eyes are identical. In other words, redundancy itself may be of value. However, the binocular advantage may also arise from artifacts of far less theoretical significance. Such uninteresting factors as simple distraction resulting from the very occlusion of vision to one eye or even the presence of the eye patch itself may be involved. The resolution of this matter is left to others. It is important to us only to note that, for our observers and in this kind of experiment, the substantial advantage of binocular (as opposed to dichoptic) over monocular viewing is an empirical fact.

titatively, and not qualitatively, different. The quantitative differences among the different spatial dimensions' representations are dealt with by the perceptual nervous system without observed effect. Thus there is also no functional reason to suggest the existence of qualitatively different kinds of stimulus categories, neural codes, or even perceptual responses for the different dimensions.

I must also note that the results obtained by Fox and his associates, and by Gogel and Mershon, as well as those from this present study supporting the perceptual equivalence of the X, Y, and Z axes, represent an extraordinary outcome when considered from the historical and philosophical point of view discussed earlier. These data jointly suggest that the Z axis distance, even though constructed from an indirect and a nonisomorphic aspect (disparity) of the stimulus, is just as "real" in a perceptual sense as are the X and Y distances that do have a more direct and isomorphic physical counterpart (retinal distance).

Considering that stereoscopic depth is the indirect result of invariance computations based on the magnitude of minute retinal disparities, and that it is dealt with no differently than are width and height, the unavoidable conclusion towards which I am driven is that *the X and Y distances themselves must also be "constructs" calculated on the basis of some equally highly mediated transformation* from the retinal image to the perceived plane. It is, according to this point of view, only fortuitous that perceived space appears to be isomorphic to the stimulus space in the X and Y dimensions. Thus, the seductive isomorphism of the retina and the X and Y dimensions is irrelevant. This kind of analogic isomorphism in the highly encoded world of the perceptual system is an argument for absolutely nothing.

This line of thought goes on to suggest that there is nothing especially direct or real about the X and Y dimensions, but rather, they are as indirect as the Z dimension. To suggest otherwise that depth and width or breadth are in some fundamental way "different" from each other both resuscitates the usually misunderstood nature of Bishop Berkeley's mediate-immediate dichotomy and ignores the single most important principle taught by sensory coding theory, namely—*"Isomorphism of representation is unnecessary; any neural code can represent any dimension of the stimulus or of perception equally well as any other."*

Pursuing this line of thought, the totality of our visual experience can thus be considered to be indirect, not only the obviously constructed dimensions like depth that are computed from invariant relationships among alternative representations of the stimulus object, but also height and width that have a superficially immediate relationship to retinal distances. While this logic leads to a model of a perceptual world that is in practical terms no different than the classic deterministic stimulus-response point of view, it is substantially different in terms of the epistemological model that must be invoked to explain how we actually perceive space.

4. DISCUSSION

The Isotropy of Visual Space

Another outcome of relevance to our search for an understanding of visual perception is the data indicating the *isotropic* nature of visual space obtained in these experiments. That is, visual space seems to be nearly the same in all directions and at all orientations *for these dotted stimuli*. There is no difference in detection scores as a function of the orientation of a diagonal line of dots nor of the direction of the diagonal trajectory of a sequence of dots, nor even of the angle of orientation of a plane.[10] Furthermore, stereoscopic performance decreases nearly equally with increases in both crossed and uncrossed disparity. This suggests that equal disparities between corresponding points on the retina are encoded to represent equal depth effects in both the convergent and divergent conditions.

These findings collectively lend support not only to the hypothesis that visual space is truly processed in a way that deals with all three dimensions equivalently, but also that variations in stimulus depth in any direction create equal perceptual effects over the range of the various parameters I have studied. In other words, *visual space is homogeneous, symmetrical, and isotropic* within the limits of the spatial extent of the stimuli used in this study. The observed insensitivity to orientation and direction in these three dimensional experiments is consistent with what we have observed in two dimensional space for similar dotted patterns (Uttal, 1975), but inconsistent with what many other students of vision had previously observed for continuous stimuli (as summarized in Appelle, 1972). It is, therefore, possible that the lack of continuity of the dotted stimulus forms used here is a special property that gives rise to special effects. The extrapolation of this concept of isotropic visual space obtained with dotted forms to continuous stimuli cannot, therefore, be made with impunity. What the basis of this difference between dotted and continuous forms might be is not known, but it has also been observed by Gerald Westheimer in his experiments on hyperacuity.

We can, however, speculate why this difference between dotted and continous forms exists. One speculation suggests that the very same attributes that produce to the advantages of dotted patterns also give rise to the absence of any observed differences in orientation sensitivity. Dots are isolated entities both in the mathematical and the neurophysiological senses; they are not "connected" to other dots in the field of view in the same way as are the elements of a continuous form. Rather, we see dotted *forms* solely because of their *global arrangement*.[11] Each dot in the physical stimulus, in the projection on the retina,

---

[10]Two other key experiments have yet to be done. These experiments would compare obliquely oriented dotted lines and dotted outline polygons with similar forms oriented parallel to the frontoparallel plane.

[11]There appears to be a substantial difference between an area containing random dots and an area defined by an *outline* of nearly regular dots. The term "global arrangment" may, therefore, have

and perhaps even in the neural networks representing that dot, functions discretely and independently. These discrete points have no direction or orientation of their own or, for that matter, any physical connection to any other dots. Only the overall arrangement, an attribute that is properly appreciated to be an abstraction far removed from the reality of continuous contours, has direction and/or orientation, and that abstraction itself possesses only an intangible organizational reality. Presumably this kind of form is so intangible that it does not activate the same neural mechanisms as do physically continuous stimuli. Dotted lines are not actually lines; the lines in this case are but inferences or constructs of the perceptual system. At least that is the conclusion to be drawn from the psychophysical results of von Bekesy (1968) and Nachmias (1967) and, if the duration of the dot is brief (as they are in many of the experiments reported here), from the neurophysiological results reported by Barlow, Fitzhugh, and Kuffler (1957). It is for these reasons that the perception of dotted patterns may be insensitive to direction and orientation, in a manner quite different from the sensitivity exhibited in the perception of continuous lines and contours.

The Basic Nature of Stereoscopic Time and Space

Now consider for a moment the basic parameters of the stereoscopic space as elucidated by Experiments 7, 8, and 9. Let us consider the problem of the stereoscopic threshold first. Graham (1965) reviewed many experiments that must now be regarded as classic investigations of stereoscopic thresholds. He cites the work of Howard (1919) who, using conventional two-stick measuring devices, determined the threshold (75% correct level) to be of the order of 20 sec of angular disparity, a value very close to that obtained by Woodburne (1934). Graham goes on to remind us, however, that all of the studies used relatively long exposures and that when brief exposures were used by Langlands (1926), the thresholds were considerably elevated—up to about 40 sec of disparity.

The results of Experiment 7 points to minimum detectable disparities that lie closer to 30 sec of disparity. Furthermore, a 75% proportion of correct responses is not obtained in the present study until much greater disparities are introduced. Nevertheless, the stimulus conditions of the Julesz-type random dot stereogram used in these experiments are so totally devoid of any possible secondary cue (such geometrical factors as angular separation of the sticks and stick width substantially affect threshold measurements in the Howard-Dohlman apparatus) that the values obtained in the present experiment may be considered to be especially useful estimates of the threshold of a pure, uncontaminated stereopsis.

It is also known that stereoscopic disparity threshold for sticklike objects is a function of luminance (Mueller & Lloyd, 1948) with thresholds varying from

---

multiple meanings. I shall discuss this important difference in a few pages in the context of the autocorrelation model.

4. DISCUSSION

about 8 sec to about 25 sec of visual angle as the stimulus illuminance varies over six logarithmic units. Since the present experiment used relatively dim stimuli, this condition may be contributing somewhat to the moderately high values for the obtained thresholds even though luminance is in other regards a relatively weak determinant of stereoscopic acuity for random dot stereograms.

The experiments in which two planes must be discriminated from each other (Experiments 7 and 8) also indicate that the effect on stereopsis of the number of dots in the display depends on exposure duration. Prolonged displays are only minimally affected by simple numerosity; the differential effect of dot numerosity disappears when more than ten dots are added to the display. Thus, at these longer durations, it appears that little statistical advantage is obtained from increasing the stimulus dot density beyond relatively low values. For shorter exposure durations, however, the effect of dot density is somewhat enhanced and there are noticeable differences between the scores for the 30- to 50-dot displays. It should be noted that stereopsis is still powerfully compelling with even two dots for the shortest exposure durations and the smallest disparities if the convergence is tightly controlled.

Thus, our findings (contrary to some other results) suggest that there is relatively weak global interaction among neural mechanisms at different locations to enhance depth perception. To the contrary, whatever depth processing structures exist probably operate more or less independently to encode the depth of individual regions but do not substantially reinforce the overall response strength by collective interaction. Indeed, one is hard pressed to imagine why global interactions among objects at different disparities would be a desirable feature of stereopsis. If designing such a system, one would not wish that the depth of an object should influence the depth of another nearby one. Such a process would not be objectionable if all surfaces were in a frontoparallel orientation, but could interfere with the perception of environmental surfaces presented at other orientations. This undesirable situation would be even more seriously exacerbated if stimuli adjacent to each other in the X, Y plane were at different depths. Unless independent, the depth of each stimulus could be grossly misperceived. In other words, I believe that the processes underlying local stereopsis are relatively more powerful than are those underlying global stereopsis for good reason.

Another important inference that may be drawn from my data is that whatever kind of global or local interactive forces do exist in either two or three dimensions, they are not the result of peripheral interactions, as proposed by Julesz and Chang (1976), but rather of higher level processes in which the statistics of the distribution of elements are processed in some vastly more complicated way.

It must be understood, however, that the minimal effect of dot numerosity is true only for two-plane discrimination tasks. In those experiments in which the observer is required to detect a plane hidden in a volume of random dots, the number of dots in both the stimulus and the noise has proved to be an important factor in determining detectability. It is clear that the difference in performance between the two experiments is due to the differing nature of the two experimental tasks. It is easy to understand why the two-plane discrimination task would be only minimally affected while the plane detection task is greatly affected. Any two dots in two planes contain all necessary information for the completion of the discrimination task. In the plane-in-random-dotted-volume detection task, however, increasing the number of dots in the plane or the noise alters the signal to noise ratio in a simple statistical manner. Simply put, the latter type of experiment is a signal-in-noise task and the former is not.

Two different conclusions have emerged concerning the contribution of perception and/or viewing time to the establishment of stereoscopic depth in random dot stereograms. First, as exhibited in Experiment 7, a reduction in viewing time per se does produce a reduction in the percentage of correct depth discriminations but abruptly between durations of .4 and .2 sec. This is probably due to the fact that at the shorter exposure durations the persistence of the visual image—the temporal spread of the effective duration of the stimulus—is longer than the stimulus duration. Thus, the absence of any further decrease in performance is due to the functional persistence of the image of the stimulus even though the physical stimulus itself is progressively reduced in duration. Second, the minimum period required for the perception of stereoscopic depth, as reflected in the discontinuity observed at 50 msec in Experiment 8, is five times longer than estimates of the minimum amount of time required for perceiving and encoding two dimensional stimuli (Sperling, 1963). All of these data provide descriptive insights into the temporal and spatial properties of stereoscopic perception.

Interval Irregularity in Time and Space

Another important aspect of this study concerns the detectability of dotted lines with varying, rather than periodic, temporal and spatial properties. The question with which I am now concerned is—Given the importance of spatial periodicity on detectability in two dimensions, what is the effect of temporal and spatial interval irregularity on detectability in three dimensions?

To understand fully the significance of the interval irregularity experiments, it is necessary to briefly review the effect of regular temporal intervals. Specifically, sequences of dots with small interdot intervals are perceptually simultaneous while those with longer intervals produce percepts in which the sequential nature of the patterns becomes evident and apparent motion may be experienced. As I suggested earlier, one a priori hypothesis could have suggested that the apparent motion elicited by a sequential series of stimulus dots might at least partially compensate for the reduction in apparent simultaneity. However, the data obtained provide no evidence of such a compensatory effect. The greater the interval between the dots of the stimulus form, the less detectable the forms are, regardless of how strong a perception of a moving trajectory is reported by the

116   4. DISCUSSION

observer. The mechanism that detects coherent forms among dot patterns is better able to process information when it is presented simultaneously than when it is distributed in time. This strong effect of temporal interval has also been confirmed in two dimensional space by Falzett and Lappin (1981). Whether it is due to time itself or to the larger number of noise dots encompassed by the longer duration stimulus is yet to be determined.

In light of the high sensitivity to mean interval, it was totally unexpected to observe that the mechanism integrating temporally dispersed dots into forms seems to be virtually insensitive to the regularity of the sequence of dot intervals. Dotted stimulus lines with evenly spaced intervals are detected only slightly better, if at all, than lines with highly irregular intervals. The insensitivity to temporal irregularity exhibited in this detection task is also surprising in the context of the visual system's ability to detect brief gaps in a train of otherwise regular flashing dots (Uttal & Hieronymus, 1970).

Even more surprising was the subsequent discovery that increasing *spatial* irregularity also has only a negligible effect on detection scores for lines of dots *when* the dots are plotted at intervals long enough to produce apparent movement. When the intervals are short, however, spatial irregularity does influence detectability; more irregular patterns are, as expected, less easily detected. Indeed, even disordering the dots produced only a relatively small effect on detection scores.

In some manner, therefore, the visual system displays a powerful ability to smooth over both irregular spatial position (given moderately large temporal intervals) and temporal interval irregularities programmed into the stimulus lines. The question is—how is this accomplished? I would like to speculate that this smoothing occurs as a result of the same kind of mechanism that accounts for path smoothing in apparent motion itself. Indeed, I would propose that "path smoothing" may be considered to be nothing other than an alternative form of apparent movement. Classic and modern studies of apparent motion (e.g., Brown & Voth, 1937) have indicated that the apparent trajectory of a seemingly moving object tends to be modified in such a way that the perceived pathway is more likely to reflect a "good" form (in the Gestalt sense) or even to detour around an obstacle rather than to follow the actual spatio-temporal trajectory directly implied by the physical stimulus. This phenomenon has been formalized by Foster (1978) into a theory of apparent motion analogous to the calculus of variations used in mechanics. In his theory "perceptual forces" are minimized just as are physical forces in the physicist's calculus of variations. Insensitivity to irregularity is nothing more (nor less), from this point of view, than an expression of the minimization of "perceptual forces."

One must not make too much of the term "perceptual forces" or the metaphor of the calculus of variations. However, one should make quite a bit of the fact that perceptual smoothing occurs in this situation. The most important aspect of this structuring of the perceptual response to be logically plausible or energy minimal is the implication made about the relationship between the stimulus and that phenomenal response. It seems to me that psychophysicists designing experiments to determine the specific functional relationships between physical stimuli and perceptual dimensions frequently overlook just how often the latter are, in fact, not directly determined by the former. Vast nonveridicalities exist between the two domains because of internal processes that are only hinted at by many illusions to which we are subject. Irregularity smoothing in these detection experiments, however useful, must also be considered to be another example of a nonveridical illusion. Like other illusions (including stereoscopic depth), these phenomena illustrate the wide variety of transformations that occur between the stimulus and the perceptual response. They direct our attention to the inadequacy of deterministic stimulus-response interpretations even at this "simple" level of perceptual processing. They also emphasize the extraordinary constructive powers of the perceptual system and suggest how rare dimensional verdicality may actually be in our visual experience.

While it is not clear what role such a temporal and spatial perceptual "smoother" might play in the natural visual environment where trajectories are always smooth and continuous, one can imagine that such a property of vision could, for example, be very well utilized by those designing the next generation of digitally encoded television displays. Discrete pixel coding schemes may, under some conditions, produce exactly the same sort of irregular distortions I have intentionally generated for these experiments. The simple appreciation of the fact that they will be invisible to the viewer may produce enormous engineering economies. Video designers no longer need concern themsevles with the removal of these distortions; people can't see them even if they remain in the picture.

I should also reiterate, as I draw these conclusions, my surprise that the effect of disorder, while significant and monotonic, is so modest in absolute magnitude. In fact, our observers do remarkably well in spite of the disorder; only a 7% or 8% decrement in performance obtains from the most ordered to the most disordered stimuli used in Experiment 6. Even disorder—the most extreme violation of spatio-temporal topology—only moderately diminishes detectability.

In sum, our experiments describe a visual mechanism that has some extraordinary powers. The system seems to be extremely sensitive to mean spatial and temporal intervals. However, both spatial and temporal interval irregularity seem not to influence the detection task being used here when dot intervals are large enough to create apparent motion. Even when spatio-temporal topological constraints are violated (i.e., disorder is introduced), the effect is surprisingly modest in magnitude. This outcome is almost certainly closely intertwined with the mechanisms that account for apparent motion, a phenomenon in which discrete and intermittent stimuli are perceived as smooth and continuous under the control of constructive mental process whose origins and mechanisms still remain almost totally unknown.

The Influence of Form

Finally, I come to what I anticipated would be one of the most interesting parts of this series of experiments: That is, the effect of global shape on the detectability of the stimulus form. Our probes of the nature of the visual system in Experiments 10, 11, and 12, demonstrate that the overall form or arrangement of *irregularly* positioned dots in a plane has but the merest effect on their detectability in stereoscopic space. Experiment 10 attempted to find a form effect with relatively long exposure durations (one sec) by using four prototypical forms—a square, a triangle, a rectangle, and an irregular form. Experiment 11, attempted to degrade this stimulus viewing situation by systematically shortening the exposure duration. In Experiment 12, the shape of the stimulus forms was varied in a more systematic way than had been done in the previous two experiments: A square was progressively deformed into a more and more oblong rectangle. However, contrary to my initial expectation, all of these manipulations of stimulus forms, composed as they were of irregular arrays of randomly positioned dots constrained within the subjective contours of the prototypical forms, displayed very much the same negative result: There was a very small or a nonexistant effect of the global form of these stimuli on their detectability.

Indeed, the detectability of the pattern seems to be more a function of the raw dot density measured either in terms of the number of the stimulus dots or in terms of the ratio of the number of stimulus dots to the number of noise dots. This outcome is very much in accord with the analysis made by Barlow (1978) of the results forthcoming from an experiment involving perceived density differences between adjacent two dimensional patterns. He also noted the absence of any global stimulus form effect in his study. It is also in accord with Helson and Fehrer's (1932) observation that form had little effect on luminance, form detection, and form recognition tasks when continuous areas were used as stimuli. Furthermore, it conforms with Westheimer and McKee's (1977) discovery that stimulus form had little effect on hyperacuity, a process that may be quite closely related to all of the above tasks. It is also, in retrospect, in agreement with one implication of the results of Experiment 7. That experiment, if you recall, showed that there was little advantage gained by simply increasing the number of dots in a stereoscopic depth discrimination (as opposed to a form detection) task.

I believe that all of these experiments are sending the same message at us: In many visual processes using certain kinds of stimuli, form is, in fact, not an influential parameter. All of these experiments, including the present one, also argue that there is little global interaction among the dots of a form *when* those dots are presented as a random array and *define a form only by virtue of subjective contours*. That the dots of such arrays are seen independently of each other is the message these results force upon us; there is, in fact, little effect of global form on any detection task when stimuli are formed from random dot arrays.

The conclusion toward which I therefore am driven by these data is that global interaction among *randomly positioned dots* is a far weaker force than I had expected at the outset of this study. The reader anticipating form effects should not be disappointed, however, because this conclusion does not, it will shortly be demonstrated, hold for forms defined by dotted outlines and the difference between the two kinds of stimuli turns out to be one of the most exciting outcomes of this research program.

However weak the interaction between the dots in a random array (and, as we shall see in the next section of this chapter, this lack of interaction among randomly positioned dots is correctly predicted by the autocorrelation theory), a very strong interaction occurs among dots arranged in orderly arrays, such as dotted lines and dotted outline defined planes. In fact, the autocorrelation model itself was originally suggested by exactly this kind of interaction among the dots of a stimulus form. (As we also shall see shortly, the model also accurately predicts the strong effects exhibited by dotted lines and dotted outline planes.) For example, a square is seen better than a parallelogram even when both are defined by the same four lines. Similarly, a straight line is seen better than a curved line even when they are composed of the same number of identically spaced dots. In these cases, there clearly is an interaction among the dots of the stimulus in a way that is extremely sensitive to the global arrangement of those stimulus dots. In the experiments I have reported to you so far in these lectures, which have primarily used random dot arrays, the global arrangement had little effect, however.

How can this discrepancy be explained? Obviously there is some factor that is different in the experiments that use dotted outline stimulus forms and those in which the stimulus forms are created by random arrays of dots. Whatever this factor is, however, it is only one of the several differences introduced when the transition was made from the older two dimensional work to the newer three dimensional studies. In addition to the bare fact of adding the third dimension, most of our work on planes was done with random dot arrays rather than dotted outlines. Furthermore, many of the studies used static rather than dynamic random noise dots. Finally time was also added as a variable. The question is to determine which of these changes accounts for the difference between responses to random dot and to colinear dot stimuli. Several possible explanations could be invoked to answer this question. Two, however, are predominant. The presence of global interactions with dotted outline stimuli and their absence with random array stimuli may be attributed to either:

Hypothesis 1. A difference between stereoscopic (three dimensional) and two dimensional viewing conditions;

or

Hypothesis 2. A difference between regular dotted line forms and random dotted array forms.

120   4. DISCUSSION

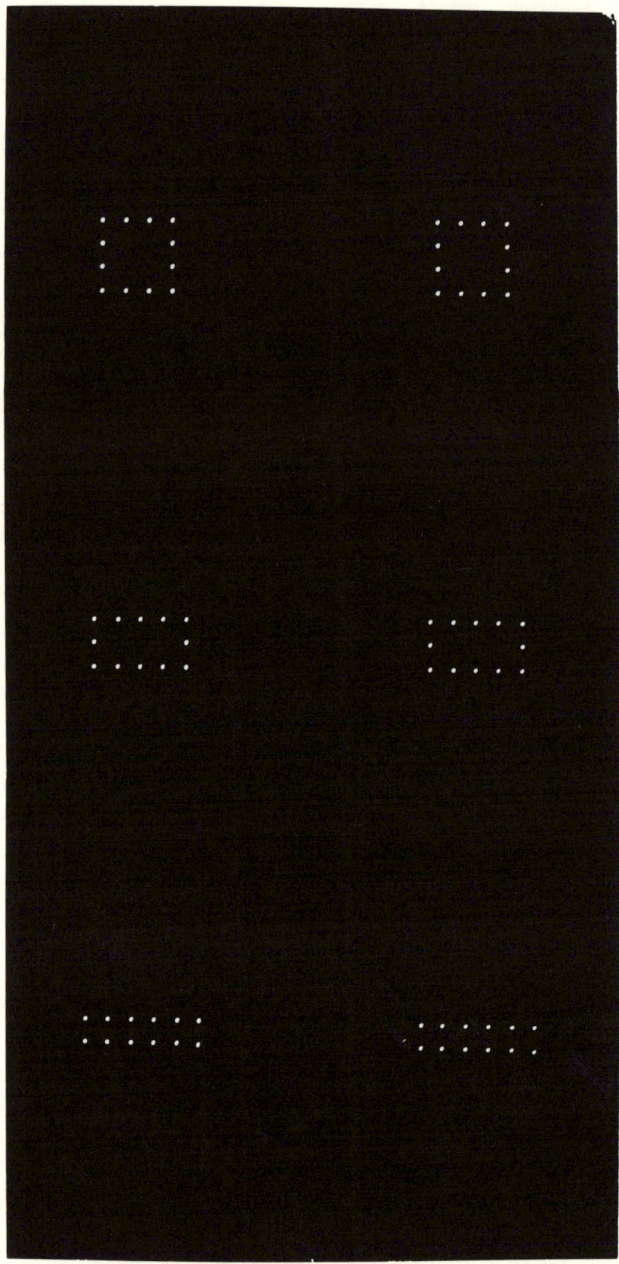

FIG. 51.   The three stimulus forms used in Supplemental Experiment 1.

Since Experiments 13 and 14 have already demonstrated how completely the Z dimension could be traded off for the X and Y dimensions, my initial impulse is to reject the first explanation and to conclude that the differences obtained are more likely to be due to the stimulus properties. However, to more rigorously test this more plausible second hypothesis two supplementary experiments have been carried out. These two experiments, both intended to help resolve this issue, respectively investigate (1) the effect of shape for dotted outline rectangles and (2) the effect of changing a regular matrix into an irregular one.

Supplemental Experiment 1

Supplemental Experiment 1 repeats Experiment 12 in which a square was deformed into a progressively more oblique rectangle. However, rather than using forms defined by random arrays of dots, this supplemental experiment uses dotted outline forms as the stimuli. Samples of this type of stimulus are shown in Fig. 51 which may be compared with those shown in Fig. 40. These stimuli are always centered in stereoscopic space in a frontoparallel position and masked by dynamic random noise. Only three stimulus prototypes are used in this experi-

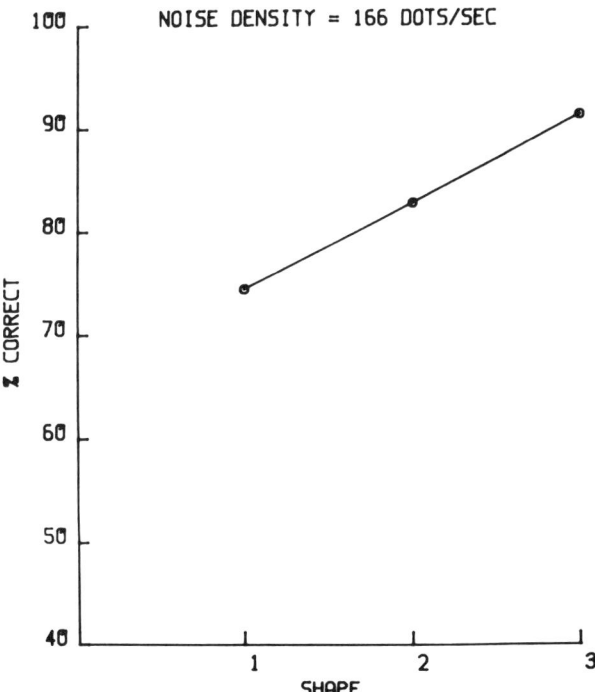

FIG. 52. The results of Supplemental Experiment 1.

122   4. DISCUSSION

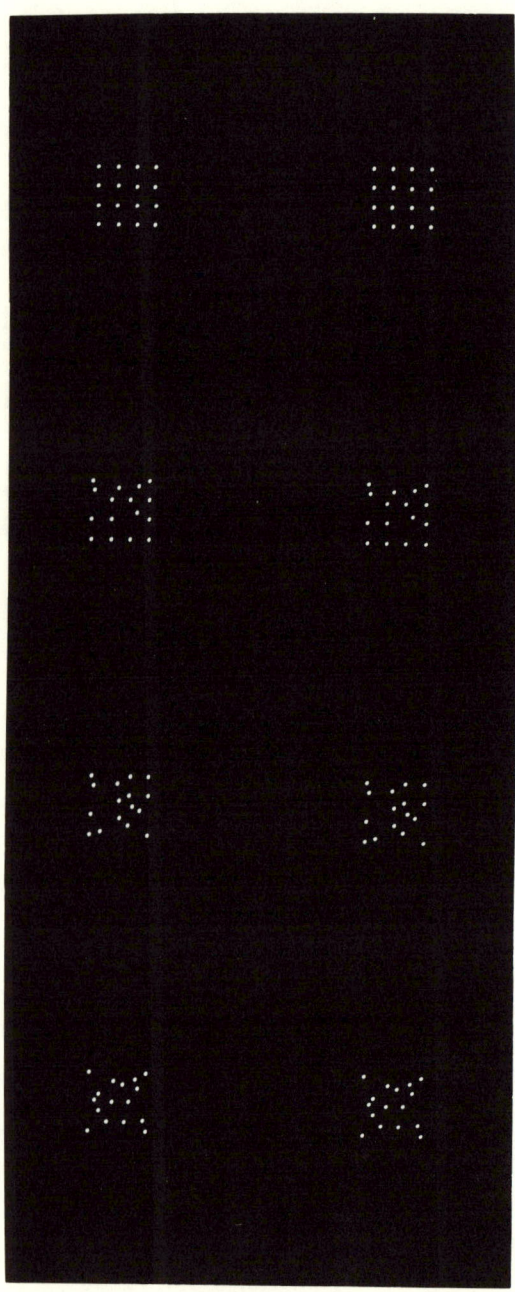

FIG. 53. The stimuli used in Supplemental Experiment 2.

ment in order to maintain constant perimeter, dot spacing, and dot numerosity: Only the three used fulfilled this criterion. The three stimuli are rotated to any of five evenly spaced rotational orientations (varying from 0 to 90 deg in 22.5 deg steps) about the Z axis to add positional uncertainty to the task. A single noise density of 166 dots/sec is used in this experiment.

The results of this experiment are plotted in Fig. 52 with all orientations pooled. (An independent analysis showed that there is no effect of orientation in this experiment.) In this case, unlike the situation in which forms created by a random array of dots are used, there is a very strong effect of form. The more oblong rectangles are detected with progressively greater accuracy. The effect is not only stronger than that of Experiment 12, but most interestingly, *in the opposite direction!* Clearly, given the results of these two experiments, the difference between random dot array forms and dotted outline forms should be ascribed to the nature of the stimuli and not the nature of stereoscopic space.

Supplemental Experiment 2

In the second supplementary experiment the question asked is: What is the effect on the detectability of a plane (as opposed to a line) of the spatial regularity of its constituent dots. In this case, stimuli similar to those shown in Fig. 53 (but which are rotated in seven 15 deg steps—from 0 to 90 deg—about the Z axis) are used. The stimulus forms can be seen in this figure to vary from a perfectly regular 4 by 4 matrix of 16 dots arranged in a plane to increasingly irregular arrays of 16 dots arranged in the same plane. Seven such patterns of increasing irregularity are used at four orientations. While the four corner dots are always kept in place, increasing numbers of the other twelve dots are displaced by discrete units equal to half of the interdot spacing between the dots in the regular array. The independent variable in this case is the cumulative number of displacements of all displaced dots. These arrays are positioned at the center depth (i.e., the depth of the fixation point) and viewed stereoscopically in dynamic visual noise consisting of 250 dots per sec distributed throughout the cubical viewing space.

The results of this examination of the effect of regularity on a plane are shown in Fig. 54. This figure displays a progressive decline in detection scores as more dots are displaced greater amounts. The only exception to this generalization is the point representing the most "irregular" stimulus form. In fact, inspection showed that, by chance, some pseudo organization has been generated in this form that made it spuriously more detectable than it should have been.

The general conclusion towards which the findings from these two supplemental experiments propel me is that the global form and periodicity sensitive mechanism, whatever it is, requires periodically spaced dotted lines or linear arrays to be activated. The merely subjective global contours defined by the statistical distribution of randomly arrayed dots are not sufficient to activate this mysterious mechanism. Indeed, as we saw in Supplemental Experiment 1, the

4. DISCUSSION

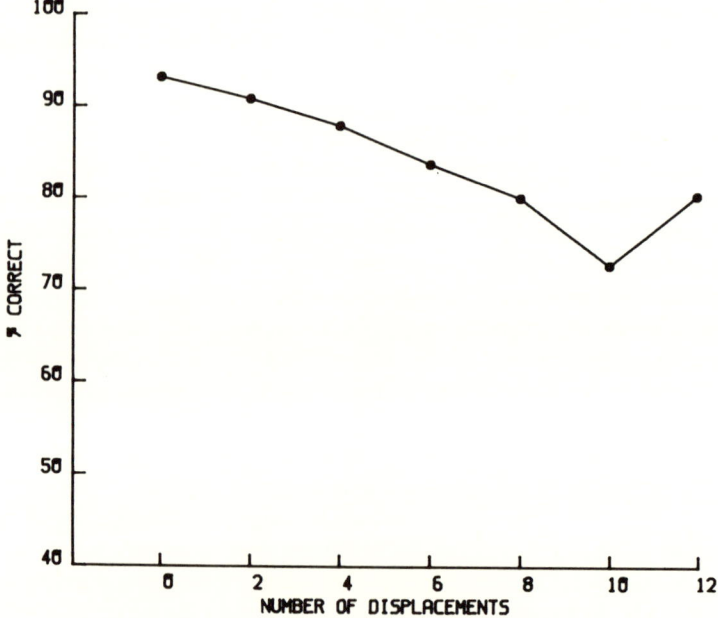

FIG. 54. The results of Supplemental Experiment 2.

effects are not just enhanced, but are actually reversed when outline forms are compared to random dot forms. In the former case, the rectangles are seen better than the square. In the latter, the square is seen better than the rectangle. The difference in the magnitude of the change in each case is also enormous; in the former case, large differences occur; in the latter only small differences occur.

On the basis of these new data, and in particular, the comparisons made between the supplemental experiments and the earlier experiments, I now am confident that I can elaborate upon the main generalization that emerged from those older two dimensional studies of form—a concept that can be briefly summarized as *the rule of linear periodicity*. Using simultaneously presented, two dimensional, dotted line stimuli, the single most important variable in determining detectability is shown to be the *spatial periodicity of dotted lines*. That was the original reason for choosing autocorrelation as the algorithm to model these data and the basis of the high degree of predictive power of the model. Global form *is* a powerful determinant of psychophysical detectability, but only with dotted line defined forms. If one uses global forms formed from random dot arrays, global form is, at best, a weak determinant of the psychophysical detectability of a plane.

Thus, random arrays of dots, no matter how well they define a form, do not provide the necessary cues to activate the periodicity and global form sensitive process assayed with stimuli formed from dotted lines. The measured influence of dot numerosity or form in those experiments using random dotted forms is simply a matter of probability summation or some other similar statistic not following the rule of linear periodicity.

The answer to the question—Is this difference in global form effect due to depth or to stimulus material?—can now be given. It is unequivocally the stimulus material. The main influence in this case is the difference between a form defined by random dot arrays and a form defined by more or less regularly spaced dotted *lines*. The difference between two and three dimensions is incidental, as is the procedural difference between dynamic and static noise. The perceptual mechanism I have been studying is so characterized and as we shall shortly see, much to my delight in my role as a theoretician, so is the mathematical model invoking the autocorrelation transform.

In conclusion, the visual system has been shown, once again, to depend heavily on linear periodicity in three as well as two dimensions. I must acknowledge, however, that there still are many unknowns and uncertainties concerning the rich array of data that has been obtained using dotted stimuli in this experimental context. Furthermore, I appreciate that my experiments are not totally unconfounded. In some cases, other attributes than linear periodicity may be changing simultaneously. However, the preponderance of the evidence on the side of the rule of linear periodicity seems to me to be overwhelming.

The next step in this analysis is to pass from the verbal discussions of this section to the more precise language of mathematics and computer simulation in the hopes of providing further illumination. That is the function of the next section of these lectures.

A FORMAL MODEL

The discussion I have just presented of the nature and general perceptual significance of the data obtained in this study sets the stage for the final part of my presentation. In the following few pages, I will consider the appropriateness of the autocorrelation model as an analytic description of these findings. My tests of the model, however, must be limited to the issue of global form, time at last having run out.

Before I begin, however, some background is necessary. It is important to understand why have I invoked the autocorrelation model to describe these detection data in the first place. As I have noted, one of the major hypotheses initially emerging from the earlier two dimensional study (Uttal, 1975) was that spatial periodicity of the dots of a linear stimulus form is a powerful determinant of detectability. A plausible extrapolation suggested that spatial and temporal periodicity should also be influential in the dynamic three dimensional space-time environment of the present study. As we have seen, however plausible, this extrapolation turned out not to be completely correct.

126   4. DISCUSSION

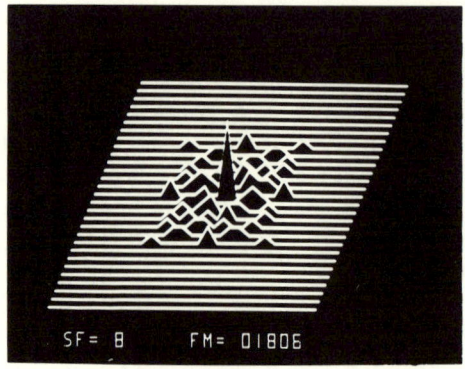

FIG. 55A.

FIG. 55 (A, B, C).   The autocorrelograms and simulated stimuli for the stimuli shown in Fig. 40.

There was, however, another very serious difficulty that loomed on the horizon of such an extension of the model from two dimensions (X and Y) to four dimensions (X, Y, Z, and t). Any future three or four dimensional mathematical model based on a processing algorithm similar in concept to the two dimensional autocorrelation model is likely to be extremely demanding of computer time. The demand for computing power required to evaluate an autocorrelation is a simple power function of the number of dimensions used in the simulated stimulus space. Thus, the extension of this model to additional dimensions could prove to be a computational disaster, particularly since all evaluations of the model have been done on the same small scale microcomputer used to run the experiments.

Very fortunately, the psychophysical data that was obtained quickly made it

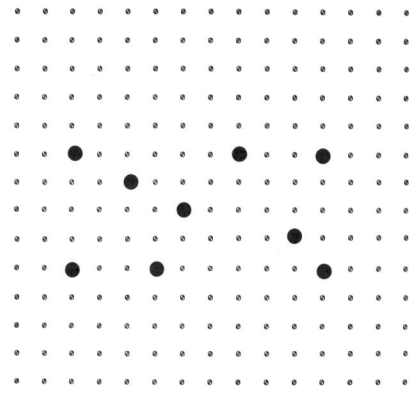

FIG. 55B.

clear that the computational requirement is not likely to be as devastating as it initially seemed. Some dimensions turned out to be psychophysically redundant. Indeed, redundancy is one specific interpretation of the results of Experiments 13 and 14; those studies demonstrated, if you recall, the ineffectiveness of rotation on the detectability of a plane. Both mathematically and psychophysically speaking, therefore, this result may assert that much of what need be said about the detectability of dotted *planes* in three dimensions can be equally well said by evaluating stimulus planes in two dimensions. Similarly, insensitivity to temporal irregularity can be interpreted as evidence that the temporal dimensions can be ignored to at least a first approximation when modeling the perceptual properties of dotted forms. However, this is obviously not the full story. The loss of sensitivity to spatial irregularity at long interdot intervals suggests that some important temporal-spatial interactions are glossed over when one uses the two dimensional autocorrelation as a reduced model of full four dimensional percep-

128   4. DISCUSSION

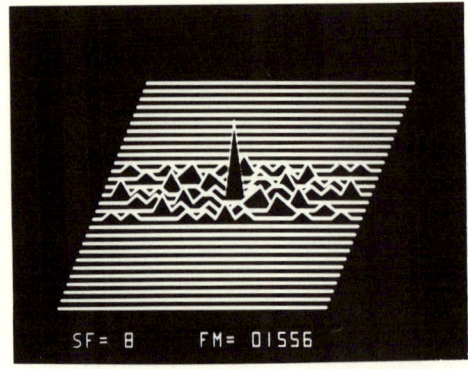

FIG. 55C.

tual processing. Therefore, this first pass at applying the two dimensional model to the four dimensional phenomena is obviously incomplete. Be that as it may, clearly the simple two dimensional autocorrelation model can be used to produce at least a partial analysis of some aspects of the detection of dotted forms.

To bring this possibility into sharper focus, let's tabulate some metaconclusions that emerge from the data and from my earlier discussion of them. These metaconclusions represent a higher level of generalization about the visual processes assayed in the present experiments than heretofore presented. They include:

1. Throughout all of these experiments, it was repeatedly observed that the signal-to-noise ratio exerts a powerful and monotonic influence on the detectability of dotted patterns.

2. Distributing noise dots in depth reduces their effectiveness as maskers in the same way as reducing their density in the X, Y plane. In fact, distributing them in depth can be considered equivalent to reducing their density.

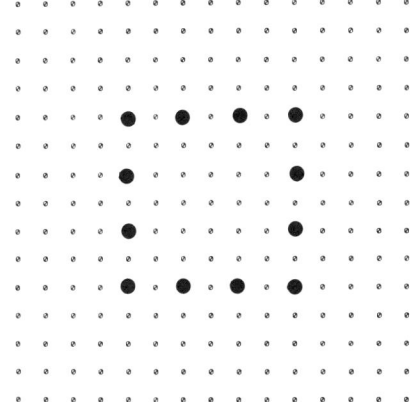

FIG. 56A.

FIG. 56 (A, B, C). The autocorrelograms and simulated stimuli for the stimuli shown in Fig. 51.

3. Visual space is to at least a first approximation[12] isotropic, uniform, and homogeneous throughout the entire 5.4 deg by 5.4 deg by 28 min (of retinal disparity) region that defined the apparent cubical space. Direction and orientation do not matter to any significant degree.

4. A corollary of metaconclusion 3 is that the two "direct" dimensions (X and Y) can be traded off against the "indirect" dimension (Z) with impunity. A frontoparallel oriented stimulus form consisting of random dot arrays is detected no better than one rotated in complex combinations about the X, Y, and Z axes.

---

[12]Obviously this approximation will not hold at greater retinal eccentricities. Since the time of Helmholtz, perceptual scientists have known that visual field curvature occurs in the peripheral retinal image. There, the uniformity, isotropy, and homogeneity observed in the more central regions is likely to be substantially violated in peripheral vision.

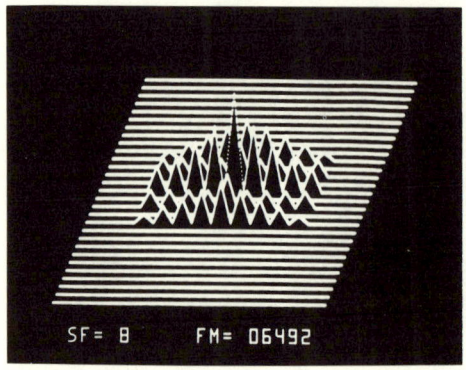

FIG. 56B.

5. Within broad limits, visual mechanisms are capable of correcting distortions in space and time, particularly at long intervals allowing apparent motion. The perceptual systems seem totally insensitive under some conditions to both temporal and spatial irregularities and modestly insensitive even to order.

6. There appears to be only a modest interaction among dotted stimuli located at different depths and thus presumably among the neural mechanisms defining those depths. In other words, global stereopsis is a weaker force than local disparity in the context of the experimental paradigm used here. In those cases in which dot numerosity does exert a significant influence on form detection, it seems to be due to simple probabilistic, rather than interactive, effects.

7. Stimulus form exerts a dual effect on detectability. The detection of planar forms produced from arrays of random dots is nearly independent of the global form of the plane. Only the texture of the plane as defined by the density, laciness, and microstructure—the three statistical moments in Julesz' (1978)

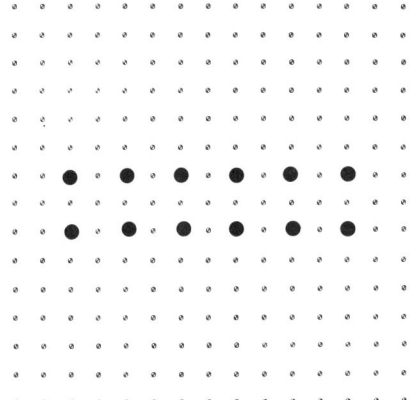

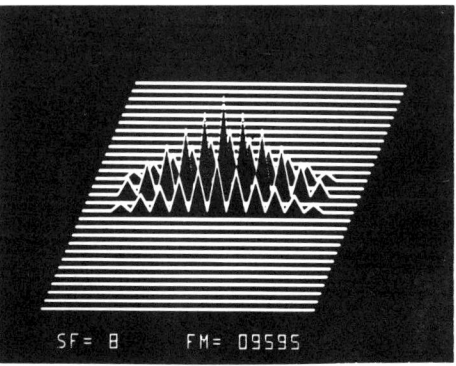

FIG. 56C.

nomenclature—is of importance in determining detectability in this case. However, the detectability of a plane defined by dotted lines is a strong function of its form, that is, of the arrangement and the nature of the dotted lines.

8. The results obtained in this series of experiments indicate it really does not matter if forms are presented dichoptically, binocularly, or monocularly; whether they are presented in dynamic or static noise, or whether they are studied at high or low signal to noise levels. Though the differential effect of form may vary in absolute magnitude, relationships among the forms remain relatively stable across all of these variable experimental conditions. These other experimental parameters, however, do play important roles in helping to understand other parameters of visual perception. It is only in light of my special emphasis on form in this theoretical section that I presently ignore them.

These metaconclusions, based upon the results obtained in this study, are not intended to summarize all of the experimental findings I have presented to you in

132   4. DISCUSSION

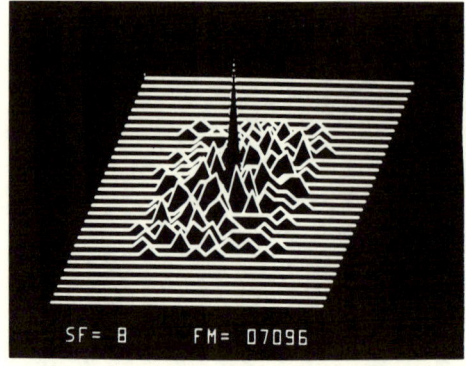

FIG. 57A.

FIG. 57 (A, B, C, D). The autocorrelograms and simulated stimuli for the stimuli shown in Fig. 35.

these lectures, nor are they themselves reductive explanations in any sense of the word. They do, however, describe the general properties of the form detection and space perception mechanisms that are assayed in my experiments. More significantly, these metaconclusions are the basis of those restrictions that will simplify the computational requirements and provide the specifications of a two dimensional model that can be used as a first approximation to the as yet unimplemented four dimensional one.

Now let us briefly summarize what evidence allows these simplifying restrictions. Three are, as I indicated, of special importance. First is the experimental result demonstrating the isotropy and interchangeability of the X, Y, and Z dimensions. Second is the finding that distributing the noise into three dimensional space simulates a reduction in two dimensional noise dot density. Both of these outcomes support the idea that any theoretical model need not necessarily incorporate all three spatial dimensions. A two dimensional analysis of stimulus

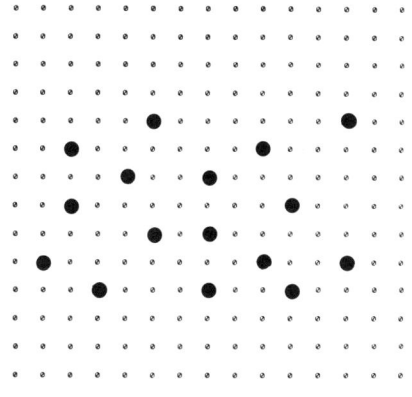

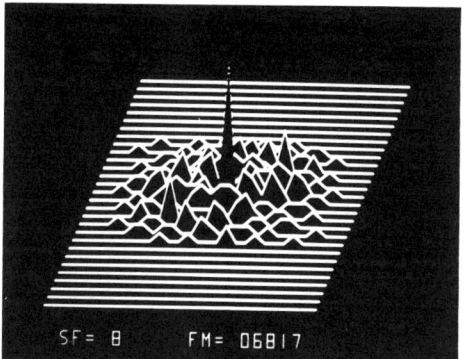

FIG. 57B.

forms should be sufficient to predict at least some aspects of dotted form detection. Third, since the detection paradigm is so insensitive to the temporal irregularity of the stimulus, it seems likely that the temporal variable can also be safely ignored in this first approximation to the proposed model. In this spirit, autocorrelation analyses similar to those described in my earlier monograph (Uttal, 1975) are now carried out to determine how well this two dimensional model fits some of the newer psychophysical data I have already presented to you.

Although I need not fully represent the details of how the autocorrelation algorithm is computed, I should briefly note that this process involves the manual construction of a simulation of one of the stimulus forms used in the experiments. This pattern is then transformed from the X, Y spatial domain to a pattern in the ΔX, ΔY autocorrelation domain by a computer implementation of the autocorrelation formula as it is expressed in Equation 1 on page 20. This X, Y domain to ΔX, ΔY domain transformation (as exemplified by those shown in Fig. 57) can then be quantified by applying another algorithm—the expression of

4. DISCUSSION

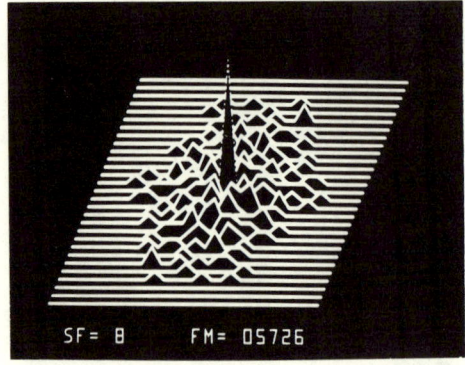

FIG. 57C.

Equation 2. This second algorithm produces a single number—the figure of merit—whose relative magnitudes have previously been shown to be a good predictor of the detectability of two dimensional dotted patterns.

In the following discussion I have concentrated on the experiments that deal explicitly with planar form effects, namely Experiments 10, 11, and 12 and Supplementary Experiments 1 and 2. The results of these autocorrelation and figure of merit computations are shown in the portfolio of photographs marked Fig. 55 through Fig. 58. Let's begin by considering Fig. 55 (simulating Experiment 12), which evaluates the effect of the shapes of the randomly dotted rectangular forms (shown in Fig. 40) on the autocorrelation. We then compare the behavior in this case with that of the autocorrelations of similar forms defined by dotted outlines shown in Fig. 51 (simulating the Supplemental Experiment 1). These autocorrelograms and simulated stimuli are shown in Fig. 56.

The figures of merit of each of these six autocorrelations are shown in the lower right hand corner of each figure. (The other number, in the lower left hand

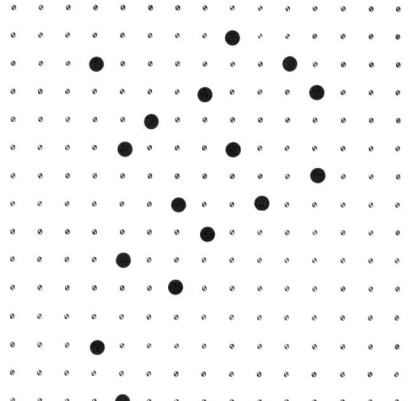

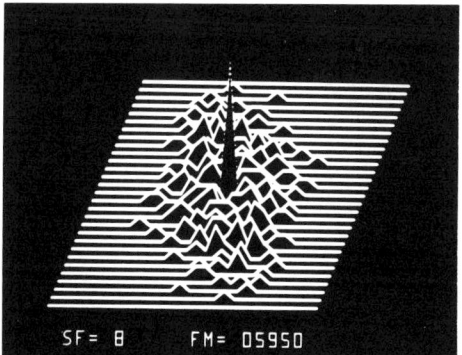

FIG. 57D.

corner indicates the display scale factor, and can be ignored for the time being since it is constant for all autocorrelations in this portfolio.) In the first series of autocorrelations (simulating the rectangular stimuli defined by random dot arrays) the figures of merit are generally small and progressively reduced by a slight amount as the rectangles become progressively more oblong. The series of figures of merit in this case is 1806, 1672, and 1556 respectively. To the contrary, in the series of autocorrelations simulating the rectangular stimuli defined by dotted outlines the sequential figures of merit progressively increase, and by considerably larger amounts, the more rectangular the simulated stimulus. The series of figures of merit in this case is 5839, 6492, and 9595 respectively.

In the earlier monograph (Uttal, 1975), I pointed out that the absolute values of the autocorrelation figure of merit for any form are not of great significance. Rather it is the *rank order* of and the *relative magnitude* of these indicators that seem to correlate well with the rank order and relative magnitude of the detec-

136   4. DISCUSSION

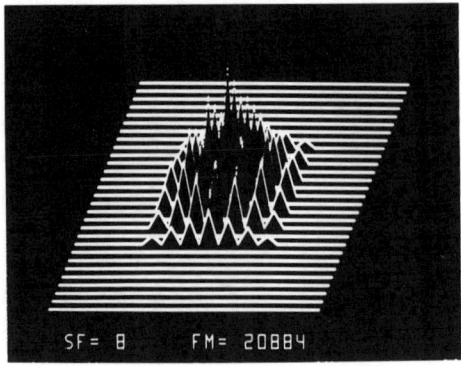

FIG. 58A.

FIG. 58 (A, B, C, D, E, F, G).   The autocorrelograms and simulated stimuli for the stimuli shown in Fig. 53.

tability scores obtained in the psychophysical experiments. In other words, I am using this model in the same way that nonparametric statistical tests sensitive to rank order are used.

Also, relatively small differences are not very significant. Slight differences in the positions of the individual dots of the simulated stimuli can produce substantial differences in the figures of merit that are not valid indicators of detectability. The autocorrelation figures of merit are rough and ready approximations. It is surprising how well they do, therefore, in so many different contexts.

It is in this same spirit that I now compare the results of the two psychophysical experiments with these two autocorrelational analyses. The first series of figures of merit predicts that the random dot array defined forms should become modestly less detectable as a square is progressively transformed into a more and

FIG. 58B.

more oblong rectangle. The second predicts, to the contrary, that the detectability of dotted outline figures should change, not only in the opposite direction, but also, that these changes should be of greater magnitude.

The actual psychophysical effects have already been presented to you in Figs. 41 and 52 respectively. I am certain that it should take no subtle statistical analysis to convince my audience that in these two experiments the predictions of the model concerning the relative detectability of these forms are confirmed in a delightful manner. This is indeed a robust and powerful test of the model and one that I frankly must admit had not been anticipated.[13]

---

[13] In this case, the "predictions" of the autocorrelation model came after the psychophysical data had been obtained. At the risk of violating the facade of modern science usually presented in technical reports, I should also note that this came as a most pleasant surprise. The interaction between theory and model provided both support for the model and further insight into the nature of the mechanisms underlying dotted form detection. Isn't this the way science is supposed to work?

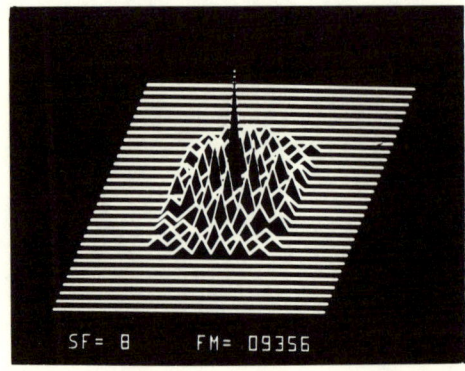

FIG. 58C.

This combination of theory and data helps us to understand the nature of the mechanisms underlying dotted form detection. The major contribution of this particular analysis is its reaffirmation of the especially important role of straight and periodic lines of dots in this kind of perceptual task. Indeed, these results raise the question of what is actually denoted by the term *global form* in these studies. Clearly both random dot arrays and dotted outline figures do define global forms. The visual system (and the autocorrelator) respond quite differently, however, to these two kinds of global form. Thus, the indiscriminate use of the term "global form" obscures important functional and formal differences between the two kinds of stimuli. Whatever the mechanism underlying the ability to carry out this task, once again we see that it shares the properties of the autocorrelation transformation. Most important of all is its extreme sensitivity to linear and periodic forms.

The next application of the autocorrelational model is to the stimulus forms used in Experiments 10 and 11. The autocorrelation figures of merit for the four forms shown in Fig. 35 in which random dot arrays defined the stimulus forms,

A FORMAL MODEL   139

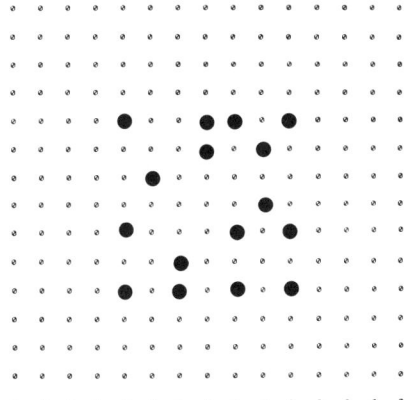

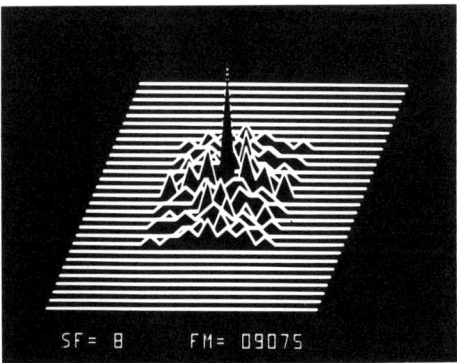

FIG. 58D.

are 7096, 6817, 5726, and 5950 respectively. The simulated stimuli and autocorrelograms are shown in Fig. 57. According to this analysis, this variation produces relatively small differences in detectability scores among the four forms and either a slight decline or irregular variations in detectability. In fact, the data shown in Figs. 37 and 39 exhibit the same trend.

Next, the psychophysical effects of disarraying a periodic array of dots, (the stimuli shown in Fig. 53) as measured in Supplemental Experiment 2, are compared with the autocorrelations of the simulated stimuli shown in Fig. 58. The psychophysical data displayed in Fig. 54 indicated a substantial and virtually linear decline in detectability as larger and larger numbers of dots were displaced. (The exception, the most disarrayed matrix—the seventh—has already been noted.) The series of autocorrelogram figures of merit for the simulated sequence is 20884, 11342, 9356, 9075, 8138, 8311, and 7747 respectively.

In this case, several discrepancies between the model's predictions and the psychophysical data should be noted. First, there is a very sharp drop in the figures of merit for the first disordered stimulus that is not reflected in the

140   4. DISCUSSION

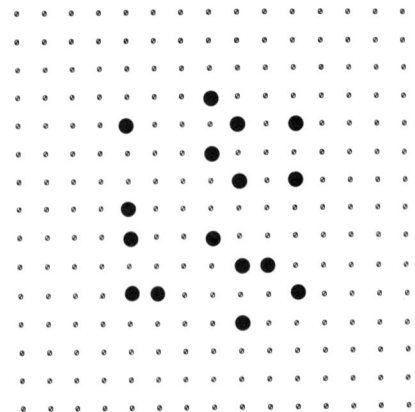

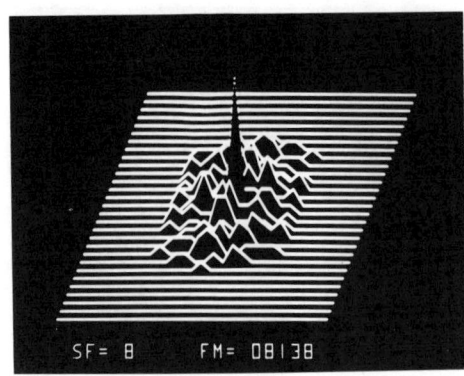

FIG. 58E.

psychophysical data. I have no explanation for this enormous difference. Second, the simulated series has one figure of merit (the sixth one) out of monotonic order. This I believe is a reflection of the generation of a spurious periodicity of the same kind producing the elevated final value in the psychophysical experiments. (The simulated and actual stimuli were not exactly the same.) In general, however, there is agreement of the trends of the experimental data and the theoretical figures of merit: Both are generally declining (each has only one exception). I must reiterate here the qualitative nature of these autocorrelation predictions. The model works only if one looks at general trends and rank orders and not at absolute values. Particularly with the multidimensional two dimensional forms used here, several attributes are changing simultaneously and the figure of merit reflects far more than single linear periodicities. The model must be accepted or rejected within these acknowledged limits. Furthermore, the simulated stimuli can not be identical to the actual stimuli because of the coarser discrete matrix of the simulation.

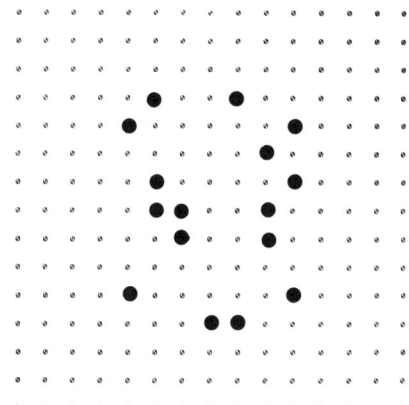

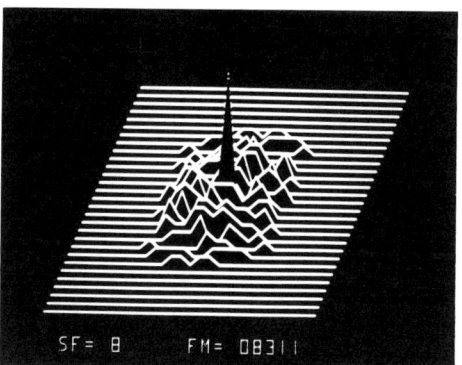

FIG. 58F.

In sum, the autocorrelational model is generally shown to be a useful predictor of human performance in a dotted stimulus within a dotted noise detection task. However, the main conclusion I wish to draw from these comparisons of psychophysical data and mathematical theory is not that there is an autocorrelator in the visual nervous system, but only that something sensitive to the same stimulus attributes as an autocorrelator is present. This is an important distinction. In my previous monograph, I proposed a specific and physiologically plausible neural network that could, in principle, autocorrelate an input stimulus form. But, I no longer feel this kind of neuroreductionism is necessary or appropriate. The very same processes performed by an autocorrelating mechanism could be carried out by any of a large number of analogous mechanisms; the specification of a particular neural mechanism is at best an exercise in unprovable speculation, given the nature of the psychophysical methodology I have used.

I shall summarize my conclusions by noting that on the basis of these data and analyses, it seems likely that there is something in the visual nervous system

4. DISCUSSION

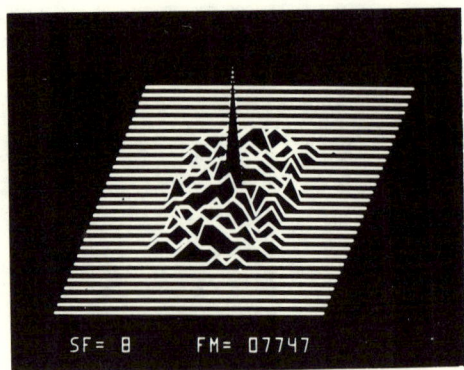

FIG. 58G.

sensitive to the same attributes—particularly linearity and periodicity—of the stimulus as is the mathematical process called autocorrelation.

FINAL COMMENTS

In discussing of the applicability of the autocorrelation model I have been able to consider only a few of the two dimensional attributes of some of the stimulus forms used in this study. The reason for this limited testing of the model is simple enough. The fixed dates of the MacEachran lectureship have allowed me neither the luxury of testing all possible two dimensional stimulus forms nor of extending the model to the multidimensional version required to model the temporal and depth aspects of this kind of visual perception. However, within limits, I feel that I have achieved some understanding of the processing of dot patterns performed by the visual nervous system. As I just noted, my main conclusion is that some kind of an analog of a periodic line sensitive, autocorrelation-like mechanism exists in the visual nervous system. I must now note certain caveats that place this conclusion in its proper context.

First, it is important to appreciate that to the extent that this particular mathematical model works, then, too, so must a large number of other models which are formally equivalent to the autocorrelation transform. After all, the autocorrelation is known to be equal to the Fourier transform of the power spectrum density of the stimulus. It seems likely, then, that other alternative formularizations containing the same information and exhibiting the same sensitivities must also exist. However, the implementations of the mechanisms may differ in ways that affect the simplicity or elegance of the interpretation. One delightfully elegant aspect of the autocorrelation model (for those of us who would like to speculate about underlying structure) is that it need not assume any specialized neural mechanism, only arrangements of unspecialized neurons in a net much like that known to exist in the nervous system.

Second, the autocorrelation process has another advantage that distinguishes it from other models of visual perception. It does not require an elaborate set of prestored (learned?) templates to accomplish its function. The detection of dotted simulus forms is completely explained in terms of processes that are carried out on the stimulus form alone by a general purpose algorithm. It may be that something more akin to a cross correlation (?) of the stimulus form with a set of learned (?) templates (?) is necessary for recognition—a perceptual process which is quite different from the detection tasks used here—but such a mechanism is clearly not necessary to describe the results of the detection task used here. Recognition experiments would have to be carried out to determine just what mechanisms are involved in such a task and I plan to pursue such research in the near future.

Third, although I have continually referred to this theory as an autocorrelation model, it is in fact not exactly equivalent to a formal autocorrelation transformation. The actual computational procedures (described in full in Uttal, 1975) are actually only a discrete approximation to an autocorrelational transform. My colleague, Wilfred Kincaid of the Mathematics Department of The University of Michigan, has pointed out to me that if these ΔX and ΔY shifts in the computational algorithm I use were not discretized, the autocorrelation would produce a function with minima and maxima rather than the monotonic function so analogous to the psychophysical data it now generates. While it is my feeling that the discrete approximation model closely simulates some real aspect of visual perception—perhaps overlapping regions of interaction in a parallel processing net, finite size receptive fields, limited visual acuity, the point spread function, or some other unknown areal smoothing aspect of perception—I must acknowledge that to call it an ''autocorrelation'' model may offend the more sophisticated mathematicians or convolutional purists among you. I do not know what the specific neurological, optical, or perceptual aspect is that is so well simulated by the discrete autocorrelation, but in the final analysis whatever it is I do on the computer works quite well. If anyone has a better name for this model, I would be delighted to substitute it for the word "autocorrelation."

Fourth, there are two metatheoretical points that I would like to make. First, it is very important for me to stress that the results of these experiments, and the theoretical context in which I have placed them, are from my point of view directly antagonistic to the biological, if not the mathematical, assumption of both the feature detecting, single cell approach and the Fourier approach that have been so popular in perceptual psychobiology in recent years. The nature of the distributed network of ungeneralized neurons that would be required to implement the autocorrelation algorithm is quite distinct mechanically from either these highly specialized neurons or spatial frequency filters. Second, the autocorrelation model is, in it most fundamental aspects, a modern manifestation and formalization of many of the classic ideas that the Gestalt psychologists professed a half century ago. The pendulum keeps swinging back and forth between wholism and elementalism and perhaps this work will give some small impetus to that pendulum back towards wholism.

Fifth, I hope that I have not given anyone the impression that I have answers to all of the questions raised by the phenomena I have studied with dots. All of this is very tentative. Explanations and even data are subject to change as more and more experiments are completed. I am firmly convinced that the dotted stimulus form detection process under investigation is a very rich and fertile paradigm. Yet, I realize I have never carried out an experiment that has fully resolved anything. Each new experiment raises more questions than it answers and none has been able to finally resolve any issue rising above the mundane trivialities of "what would happen if?" Furthermore, no matter how well the model works (and there are other discrepancies in it that I have published elsewhere, e.g., Uttal & Tucker, 1981), it is in the final analysis a descriptive rather than a reductive explanation. It may suggest, but it does not confirm. Obviously, there is much yet to be done—these lectures are but a progress report.

Finally, I would once again like to express my appreciation to Professors Lechalt and DiLollo and the MacEachran Committee for inviting me to participate in this lecture series. It has been a very useful thing for me to have had the incentive to put down on paper the experiences that I have had in the laboratory during the last year and a half.

ACKNOWLEDGMENTS

This project is currently supported by Contract #N00014–81–C–0266 from the office of Naval Research, Alexandria, Virginia. I am especially appreciative of the cooperative support of Dr. John O'Hara whose scientific contributions to this project have gone far beyond his administrative responsibilities.

I would also like to express my appreciation to Cheryl Slay, Jo Wilsmann, and Susan Robertson whose editorial and typing skills made this a far better document than it would otherwise have been. Susan, in particular, cleared up some of my grammatical vagaries in a way that only can be appreciated by those who may have seen the earlier drafts. It should not, furthermore, go unacknowledged, that the research reported here was done in collaboration with others. Judy Fitzgerald, Thelma Tucker, John Brogan, and Mark Azzato contributed much to what I have to say in this monograph. I am also grateful to Professor Wildred Kincaid of The University of Michigan's Mathematics Department for his counsel and advice concerning the evaluation of the model.

References

Anderson, J. A., Silverstein, J. W., Ritz, S. A., & Jones, R. S. Distinctive features, categorical perceptions, and probability learning: Some applications of a neural model. *Psychological Review*, 1977, *84*, 413–450.

Appelle, S. Perception and discrimination as a function of stimulus orientation: The "oblique effect" in man and animals. *Psychological Bulletin*, 1972, *78*, 266–278.

Attneave, F. & Arnoult, M. D. The quantitative study of shape and pattern perception. *Psychological Bulletin*, 1956, *53*, 452–471.

Bachmann, T. Genesis of subjective image. Acta et commentatione, Universitat Taneuensis #522 *Problems of Cognitive Psychology*, 1980, 102–126, Tartu, Estonia, U.S.S.R.

Barlow, H. B. The effenciency of detecting changes of density in random dot patterns. *Vision Research*, 1978, *18*, 637–650.

Barlow, H. B., Fitzhugh, R., & Kuffler, S. W. Change of organization in the receptive fields of the cat's retina during dark adaptation. *Journal of Physiology*, 1957, *137*, 338–354.

Barlow, H. B., & Reeves, B. C. The versatility and absolute efficiency of detecting mirror symmetry in random dot displays. *Vision Research*, 1979, *19*, 783–793.

Brown, D. R. & Owen, D. H. The metrics of visual form: Methodological dyspepsia. *Psychological Bulletin*, 1967, *68*, 243–259.

Brown, J. F. & Voth, A. C. The path of seen movement as a function of the vector-field. *American Journal of Psychology*, 1937, *49*, 543–63.

Caelli, T. *Visual perception: Theory and practice*. Oxford, England: The Pergamon Press. 1981.

Campbell, F. W. & Robson, J. G. Application of Fourier analysis to the visibility of gratings. *Journal of Physiology*, 1968, *197*, 551–566.

Coffin, S. Spatial frequency analysis of block letters does not predict experimental confusions. *Perception and Psychophysics*, 1978, *23*, 69–74.

DiLillo, V. Temporal integration in visual memory. *Journal of Experimental Psychology: Gen.*, 1980, *109*, 75–97.

DiLollo, V. & Wilson, A. E. Iconic persistence and perceptual moment as determinants of temporal integration in vision. *Vision Research*, 1978, *18*, 1607–1610.

REFERENCES

DiLollo, V. & Woods, E. Duration of visible persistence in relation to range of spatial frequencies. *Journal of Experimental Psychology: Human Perception and Performance,* 1981, *7,* 754–769.

Falzett, M. and Lappin, J. S. (1981). *Personal communication.*

Fitts, P. M. & Leonard, J. A. *Stimulus correlates of visual pattern perception: A probability approach.* Columbus: Ohio State University, Aviation Psychology Laboratory. 1957.

Foster, D. H. Visual apparent motion and the calculus of variations. In Leeuwenberg, E. L. J. and Buffant (Eds.), *Formal theories of visual perception.* Chichester: Wiley. 1978.

Fox, R. *Contour interaction in visual space* (Tech. Rep. N14–1101 81C–0003). Nashville: Vanderbilt University, Department of Psycholoy. 1981.

Fox, R. & Patterson, R. E. *The effect of depth separation on lateral interference* (Tech. Rep. N14–1101 80C–0001). Nashville: Vanderbilt University, Department of Psychology. 1980.

Garner, W. R. *The processing of information and structure.* Hillsdale, New Jersey: Lawrence Erlbaum Associates. 1974.

Garner, W. R. & Clement, D. E. Goodness of pattern and pattern uncertainty. *Journal of Verbal Learning and Verbal Behavior,* 1963, *2,* 446–452.

Gogel, W. C., & Mershon, D. H. Depth adjacency in simultaneous contrast. *Perception and Psychophysics,* 1969, *5,* 13–17.

Graham, C. H. *Vision and visual perception.* New York: Wiley. 1965.

Grossberg, S. A theory of visual coding, memory, and development. In Leeuwenberg, E. L. J. and Buffart, H. F. J. M. (Eds.), *Formal theories of visual perception.* Chichester, England: John Wiley and Sons. 1978.

Hartline, H. K. & Ratliff, F. Inhibitory interaction of receptor units in the eye of Limulus. *Journal of General Physiology,* 1957, *40,* 357–376.

Hartline, H. K. & Ratliff, F. Spatial summation of inhibitory influences in the eye of the Limulus, and the mutual interaction of receptor units. *Journal of General Physiology,* 1958, *41,* 1049–1066.

Helson, H. H. & Fehrer, E. The role of form in perception. *American Journal of Psychology,* 1932, *44,* 79–102.

Hochberg, J. E. & McAlister, E. A quantitative approach to figural "goodness". *Journal of Experimental Psychology,* 1953, *46,* 361–364.

Hoffman, W. C. The Lie algebra of visual perception. *Journal of Mathematical Psychology,* 1966, *3,* 65–98.

Hoffman, W. C. A mathematical framework for Piagetian psychology. (Preprint available from the author). Department of Mathematical Science, Oakland University, Rochester, Michigan. 1976.

Hoffman, W. C. The Lie transformation group approach to visual neurophysiology. In Leeuwenberg, E. L. J. and Buffart, J. M. (Eds.), *Formal theories of visual perception.* Chichester, England: John Wiley and Sons. 1978.

Hogben, J. H. *Perception of visual pattern with components distributed in time.* Unpublished doctoral dissertation. University of Western Australia. 1972.

Howard, H. J. A test for the judgment of distance. *American Journal of Optometry,* 1919, *2,* 656–675.

Huggins, A. W. F. & Getty, D. J. *Display-control compatibility in 3-D displays:1. Effects of orientation* (Report No. 4724). Cambridge, Mass.: Bolt Beranek and Newman Inc. 1981.

Jonides, J., Irwin, D. E., & Yantis, S. Integrating visual information from successive fixations. *Science,* 1982, *215,* 192–194.

Johansson, G. About the geometry underlying spontaneous visual decoding of the optical message. In E. L. J. Leeuwenberg and H. F. J. M. Buffart (Eds.), *Formal theories of visual perception.* Chichester: Wiley. 1978.

Julesz, B. Binocular depth perception of computer generated patterns. *Bell System Technical Journal,* 1960, *39,* 1125–1162.

REFERENCES

Julesz, B. Binocular depth perception without familiarity cues. *Science,* 1964, *145,* 356–362.
Julesz, B. *Foundations of cyclopean perception.* Chicago: The University of Chicago Press. 1971.
Julesz, B. Perceptual limits of texture discrimination and their implications to figure-ground separation. In E. L. J. Leeuwenberg and H. F. J. M. Buffart (Eds.) *Formal Theories of Visual Perception.* New York: Wiley. 1978.
Julesz, B. & Chang, J. J. Interaction between pools of binocular disparity detectors tuned to different disparities. *Biological Cybernetics,* 1976, *22,* 107–119.
Kaniza, G. Subjective contours. *Scientific American,* 1976, *234(4),* 48–52.
Kohler, I. *Uber Aufbau and Wandel lungen der wahrnehmungswelt: Insbesondere uber bedingte empfindungen.* Vienna: Rohrer. 1951.
Kubovy, M. & Pomerantz, J. R. Eds. *Perceptual organization.* Hillsdale, N.J.: Lawrence Erlbaum Associates. 1981.
Langlands, H. M. S. Experiments in binocular vision. *Transactions of the Optical Society,* 1926, *28,* 45–82.
Lappin, J. S., Doner, J. F., & Kottas, B. L. Minimal conditions for the visual detection of structure in motion. *Science,* 1980, *209,* 717–719.
Leeuwenberg, E. Quantative specification of information in sequential patterns. *Psychological Review,* 1969, *76,* 216–220.
Leeuwenberg, E. A perceptual coding language for visual and auditory patterns. *American Journal of Psychology,* 1971, *84,* 307–349.
Lehmkuhle, S. & Fox, R. Effect of depth separation on metacontrast masking. *Journal of Experimental Psychology,* 1980, *6,* 605–621.
Lindberg, D. C. *Theories of vision from Ak-kindi to Kepler.* Chicago: The University of Chicago Press. 1976.
Mershon, D. H. Relative contributions of depth and directional adjacency to simultaneous whiteness contrast. *Vision Research,* 1972, *12,* 969–979.
Mueller, C. B. & Lloyd, V. V. Stereoscopic acuity for various levels of illuminance. Proceedings of the National Academy of Science, 1948, *34,* 223–227.
Muller, J. *The physiology of the senses, voice, and muscular motion and with the mental faculties.* Trans. by W. Baly with notes. London: Taylor, Walter, and Maberly. 1848.
Nachmias, J. Effect of exposure duration on visual contrast sensitivity with square-wave gratings. *Journal of the Optical Society of America,* 1967, *57,* 421–427.
Nakayama, K. Psychophysical isolation of movement sensitivity by removal of familiar position cues. *Vision Research,* 1981, *21,* 1475–1481.
Newhouse, M. & Uttal, W. R. Distribution of stereoanomalies in the general population. *Bulletin of the Psychonomic Society,* 1982, *20,* 48–50.
Patterson, R. E. & Fox, R. *Information processing in global stereopsis.* Paper presented at Psychonomics Society Meeting, Philadelphia. 1981.
Pepper, R. L., Cole, R. E., Merritt, J. O., & Smith, D. Operator performance using conventional or stereo displays. *Optical Engineering,* 1978, *17,* 411–415.
Pitts, W. & McCulloch, W. S. How we know universals: The perception of auditory and visual forms. *The Bulletin of Mathematical Biophysics,* 1947, *9,* 127–147.
Pomerantz, J. R. Pattern goodness and speed of encoding. *Memory and Cognition,* 1977, *5,* 235–241.
Pomerantz, J. R. Are complex visual features derived from simple ones. In Leeuwenberg, E. L. J. and Buffart, H. F. J. M. (Eds.), *Formal theories of visual perception.* Chichester, England: John Wiley and Sons. 1978.
Richards, W. Stereopsis and stereoblindness. *Experimental Brain Research,* 1970, *10,* 380–388.
Robinson, D. N. *Towards a science of human nature.* New York, Columbia University Press. 1982.
Rock, I. *Orientation and form.* New York: Academic Press. 1973.

REFERENCES

Rogers, B. & Graham, M. Similarities between motion parallax and stereopsis in human depth perception. *Vision Research,* 1982, *22,* 261–270.

Rogers, T. D. & Trofanenko, S. C. On the measurement of shape. *Bulletin of Mathematical Biology,* 1979, *41,* 283–304.

Rosenblatt, F. *Principles of neurodynamics: Perceptions and the theory of brain mechanisms.* Washington, DC: Spartan Books. 1963.

Sher, L. *The spacegraph display: Principles of operation and application* (Internal Rep.). Cambridge, Mass.: Bolt Beranek and Newman. 1979.

Shetty, S. S., Brodersen, A. J., & Fox, R. *System for generating dynamic random element stereograms* (Tech. Rep. N14–1101 79C–0003). Nashville: Vanderbilt University, Department of Psychology. 1979.

Smith, D. C., Cole, R. C., Merritt, J. O., & Pepper, R. L. *Remote operator performance comparing mono and stereo TV displays: The effects of visibility, learning and task factors* (Report NOSC TR 380). Kailua, Hawaii: Naval Ocean Systems Center. 1976.

Snyder, F. W. & Pronko, N. H. *Vision with spatial inversion.* Wichita, Kansas: University of Wichita Press. 1952.

Sperling, G. A model for visual memory tasks. *Human Factors,* 1963, *5,* 19–31.

Stratton, G. Some preliminary experiments on vision without inversion of the retinal image. *Psychological Review,* 1896, *3,* 611–617.

Stratton, G. Upright vision and the retinal image. *Psychological Review,* 1897, *4,* 182–187.

Sutherland, N. S. Comments on the session. In W. Wathen-Dunn (Ed.), *Models for the perception of speech and visual form.* Cambridge: MIT Press. 1967.

Tormey, A. & Tormey, J. F. Renaissance Intarsia: The art of geometry. *Scientific American,* 1982, *247,* 136–143.

Uttal, T. *Personal communication.* 1982.

Uttal, W. R. The effect of interval and number on masking with dot bursts. *Perceptual Psychophysiology,* 1971, *9,* 469–473.

Uttal, W. R. Chromatic and intensive effects in dot pattern masking: Evidence for different time constants in color vision. *Journal of the Optical Society of America,* 1973, *63,* 1490–1494.

Uttal, W. R. *An autocorrelation theory of form detection.* Hillsdale, N.J.: Lawrence Erlbaum Associates, 1975.

Uttal, W. R. *A taxonomy of visual processes.* Hillsdale, N.J.: Lawrence Erlbaum Associates, 1981.

Uttal, W. R., Fitzgerald, J. & Eskin, T. E. Parameters of tachistoscopic stereopsis. *Vision Research,* 1975(a), *15,* 705–712.

Uttal, W. R., Fitzgerald, J. & Eskin, T. E. Rotation and translation effects on stereoscopic acuity. *Vision Research,* 1975(b), *15,* 939–944.

Uttal, W. R. & Hieronymus, R. Spatio-temporal effects in gap detection. *Perception and Psychophysics,* 1970, *8,* 321–325.

Uttal, W. R. & Tucker, T. E. Negligible symmetry effects in dot pattern recognition. In Getty, D. J. and Howard J. H. Jr. (Eds.) *Auditory and Visual Pattern Recognition,* Hillsdale, N.J.: Lawrence Erlbaum Associates, 1981.

Vernon, M. D. *A further study of visual perception.* Cambridge, England: Cambridge University Press, 1952.

von Bekesy, G. Mach- and Hering-type lateral inhibition in vision. *Vision Research,* 1968, *8,* 1483–1499.

Westheimer, G. & McKee, S. P. Spatial configurations for visual hyperacuity. *Vision Research,* 1977, *17,* 941–947.

Woodburne, L. S. The effect of a constant visual angle upon the binocular discrimination of depth differences. *American Journal of Psychology,* 1934, *46,* 273–286.

Zusne, L. *Visual perception of form.* New York: Academic Press, 1970.

THE AUTHOR'S PUBLICATIONS

Books

1. Uttal, W. R. *Real-Time Computers: Technique and Applications in the Psychological Sciences.* New York: Harper & Row, 1968.
2. Uttal, W. R., Rogers, M., Hieronymus, R., & Pasich, T. *Generative Computer Assisted Instruction in Analytic Geometry,* Newburyport, Mass.: Entelek Press, 1970.
3. Uttal, W. R. (Ed.). *Sensory Coding: Selected Readings.* Boston: Little, Brown & Co., 1972.
4. Uttal, W. R. *The Psychobiology of Sensory Coding.* New York: Harper & Row, 1973.
5. Uttal, W. R. *Cellular Neurophysiology and Integration: An Interpretive Introduction.* Hillsdale, NJ: Lawrence Erlbaum Associates.
6. Uttal, W. R. *An Autocorrelation Theory of Form Detection.* Hillsdale, N.J.: Lawrence Erlbaum Associates, 1975.
7. Uttal, W. R. *The Psychobiology of the Mind.* Hillsdale, N.J.: Lawrence Erlbaum Associates, 1978.
8. Uttal, W. R. *A Taxonomy of Visual Processes.* Hillsdale, N.J.: Lawrence Erlbaum Associates, 1981.
9. Robinson, D. N., & Uttal, W. R. *Principles of Psychobiology.* New York: MacMillan, 1983.
10. Uttal, W. R. *The Detection of Forms in Space.* Hillsdale, N.J.: Lawrence Erlbaum Associates, 1983.

Articles

1. Uttal, W. R. A comparison of neural and psychophysical responses in the somesthetic system. *Journal of Comparative and Physiological Psychology,* 1959, *52,* 485–490.
2. Uttal, W. R. Cutaneous sensitivity to electrical pulse stimuli. *Journal of Comparative and Physiological Psychology,* 1958, *51,* 549–554.
3. Uttal, W. R. Neural responses to long duration electrical pulse stimuli in the somesthetic system of man. *IBM Information Research Reports,* 1958, IR-00195.
4. Uttal, W. R. Computer studies of neurophysiological phenomena in man and crayfish. *Proceedings of the 2nd Annual IBM Symposium,* September 1960, pp. 26–30.
5. Uttal, W. R. Computers and Sensory Neurophysiology. *Proceedings of the Aeronautics Electronics Conference, NAECON,* 1960, 221–226.
6. Uttal, W. R. The IBM Biophysical Research System. *IBM Research Reports,* 1960 RC-195.
7. Uttal, W. R. Inhibitory interaction of responses to electrical stimuli in the fingers. *Journal of Comparative and Physiological Psychology,* 1960, *53,* 47–51.
8. Uttal, W. R. The neural coding of somesthetic sensation: A psychophysical-neurophysiological comparison. *USAMRL Symposium on Cutaneous Sensitivity* (G. R. Hawkes, Ed.), February 1960, pp. 11–13, Ft. Knox, KY.
9. Uttal, W. R. The three stimulus problems: A further comparison of neural and psychophysical responses in the somesthetic system. *Journal of Comparative and Physiological Psychology,* 1960, *53,* 42–46.
10. Uttal, W. R., & Cook. L. On the absense of contralateral inhibitory interaction to electrical stimuli in the fingers. *IBM Research Reports,* 1960, RC-243.
11. Uttal, W. R., & Roland, P. A. A terminal device for entry of neuro-electric data into an electronic data processing machine. *EEG & Clinical Neurophysiology,* 1961, *13,* 637–640.
12. Uttal, W. R. My teacher has three arms. *IBM Research Reports,* 1962, RC-788.

REFERENCES

13. Uttal, W. R. On conversational interaction. In J. Coulson (Ed.), *Programmed Learning and Computer Based Instructions.* New York: Wiley, 1962, pp. 171–190.
14. Uttal, W. R. Use of summary card punch as simultaneous stimulus generator and data collecter. *American Journal of Psychology,* 1962, *75,* 150–151.
15. Uttal, W. R., Charap, M., & Maher, A. The computer tutoring of stenotype: A preliminary report. *IBM Research Reports,* 1962, RC-663.
16. Uttal, W. R., Dickinson, C. A., Hom, C., Bernard, F. H., Selfridge, L. P., Cook, L., & Phillips, M. L. A modular, fully buffered multiplexer system for real time man-machine applications. *IBM Research Reports,* 1962, RC-885.
17. Uttal, W. R., & Kasprzak, H. The caudal photoreceptor of the crayfish: A quantitative study of responses to intensity, temporal and wavelength variables. *AFIFPS Conference Proceedings,* 1962, *21,* 159–169.
18. Uttal, W. R. Computers and the future. *Proceedings of the Midwest Human Factor Society Symposium on Human Factors & Computers,* August 1963.
19. Uttal, W. R., & Kasprzak, H. Stimulus-intensity response amplitude relations for monochromatic stimulation of the crayfish caudal photorecpetor. *IBM Research Reports,* 1963, RC-889.
20. Uttal, W. R. On relations between men and machines. In *Digital Computers in Real Time—A Course Outline for The University of Michigan Engineering Summer Conference,* 1964.
21. Uttal, W. R. The automated laboratory. MHRI Preprint #130, 1964, The University of Michigan.
22. Uttal, W. R., & Cook. L. Systematics of the evoked somatosensory cortical potential. *Annals of the New York Academy of Sciences,* 1964 *112,* 60–81.
23. Uttal, W. R., Cook, L., & Kasprzak, H. Computer studies of neurophysiological and psychological envents. *Annals of the New York Academy of Sciences,* 1964, *115,* 776–796.
24. Uttal, W. R. Do compound evoked potentials reflect psychological codes? *Psychological Bulletin,* 1965, *64,* 377–392.
25. Uttal, W. R. Acdemic freedom and corporate influence. *Educational Technology,* 1966, 6(23), 1–12.
26. Uttal, W. R. Oscillations in the amplitude of human peripheral nerve impulses during repetitive stimulation. *Kybernetik,* 1966, *3,* 24–27.
27. Uttal, W. R., & Krissoff, M. The effect of stimulus pattern on temporal acuity in the somastosensory system. *Journal of Experimental Psychology,* 1966, *71,* 878–883.
28. Uttal, W. R. Computer reaching machines—real time stimulation of the tutorial dialogue. MHRI Preprint #184, 1966, University of Michigan. Also published in part in *Psychology Today,* August 1967, under title: Teaching and machines. Reprinted in *Readings in Psychology Today,* Eds. I & II.
29. Uttal, W. R. The effect of ischemia on the peripheral nerve action potential and its relation to somatosensory magnitude coding. *Perception & Psychophysics.* 1967, *2,* 137–140.
30. Uttal, W. R. Evoked brain potentials: Signs or codes? *Perspectives in Biology & Medicine,* 1967, *10,* 627–639.
31. Uttal, W. R., & Krissoff, M. On the refractoriness of somasthetic temporal acuity. *Perception & Psychophysica,* 1967, *2,* 115–118.
32. Uttal, W. R., & Smith, P. Contralateral and hetermodal interaction effects in somastosensation: Do they exist? *Perception and Psychophysics,* 1967, *2,* 363–368.
33. Uttal, W. R., & Smith, P. On the psychophysical discriminability of somatosensory nerve action potential patterns with irregular intervals. *Perception & Psychophysica,* 1967, *2,* 341–348.
34. Beatty, J., & Uttal, W. R. The effect of grouping visual stimuli on the cortical evoked potential. *Perception & Psychophyscis,* 1968, *4,* 214–217.
35. Uttal, W. R. Basic black in computer interfaces for psychological research. *Behavior Research Methods & Instrumentation,* 1968, *1,* 35–40.

36. Uttal, W. R. Reaction paper. In *Computer-assisted Instruction and the Teaching of Mathematics*, proceedings of the September 1968 National Conference on Computer-assisted Instruction. *National Council of Teachers of Mathematics*, 1969, 100–117.
37. Uttal, W. R., & Krissoff, M. The response of the somesthetic system to patterned trains of electrical stimuli: An approach to the problem of sensory coding. In D. R. Kenshalo (Ed.), *The Skin Senses*. Springfield, IL: C. C. Thomas, 1968, pp. 262–303.
38. Uttal, W. R., & Smith, P. Further studies on the psychophysics of irregular nerve action potential patterns. *Perception & Psychophysics*, 1968, *3*, 341–345.
39. Uttal, W. R., & Smith, P. Recognition of alphabetic characters during eye movements. *Perception & Psychophysics*, 1968, *3*, 257–264.
40. Uttal, W. R. Buggywhips, whalebones and clipboards: Some notes on generating complex stimuli with small computers. *American Psychologist*, 1969, *24*, 202–206.
41. Uttal, W. R. Emerging principles of sensory coding. *Perspectives in Biology & Medicine*, 1969, *12*, 344–368.
42. Uttal, W. R. Masking of alphabetic character recognition by dynamic visual noise (DVN). *Perception & Psychophysics*, 1969, *6*, 121–128.
43. Uttal, W. R. Masking of alphabetic character recognition by ultrahigh density dynamic visual noise. *Perception & Psychophysics*, 1970, *7*, 19–22.
44. Uttal, W. R. Interaction of forward and backward masking of alphabetic character recognition by dynamic visual noise (DVN): The character in the hole experiment. *Perception & Psychophysics*, 1969, *6*, 177–181.
45. Uttal, W. R. On the physiological basis of masking with dotted visual noise. *Perception & Psychophysics*, 1970, *7*, 321–327.
46. Uttal, W. R. Violations of visual simultaneity. *Perception & Psychophysics*, 1970, *7*, 133–136.
47. Uttal, W. R., Bunnell, L. M., & Corwin, S. On the detectability of straight lines in visual noise: An extension of French's paradigm into the millisecond domain. *Perception & Psychophysics*, 1970, *8*, 385–388.
48. Uttal, W. R., & Hieronymus, R. Spatio-temporal factors in visual gap detection. *Perception & Psychophysics*, 1970, *8*, 321–325.
49. Uttal, W. R. The effect of interval and number on masking with dot bursts. *Perception & Psychophysics*, 1971, *9*, 469–473.
50. Uttal, W. R. A masking approach to the problem of form perception. *Perception & Psychophysics*, 1971, *9*, 296–298.
51. Uttal, W. R. Neurophysiology. *McGraw-Hill Yearbook of Science and Technology*, 1971, pp. 284–285.
52. Uttal, W. R. The psychobiological silly season, or what happens when neurophysiological data become psychological theories. *Journal of General Psychology*, 1971, *84*, 151–166.
53. Uttal, W. R. A reply to Robinson. *Perception & Psychophysics*, 1971, *10*, 36–37.
54. Uttal, W. R. A reply to Walsh. *Perception & Psychophysics*, 1971, *10*, 267–268.
55. Uttal, W. R. Computer aided psychological studies concerning human pattern recognition and its physiological substrates. *Proceedings of the Vth Hawaii International Conference on Systems Sciences*, 1972.
56. Uttal, W. R. A minor perturbing effect of retinal locus on dot pattern recognition: Rejection of a possible artifact. *Psychonomic Sciences*, 1972, *29*, 100–102.
57. Uttal, W. R. Misuse, abuse, overuse, and unuse of on-line computer facilities by psychologists. *Behavior Research Methods & Instrumentation*, 1972, *4*, 55–60.
58. Chinnis, J. O., Jr., & Uttal, W. R. Effects of random and nonrandom visual noise on discrimination of a dotted target line. *Journal of Experimental Psychology*, 1973, *100*, 335–340.
59. Uttal, W. R. Analogy or homology? (Review of Peter Dodwell, *Perceptual Processing: Stimulus Equivalence and Pattern Recognition*) *Contemporary Psychology*, 1973, *18*, 459–460.

154 REFERENCES

60. Uttal, W. R. Chromatic and intensive effects in dot pattern masking: Evidence for differential time constants in color vision. *Journal of the Optical Society of America*, 1973, *63*, 1490–1494.
61. Uttal, W. R. The effect of deviations from linearity on the detectability of dotted patterns. *Vision Research*, 1973, *13*, 2155–2163.
62. Uttal, W. R. Real-time, on-line computer applications in the psychophysical laboratory. In B. Weiss (Ed.), *Digital Computers in the Behavioral Laboratory*, 1973.
63. Uttal, W. R. Variable manufacturing characteristics of the P-15 phosphor: A warning. *Behavior Research Methods & Instrumentation*, 1973, *5*, 60.
64. Uttal, W. R., Pasich, T., Rogers, M., & Hieronymus, R. Generative computer assisted instruction. In B. Weiss (Ed.), *Digital Computers in the Behavioral Laboratory*, 1973.
65. Chinnis, J. O., Jr., & Uttal, W. R. Tachistoscopic detectability of dotted lines in dotted visual noise: The effect of the signal-to-noise ratio. *American Journal of Psychology*, 1974, *87*, 83–93.
66. Gourlay, K., Uttal, W. R., & Powers, M. . VRS—A programming system for visual electrophysiological research. *Behavior Research Methods & Instrumentation*, 1974 *6*(2), 281–287.
67. Uttal, W. R. The neuropsychology of pain. In *International Encyclopedia of Psychobiology, Psychology, and Psychoanalysis*. Glencoe, IL: MacMillan, 1977.
68. Uttal, W. R. An R. C. model of response time differences in human color vision. In Day, R. H., & Stanley, G. V. *Studies in Perception*. Perth: University of Western Australia Press, 1977.
69. Uttal, W. R., Fitzgerald, J., & Eskin, T. E. Parameters of tachistoscopic stereopsis. *Vision Research*, 1975, *15*, 705–712.
70. Uttal, W. R., Fitzgerald, J., & Eskin, T. E. Rotation and translation effects on stereoscopic acuity. *Vision Research*, 1975, *15*, 939–944.
71. Uttal, W. R. An autocorrelation theory of visual form detection: A computer experiment and a computer model. *Behavior Research Methods & Instrumentation*, 1975, *7*(2), 87–91.
72. Uttal, W. R. Visual spatial interactions between dotted line segments. *Vision Research*, 1976, *16*, 581–586.
73. Uttal, W. R. Can mind modeling not be mind boggling? (Review of Schank, R. C., & Colby, K. M. (Eds.). *Computer Models of Thought and Language*) *Contemporary Psychology*, 1975, *20*, 869–870.
74. Lappin, J. S., & Uttal, W. R. Does prior knowledge facilitate the detection of visual targets in random noise? *Perception & Psychophysics*, 1976, *20*, 367–374.
75. Uttal, W. R., & Eskin, T. Complexity effects in form perception. *Vision Research*, 1977, *17*, 359–365.
76. Uttal, W. R. (Review of Szentagothai, J., & Arbib, M. A. *Conceptual Models of Neural Organization*) *Brain, Behavior & Evolution*. 1977, *14*, 238–240.
77. Uttal, W. R. Too much data: Too little integration. (Review of Granit's R. *The Purposive Brain*) *Contemporary Psychology*, 1978, *23*, 391–392.
78. Uttal, W. R. Experimental psychology from long ago and far away. (Review of Obonai, T. *Perception, Learning and Thinking*), *Contemporary Psychology*, 1978, *23*, 673–675.
79. Uttal, W. R. Codes, sensations, and the mind-body problem. Commentary in *The Behavioral and Brain Sciences*, 1978, *1*, 368.
80. Uttal, W. R., & Tucker, T. E. Negligible symmetry effects in dot pattern detection in Getty, D. J. and Howard, J. H. Jr. (Eds.) *Auditory and visual pattern recognition*, Erlbaum, Hillsdale, N.J., 1981.
81. Uttal, W. R. Do central nonlinearities exist? Commentary in *The Behavioral and Brain Sciences*, 1979, *2*, 286.

82. Uttal, W. R. Review of Bibbero, Microprocessors in instrumentation and control. *Behavior Research Methods and Instrumentation,* 1979, *11,* 614–615.
83. Uttal, W. R. Neuroreductionistic dogma: A heretical counterview. In Albrecht, D. G. (Ed.) Lecture Notes in Biomathematics *Recognition of pattern and form.* Berlin: Springer-Verlag, 1982.
84. Uttal, W. R. Codes, messages, and media. Commentary in *The Behavioral and Brain Sciences,* (In Press).
85. Uttal, W. R. Psychology and Biology. In Bornstein, M. H. (Ed.) *Psycholgy in relation to the allied disciplines* (In Press).
86. Uttal, W.. R. Internal representation and indeterminacy: A skeptical view. Commentary in The *Behavioral and Brain Sciences,* (In Press).
87. Uttal, W. R., Azzato, M., and Brogan, J. Dot and line detection in stereoscopic space. In Getty, D. J. (Ed.) *Three dimensional displays: Perceptual research and applications to military systems.* Proceedings of a symposium, Washington, D.C., January 29, 1982.
88. Uttal, W. R. An elegant misnomer. (Review of Pompeiano and Ajmone Marsan's *Brain Mechanisms of Perceptual Awareness and Purposeful Behavior.*) *Contemporary Psychology,* 1982, *27,* 687–688.
89. Newhouse, M. and Uttal, W. R. Distribution of stereoanomalies in the general population. *Bulletin of the Psychonomic Society,* 1982, *20,* 48–50.
90. Uttal, W. R. Don't exterminate perceptual fruit flies!! Commentary in *The Behavioral and Brain Sciences,* (In Press).
91. Uttal, W. R. On the limits of sensory neuroreductionism. In *Relating physiology to psychophysics: Current problems and approaches.* Center for Visual Science, The University of Rochester, Proceedings of the 12th Symposium, June 18–20, 1981.
92. Uttal, W. R. Another view of the mind-brain problem. (Review of Miller's Meaning and Purpose in the Intact Brain.) *Contemporary Psychology,* (In Press).

Author Index

A

Anderson, J. A., 31, *147*
Appelle, S., 112, *147*
Arnoult, M. D., 3, 9, 10, *147*
Attneave, F., 3, 9, 10, *147*

B

Bachmann, T., 13, *147*
Barlow, H. B., 8, 113, 118, *147*
Brodersen, A. J., *150*
Brown, D. R., 2, 10, *147*
Brown, J. F., 116, *147*

C

Caelli, T., 31, *147*
Campbell, F. W., 30, *147*
Chang, J. J., 114, *149*
Clement, D. E., 8, 30, *148*
Coffin, S., 11, *147*
Cole, R. E., 108, *149, 150*

D

DiLollo, V., 8, *147, 148*
Doner, J. F., 8, *149*

E

Eskin, T. E., 71, 91, *150*

F

Falzett, M., 8, 116, *148*
Fehrer, E., 13, 118, *148*
Fitts, P. M., 3, 9, *148*
Fitzgerald, J., 71, 91, *150*
Fitzhugh, R., 113, *147*
Foster, D. H., 116, *148*
Fox, R., 7, 8, 40, 109, *148, 149*

G

Garner, W. R., 2, 8, 30, *148*
Getty, D. J., *148*
Gogel, W. C., 7, 109, *148*
Graham, C. H., 113, *148*
Graham, M., 8, *150*
Grossberg, S., 31, *148*

H

Hartline, H. K., 31, *148*
Helson, H. H., 13, 118, *148*
Hieronymus, R., 116, *150*

Hochberg, J. E., 10, *148*
Hoffman, W. C., 32, *148*
Hogben, J. H., 8, *148*
Howard, H. J., 113, *148*
Huggins, A. W. F., *148*

I

Irwin, D. E., 8, *148*

J

Johansson, G., 8, *148*
Jones, R. S., 31, *147*
Jonides, J., 8, *148*
Julesz, B., 40, 46, 77, 78, 114, 130, *148, 149*

K

Kaniza, G., 83, *149*
Köhler, I., 28, *149*
Kottas, B. L., 8, *149*
Kubovy, M., 3, 8, *149*
Kuffler, S. W., 113, *147*

L

Lappin, J. S., 8, 116, *148, 149*
Langlands, H. M. S., 113, *149*
Leeuwenberg, E., 3, 9, *149*
Lehmkuhle, S., 109, *149*
Leonard, J. A., 3, 9, *148*
Lindberg, D. C., 25, *149*
Lloyd, V. V., 113, *149*

M

McAlister, E., 10, *148*
McCulloch, W. S., 32, *149*
McKee, S. P., 118, *150*
Merritt, J. O., 108, *149, 150*
Mershon, D. H., 7, 109, *148, 149*
Mueller, C. B., 113, *149*
Müller, J., 29, *149*

N

Nachmias, J., 113, *149*
Nakayama, K., 8, *149*
Newhouse, M., 40, *149*

O

Owen, D. H., 2, 10, *147*

P

Patterson, R. E., 7, 40, *148, 149*
Pepper, R. L., 108, *149, 150*
Pitts, W., 32, *149*
Pomerantz, J. R., 3, 8, 30, 31, *149*
Pronko, N. H., 28, *150*

R

Ratliff, F., 31, *148*
Reeves, B. C., 8, *147*
Richards, W., 40, *149*
Ritz, S. A., 31, *147*
Robinson, D. N., 5, *149*
Robson, J. G., 30, *147*
Rock, I., 2, *149*
Rogers, B., 8, *150*
Rogers, T. D., 9, *150*
Rosenblatt, F., 32, *150*

S

Sher, L., *150*
Shetty, S. S., *150*
Silverstein, J. W., 31, *147*
Smith, D. C., 108, *149, 150*
Snyder, F. W., 28, *150*
Sperling, G., 78, 115, *150*
Stratton, G., 28, *150*
Sutherland, N. S., 2, *150*

T

Tormey, A., 26, *150*
Tormey, J. F., 26, *150*
Trofanenko, S. C., 9, *150*
Tucker, T. E., 144, *150*

U

Uttal, W. R., 7, 8, 11, 15, 16, 20, 21, 22, 31, 32, 40, 47, 55, 62, 64, 71, 78, 89, 90, 91, 95, 112, 116, 125, 133, 135, 143, 144, *149, 150*

V

Vernon, M. D., 13, *150*
von Bekesy, G., 113, *150*
Voth, A. C., 116, *147*

W

Westheimer, G., 118, *150*
Wilson, A. E., 8, *147*

Woodburne, L. S., 113, *150*
Woods, E., 8, *148*

Y

Yantis, S., 8, *148*

Z

Zusne, L., 2, 9, 10, *150*

Subject Index

A, B, C

Anaglyphic screening, 40
Analog subsystem, 41, 43
Analog voltage, 41, 43
Apparent motion, 58, 60, 67, 107, 115, 116, 130
Apparent volumetric distance, 109
Autocorrelation, 134, 136, 137, 138, 139
Autocorrelation algorithm, 133, 144
Autocorrelation approach, 32
Autocorrelation formula, 20, 133
Autocorrelation model, 8, 15, 20, 22, 119, 124, 126, 127, 128, 141, 142, 143, 144
Autocorrelation predictions, 140
Autocorrelation transform, 143
Backward masking, 78
Behaviorism, 14
Binocular viewing, 38, 51, 106, 108–109, 131
Cognitive manipulation, 19
Contour interaction, 109
Convergence dot, 39, 45
Convergence point, 49
Convolution integrals, 30–31
Critical levels, 15
Cross correlation, 31

D

Depth difference, 73
Detection, definition, 12, 14

Dichoptic images, 36
Dichoptic viewing, 38, 58, 59, 60, 66, 70, 83, 86, 96, 99, 106, 131
Digital to analog converters, 43
Discrimination, definition, 12, 14
Disparity, 8, 41, 45, 55, 71–72, 73, 105, 109, 111, 113, 114
Dot, depth differences, 79, 80
Dot, detection, 7
Dot, disparity, 80
Dot, flash interval, 46, 48, 52, 53, 54, 55, 106
Dot, global arrangement, 4–5
Dot, numerosity, 23
Dot, position, 46, 48, 51, 54, 106
Dot, single flashing, 48, 50–51, 52
Dot, spacing, 23
Dotted form detection, 105
Dotted forms, attributes and detection, 8
Dotted forms, global arrangement, 112
Dotted line, order of presentation, 68–69, 71
Dotted line, orientation, 55, 61–62, 71, 107, 112
Dotted line, plotting interval, 56, 58, 59, 60, 61, 66–67, 69–70, 71, 107
Dotted line, spatial irregularity, 64–66, 67, 107
Dotted line, temporal irregularity, 62–63, 64, 107
Dotted line, temporal sequence, 46
Dotted outline form, deformation, 121

161

Dotted outline form, orientation, 123
Dualism, 26
Dummy dots, 38
Dynamic mode, 39, 43, 44, 46, 119, 121, 123

E, F, G

Elementalism, 3, 29, 30, 31, 34
Empiricism, 27
Epistemology, 1, 27, 28, 35
Exposure duration, 114
Eye movement, 28
Figural goodness, 23
Figure of merit, 22, 23, 124, 134, 135, 136, 138, 139, 140
Forced choice detection, 36
Form, attributes and detection, 2-3, 23
Form, classification, 14
Form, definitions, 3-4, 9, 10, 11, 12
Fourier analysis, 11, 30, 31
Fourier approach, 144
Fourier transform, 143
Frequency domain, 3
Gestalt, psychologists, 29, 31, 144
Gestalt, psychology, 3, 4, 9-10
Global form, 138
Global form effect, 81, 85, 86, 87, 89, 90, 107, 118, 119, 123, 124-125, 130-131
Global interaction, 119
Global neural interaction, 114
Global stereopsis, 130
Global theories, 2
Graphic input digitizer, 83

H, I, K

Hermann grid, 18
Hybrid computer, 41, 43, 45
Hyperacuity, 112
Idealism, 27-28
Immediate stimuli, 27, 28
Information saturation, 16
Intarsia, 26
Irregular form, detectability, 89
Isomorphic space, 111
Isotropic space, 56, 62, 107, 112, 129
Kaniza triangle, 83
Lateral inhibitory interaction, 31, 109
Lie group, 32
Line, orientation, 23
Linear periodicity, 124, 125

Local feature theory, 32
Luminance, 44, 113-114

M, N

Mach band, 18
Materialism, 29
Mediate stimuli, 27, 28
Metacontrast, 109
Molar processes, 16
Monism, 29
Monocular cues, 38, 108
Monocular viewing, 38, 58, 60, 63, 106, 108-109, 131
Multi-level processing, 16
Neo-Gestaltism, 3, 30
Neural autocorrelator, 141
Neural coding, 110
Neural net theories, 109
Neural networks, 29, 31, 32, 113
Neural processing, 105
Neurophysiology, 29
Neuroreducationism, 16, 30, 31

O, P

Operationalism, 14
Oscilloscope, 36, 41, 43, 44
Path smoothing, 116
Pattern, 11
Pattern degradation, 20, 23
Perception, definition, 12-13, 14
Perception, levels of, 13-20
Periodicity, 47
Peripheral interaction, 109
Persistence, 8, 58, 77, 115
Pixel coding, 117
Plane, disparity, 71-72, 73, 74, 75, 76, 77, 79, 100-101, 103, 107, 108, 130
Plane, dot numerosity, 73, 74, 75, 76, 77, 83, 84, 86, 87, 91, 93-94, 95, 101, 102-103, 107, 108, 114
Plane, exposure duration, 71-72, 73, 76, 77, 78, 86, 87, 107
Plane, masking burst interval, 77, 78
Plane, orientation, 112, 123
Plane, rotation, 89, 91, 93, 94, 95, 96, 97, 99, 100, 108, 110
Plane, spatial irregularity, 123
Plane, transformation, 89, 107
Platonic emanations, 23

Polygon, detectability, 84
Preattentive responses, 19
Presentation, 38, 39

Q, R, S

Quality area, 90
Real time clocks, 43–44
Realism, 29
Receptor cells, 17–18
Recognition, definition, 12, 14
Rectangle, detectability, 85, 89, 123, 124
Reductionism, 29
Sensory coding theory, 111
Signal-to-noise rato, 118, 128
Simultaneous contrast, 109
Spatial domain, 3
Spatial frequency, 30, 31
Spatial irregularity, 115, 116, 117
Square, detectability, 85, 89, 124
Static mode, 39, 43, 44, 46, 83, 93, 96, 99, 102, 119
Stereoscopic depth, 45
Stereoscopic discrimination, 79
Stereoscopic space, 7
Stereoscopic stimuli, 41
Stereoscopic threshold, 113
Stereoscopic time, 77, 115
Stereoscopic viewing, 39, 51, 54, 108–109
Stimulus dot density, 118
Stimulus form, 36, 38
Symbolic processing, 18–19

T, V

Taxonomy, 15–19
Taxonomy, Level 0, 16
Taxonomy, Level 1, 16
Taxonomy, Level 2, 17
Taxonomy, Level 3, 17, 35
Taxonomy, Level 4, 17
Taxonomy, Level 5, 18
Temporal irregularity, 115, 116, 117
Threshold, 18
Trial, 38, 39
Triangle, detectability, 84, 89
Trigger, 44
Trompe l'oeil, 26
Vector field analysis, 32
Vergence aid, 73, 76
Vergence pattern, 79
Visual angle, 24
Visual noise, 36, 38, 44, 48
Visual noise, density, 50, 51, 55, 56, 58, 59, 60, 63, 66, 83, 84, 86, 89, 91, 94–95, 96, 106, 128, 132
Visual noise, distribution, 83, 92, 102, 104
Visual noise, effect as masker, 109
Visual noise, masking burst interval, 107

W, X

Wholism, 3, 29, 30, 34
X, Y, Z equivalence, 110–111, 120, 129, 132